The God of LOVE Divided By Three Equals One

Introduction

Although I am just the physical author of this book, His Majesty God the Father, and His Majesty God our Lord and Savior Jesus the Christ, the Messiah, and His Majesty God the Holy Spirit is the spiritual Author and complete finisher of all of our faith; for this same faith cometh by hearing and understanding all that God the Father and God the Lord Jesus and God the Holy Spirit had been doing for all of mankind's salvation; for in the beginning was this Salvation plan of God, and this Salvation plan of God was with God at the time and creation of Adam and Eve, and this salvation plan of God was God in the form of a flesh and blood man named Jesus. Everything that Jesus had said and had accomplished for all of mankind's salvation is what we put our hope and trust into by faith; for it's not by any of our own works that we could do on our own; but it's by all of the works that God the Father, and God the Holy Spirit had accomplished through the complete works that God the Lord Jesus, as a physical flesh and blood man named Jesus, had performed and completed to legally remove and separate all of our sins from us, so that our sins can be cast into hell by themselves, setting us free from that bondage that the slavery of our sins had against us, making all of us free and clear of any sins, that was keeping us from entering God's heaven; for by the Grace of God are we saved from the eternal pits of hell, through hope, trust and faith of all of the works that Jesus had accomplished for our salvation and not by any of your own works: all we have to do is just freely accept this free offer of God by faith.

I highly recommend that you read this book through completely at least three times, or more; so that you can gain a greater understanding of God's salvation plan for all of mankind; for the eyes of your spirit will either gain sight through the light of understanding; or remain in the darkness and blindness of misunderstanding.

© by the author of this book.

The book author retains sole copyright to his or her contributions to this book.

ISBN-13:978-0-9907342-1-5

Author
Neal O. McAfee
NOM777mailbox@gmail.com

Preview

Do you want to know why God had created this earth? Do you want to know why this earth, that is in this dark and empty universe, is the only planet that has life on it and the other planets in our solar system and universe don't? Do you want to know the size of this universe? Do you want to know where sin had originally come from? Did you know that all of mankind is conceived, formed and born into this world with that same sinful nature and sin of Adam that has already damned us all to hell? Did you know that we are all on this path to hell and it's not by choice but by the sin of Adam's sin that has been passed unto all of us at conception? Did you know that God had provided for all of us, a free choice to choose and accept His salvation plan to have your sins removed from you so that your sins go to hell and you are then free and clear to go to God's heaven? This book will answer all of these questions and more. This book will give you an overall view starting at the timeline where God is about to make and create the angels of heaven; and when the first sin entered into God's heaven for the first time; and the restoration of this earth; and the reason why God had decided to make and create the first man Adam; and to the point, at that very moment, that Jesus had made that powerful statement, "It Is Finished!", when He was on that cross, for our salvation, and just before, Jesus had laid down His life for us and died. This book will set you free, from the darkness of misunderstanding, and lies, by the understanding of the light of the Truth; for the eyes of our spirit, will either walk and believe in misunderstanding or understanding; the darkness of lies or the light of the Truth; the lies of Satan or the Truth of Jesus; for Satan is the father of all lies; but Jesus is the only Way, and the only Truth, and the only Eternal Life.

001 In the book of Genesis chapter one, and verse one; we read that in the beginning God created the heaven and the earth. This is a true statement. But not in the way that it has been, and is still being taught today. And what I mean by this statement, is that we have been, and we are still being taught that God had created the heaven and this earth, and then He created Adam and Eve and the Garden of Eden, and then God had placed them in that garden, and so on and so on. But this type of biblical teaching is not completely correct or accurate. This teaching that God had created the heaven and the earth, and then jumping to God creating Adam and Eve, is not a complete and accurate picture of what had actually taken place, and leaves out a major event that had taken place between verse one, and verse two, of Genesis chapter one. In other words; in verse one, this is when God had created all of the heaven and this earth, and brought them into existence, from nothing, for the first time. This dark universe that we see today did not exist, as we see it today when all of this universe was brought into existence by God, from nothing, for the first time, as stated in verse one of Genesis chapter one. For when we read verse one; In the beginning God created the heaven and the earth: and then we read verse two; And the earth is without form, and void, and darkness was upon the face of the deep. And the Spirit of God moved upon the face of the waters. In short, verse one, is when God had originally made this earth brand new from nothing, and was brought into existence for the first time. But then in verse two, we now are shown that this same earth that was made in verse one is now without form, and void, and darkness was upon the face of the deep; and this is where God has come to restore this earth from a destructive state, to like or similar to its original created form. And then this is where God Creates Adam and Eve, etc., etc. For you see that in verse two God did not create the earth at this time but has come back to this earth to restore it from a destructive state. For in verse one, this earth didn't exist and was brought into existence by God

from nothing that had already existed: for through faith we understand that the worlds were framed by the word of God, so that things which are seen were not made of things which already do appear.

002 For you see, that in order for this earth to even be in a distructive state as stated in verse two; "And the earth is without form, and void, and darkness was upon the face of the deep." It would have already had to be created into existence by God first; for just plain common sense would tell you that you cannot have even a destructive earth or an earth without its original form unless it had already been created for the first time. And that second part of verse two where, "And the Spirit of God moved upon the face of the waters." God had come back to this formless and destructive earth to restore it from this destructive state. This is not where God is creating this earth for the first time; for this earth is already here in existence but in a destructive and formless existence. But God had come back to restore it from its destructive state to like or similar to its original created form and appearance.

003 In verse two this same earth that was created in verse one by God is already in existence but is for some reason now without its original form, and void or empty of any life, and now completely surrounded in a thick and total darkness that this darkness even engulfed the very depth of this whole universe. Jeremiah 4:23 I beheld the earth, and, lo, it was without form, and void, and the heavens, and they had no light. And in verse two God has come back to this earth to restore it from this destructive state. For when this earth was created for the first time in verse one, it was originally created for the angels of heaven.

004 So when God had created this earth and all of his heaven, this was when God had decided to make or create all the angels of heaven. And

before verse one of Genesis chapter one; there were no angels in God's heaven. But yet God has still always existed: And since all of the angels of heaven were created by God; that means that there was a time that all of the angels of heaven did not exist until God had decided to create them and bring them into existence for the first time. And that also means that there was a point in God's eternal timeline that He had decided to make the angels in His heavenly kingdom. And at this point of time in God's eternal timetable; Evil, sin, death, and darkness did not exist anywhere in God's heavenly kingdom. And this means that this dark and desolate universe including all of the planets, galaxies, stars, suns, and including this planet earth did not exist yet; there were no angels; there were no fallen angels; no Satan; no demons or evil spirits and no hell: and this was before God had made Adam and Eve. So when God created the heaven and including this earth; as stated in verse one, this was the timeline in God's eternal timetable that He had decided to create all the angels of heaven for the first time. Also at this point in God's eternal timetable there has never ever been any evil, sin, death, or darkness anywhere in God's eternal heaven. There was eternal light everywhere in God's heaven and all of the angels and their positions of power and authority that they were placed into were made in that eternal light of God's heaven and not in any darkness. This whole dark universe, including this earth, was originally made in the eternal light of God and His heaven.

005 This was when God had or was making the angels of heaven for their first time. In other words, God had made all of the positions of power and authority throughout His heavenly kingdom, for all of the angels of heaven; and then God had made the angels of heaven, and He then had placed each of them into their position of power and authority; And this is when this earth, that we are on today, was originally made, from nothing, by God and brought into existence for the first time. And then God had originally

made and placed angels on this earth and on all of the other planets throughout this whole universe, that we see today, and throughout His entire heavenly kingdom. So you see that this earth and this entire universe, that we see today was originally part of the eternal state of God's heavenly kingdom. But in order to get a clearer picture and help you to get a better understanding of a major event that had taken place; we need to go back into God's past to the point in time just before God has decided to create and make the angels of heaven for the first time.

006 But first; and in order for you to fully understand a lot of the events that had taken place throughout the bible, you have to first get a grasp or try to fully understand the true image of who God really is. In other words, there are certain attributes of God that qualifies Him for being a true and living God. And these attributes are: That God has always existed right now and has always existed in the past; and will always exist in the future. In other words, God was never conceived or born into existence; and He was not created by anyone or anything. He has always existed in the past far more than we can comprehend. And He will always exist in the future far more than we can comprehend that either. And He has, basically, existed forever in the eternal present. And the other attributes too is that God will never die, and He cannot be destroyed. He is all powerful and everlasting; He is a One, True, and Living God. But yet this One, True and living God has also three distinct and separate forms that make up the Godhead: You have God the Father, and you have God the Lord Jesus, and you have God the Holy Spirit: these three are the three forms or persons of the One God; not three separate gods. You have God the Father that is truly, 100% and fully God; And you have God the Lord Jesus that is truly, 100% and fully God also; And you have God the Holy Spirit that is truly, 100% and fully God also; these three are not three separate gods; but one God as stated in 1John 5:7; For there are three that bear record (witness) in

heaven, the Father, the Word (Jesus), and the Holy Ghost: and these three are one.

007 You have God the Father that is one distinct and separate form that is different from God the Lord Jesus and God the Holy Spirit: And this is also the same with God the Lord Jesus that is also one distinct and separate form that is different and separate from God the Father and God the Holy Spirit: And this is also the same with God the Holy Spirit, that is also one distinct and separate form that is different from God the Father and God the Lord Jesus; but all three forms are the One, True and Living God.

008 Now there is a better way to help illustrate and to help us to get a clearer picture or a greater understanding of this three divine and distinct forms of one God. Jesus had referred to himself as the bread of life and the living waters of everlasting life: Jeremiah 2:13 For my people have committed two evils; they have forsaken Me the fountains of living waters, and hewed them out cisterns, broken cisterns, and can hold no water. John 4:14 "But whosoever drinketh of the water that I shall give him shall never thirst; but the water that I shall give him shall be in him a well of water springing up into everlasting life"; for God is Eternal life. John 6:35 "I am the bread of life: he that cometh to Me shall never hunger; and he that believeth on Me shall never thirst". John 7:38 "He that believeth on Me, as the scripture hath said, out of his belly shall flow rivers of living waters". Proverbs 10:11 the mouth of a righteous man is a well of life: but violence covereth the mouth of the wicked.

009 Basically, God is the Living water of Heaven. And just like the living water of heaven, we have the physical water here on this earth. Now we only have one kind of water on this earth. But I have had many people try to correct me and say that there are two different kinds of water on this

earth; salt water and fresh water. But that's not two different kinds of water; for water is a mineral, and salt is also a mineral. You can remove the mineral salt from salt water to make it into fresh water; and you can take fresh water and add salt to it and make it into salt water. So you see salt water and fresh water is not two different kinds of water. There is only one kind of water here on this earth. Its just that some of this water on earth has salt in it and some of it don't.

010 Now in order to help illustrate a point here and what we are going to do is to use our imagination. We are going to temporary suspend all marine life that is in all the waters here on earth: we are going to separate all dirt and debris. Basically, remove all the water from off this earth; and that would be all of the water that is in the ground; in the rivers, creeks and lakes; in the oceans and seas; in the clouds of the air and on the mountain tops and both the north and south poles. We are going to take all of this water from off this earth so that all we have is just the mineral water only and nothing else. And then we are going to suspend it out here in space from this earth temporarily. Then as you turn back to the earth, you will see that there is no other kind of water on this earth. So now you can see that as we then turn back to that one water that we had removed from this earth and had suspended it out in space; you now can see that we have only one kind of water on this earth. Just like there is only one kind of water in heaven, the living water of God himself. But now we are going to take that one water that we had removed from off this earth, and we had suspended it out in space; and we are now going to divide it into three equal amounts: we are going to take the first amount and turn it into the solid form of water, Ice; and then we are going to leave the second amount in the liquid form of water; and then we are going to take the third amount and turn it into the vapor form of water, steam. So you can now see that this one kind of water that we had removed from off this earth is

only one water and yet it can have three distinct and separate forms from each other and still remained one water; Ice is the solid form of water, the liquid form of water, and steam, is the vapor form of water: and yet each form of water is distinctly different from its other two forms of water. The solid form of water is distinctly different from the liquid form and the vapor form of water. And the liquid form of water is distinctly different from the solid form and the vapor form of water. And the vapor form of water is distinctly different from the liquid form and the solid form of water. Each form is distinctly different from each other; but yet all three forms are water. In other words, these three forms of water are not three different kinds of water but the three distinct, separate and different forms of that one water.

011 This is the same with God; for God is that living water of heaven. And just like this physical water of earth has three distinct, separate and different forms of this one water of earth; God the living water of heaven also has three distinct, separate and different forms of this living water of heaven: God the Father represents the solid form of the true and living Godhead; just like ice represents the solid form of water: God the Lord Jesus represents the liquid form of the true and living Godhead; just like the liquid form of water: and God the Holy Spirit represents the vapor form of the true and living Godhead; just like steam represents the vapor form of water. In other words, the three distinct, separate and divine forms of the true and living Godhead is not three different and separate gods; But the three distinct, separate and divine forms of the one true and living God.

012 You need to fully understand this in order for you to gain a better understanding of God's plan to eliminate all evil, sin, and death from his heavenly kingdom once and forever. God is not going to let any sin back into his heavenly kingdom again. Also you need to fully understand this in order for you to know and understand the events that had taken place;

because God the Father does certain things and God the Lord Jesus does certain things and God the Holy Spirit does certain things independently from each other. In other words, you have God's throne that is the center most highest position of God's heaven. Well God the Father can go to one section of heaven; and God the Lord Jesus can go to another section of heaven; and God the Holy Spirit can go to another section of heaven independently and yet each is still on the throne as though he had never left it. God is always on his throne even though he would leave his throne and go anywhere in his heaven. He is always on his throne; for God is a part of his throne and his throne is a part of him. God can never be removed or separated from his throne by anyone or anything; and it would be impossible for God to remove himself from his own throne.

013 I need to side step here while on this thought path of the three-in-one Godhead, so as to clarify our modern day doctrine of the Trinity. And as stated above; God the Father, and God the Lord Jesus, and God the Holy Spirit are the three divine, distinct, and separate forms or persons of the one and only true and living Godhead; which clearly shows us that God is not three separate Gods but three separate forms of the One God. And this is also known as our modern day doctrine of the Trinity; even though that this word, "Trinity:, is not in our English version bibles. This modern day word "Trinity" that we have today in our English language, means, and by definition, "The three divine and separate forms or persons of one God". And this is clearly stated in the bible, by definition, in 1John 5:7: "For there are three that bear record, (witness), in heaven, the Father, the Word, (Jesus), and the Holy Ghost: and these three are one". Our modern day word, Trinity", which in our English language that exists today and didn't exist when only Greek, Hebrew, and Aramaic languages existed when the original scriptures were written; and when these same scriptures were translated into our English language, the modern day word Trinity

didn't exist at that translation to English. But that word Trinity exists today with its definition that means; three divine and separate forms or persons of one God. For a word and its definition is one and the same; a word doesn't exist by itself without its definition and a definition doesn't exist by itself either without its word. So when you read a given word in a sentence; it's the same as if the definition is there also; or, on the other hand, if you were to read the definition of that word in a sentence; it's also the same as if that word was there also.

014 Now I had said all that to say this. Our modern day word, "Trinity", is not in our English translated version or bibles, of the original Greek, Hebrew, and Aramaic languages or scriptures; but its definition is there as clearly stated in 1John 5:7: and the simple reason that the word Trinity is not in our English translated bibles is that the word Trinity did not exist in the English language at that time when the first English bibles were being translated into our English language from the Greek, Hebrew, and Aramaic scriptures. For the word Trinity is our modern day word for the meaning and definition of the three divine and separate forms or persons of one God. And as I had stated above, a word and its definition is one and the same. If the word is there in a sentence, then it's the same as if the definition is there also; or if the definition of a word is in a sentence, it's the same as if the word is there also; you cannot separate a word and its definition; one or the other will be there and sometimes both will be there. And since the definition of our modern day word, "Trinity", is there in our English translated version of our bibles; and as stated in 1John 5:7; it's the same as if our modern day word "Trinity" is there also: and if you will just flat out and stubbornly refuse to believe in the Trinity Doctrine just because the word Trinity is not in our English bibles; then you are a fool because all of our English translated bibles is not the original scriptures but a translation of the original scriptures from the Greek, Hebrew, and Aramaic languages

that only existed at the time and writing of the scriptures; and the simple reason that there were no writings of the scriptures in the our English language is that the English language did not exist then; for it had come into existence later and basically branched out from the Greek language. So the Trinity doctrine is a modern day doctrine that is backed up by scripture, even though our modern day word, "Trinity", is not in our English translated and transcribed bibles.

015 God the Father and God the Lord Jesus and God the Holy Spirit have been on His throne for all of eternal past, present and future. His throne has been in the center most high position of His heaven forever. And God's entire heavenly kingdom extends out and away, in all directions from His throne forever. A graphical outline of God's throne would be similar to drawing a circle on a piece of paper and then divide that circle into three equal sections such as one would cut a whole pie into three equal pieces. And I had made this circle with the three sections on a piece of paper so that one section, or one piece of the pie was at the top; and one section or one piece of the pie was down and over to the left of that top section; and one section, or one piece of the pie was down and over to the right of that top section: And in that top section of that circle I had put God the Father: And in that section of that circle that was down and over to the left, I had put God the Lord Jesus: And in that section of that circle that was down and over to the right, I had put God the Holy Spirit. Now this is not an actual picture of God's throne, but a graphical outline of God's throne. Also, see Drawing #1 on page 253.

016 Again, I am going to side step here, off this main thought path, so as to clarify another point. And like I had said above that a graphical outline is not an actual picture of something similar to when a child makes a stick figure drawing of mommy and daddy. The stick figure drawing of mommy

and daddy, is not an actual picture of mommy and daddy, but a graphical outline using lines and circles as a symbol that represents mommy and daddy. Another example of a graphical outline is the use of city and state road maps. For example, a road atlas of the united states will display the highways and roads, cities and towns, counties, water ways, rivers, and lakes, etc. as graphical symbols and not as an actual picture of them. For example, if you live in a small town on a US highway in any state in the USA, your town will appear on that map as a small black dot. That map will not show your house and the street that it is located on; it will not show you the trees that are in the front and back yards; it will not show your cars parked in the drive way, etc.; Basically, a state map will show you a graphical outline of all major highways, interstate freeways, state roads, and secondary roads and country roads, etc.; but also, a state map will not show you or display every road that there is in that state; such as, the small little local streets that is in your town and small county roads and private roads.

017 So you see that a state map is a graphical out line of cities, towns, and the major roads, US highways, interstates freeways that is used to route anyone to anywhere in a state that they would plan to go to. This state map is not an actual picture of everything that is in that state, but a graphical outline of that state that shows only what is needed to, through graphical symbols, lines, and color, etc.; so that anyone can route themselves through or to a specific city, town, or point. So a graphical outline is simply used to illustrate an event, or main point without going into exact detail like an actual picture would be able to do; and a graphical outline is a much faster way of making a point or illustrating the main points of an event or to show a generalized path that leads up to an event; where trying to make an exact picture would be impossible to do and would also take too much time and effort to make and present it to anyone.

018 Now in order to get a clearer picture and to gain a better understanding of some of the main events that has taken place in God's past; and has also taken place before mankind's existence or before God had created Adam and Eve: I will be using a graphical outline to illustrate a sequence of events that will lead up to a major event that had taken place in God's heaven that will show us how God has and is dealing with Evil, sin, death and darkness. And this graphical outline in not an actual picture of God's heaven or events that had taken place; but is a graphical outline of God's heaven and events that had taken place since we have no actual picture of this except the picture that the bible gives us; for it is has been said that a picture it worth a thousand words; but also, a thousand words is worth a picture; and as we study and read God's word to us, or the bible; these words, verses, chapters and books of the bible paint a picture in our minds as to what God wants us to understand of him and his heaven and the things that he is doing for us and our salvation and to bring us back to his heaven and not go to hell.

019 Now back to that graphical outline of that circle that I had drawn on a piece of paper earlier, and where I had divided that circle into three equal sections similar to like cutting a whole pie into three equal pieces of pie. And in that top section of that circle I had put God the Father: And in that section of that circle that was down and over to the left, I had put God the Lord Jesus: And in that section of that circle that was down and over to the right, I had put God the Holy Spirit. And like I had said before, this is just a graphical outline that represents God's throne and not an actual picture of his throne. This complete circle represents God's one and only throne for a one, true and living Godhead. And the three sections inside that circle represent the three distinct, separate and divine positions of power and authority of that one, true and living Godhead. So you see that inside of that circle is God's eternal throne. And God's throne has always been in the

center most high position of his heavenly kingdom forever. In other words, his throne has always been there in all of God's eternal past; and still is, even to this very day; and will always be in that same position for all of God's eternal future; and will never be moved or removed.

020 And since God's throne is in the center most high position of his heavenly kingdom. All of God's heaven exists and extends out and away and in all and every directions, 360 degrees from God's throne forever. And God's heaven is not a physical existence but a spiritual and eternal type of existence or place. So you see that if it were possible for you to build a big enough space ship and take off from this physical earth and fly your physical space ship and try to find God's heaven through this physical universe you would never be able to find God's spiritual and eternal heaven. But God can transfer himself from his spiritual and eternal heaven and into this physical realm of this earth without a physical space ship and back in just a twinkling of an eye. And God can also be on his throne in his spiritual and eternal heaven and be on this physical earth at the same time. So you see that you would never be able to find God's heaven on your own. It would be physically impossible and a waste of time.

021 Mankind has a spirit, soul, and body that complete us as individual human beings. Our spirit and body are similar in all of us even though we all don't have the same color of hair, skin, or facial appearances, etc. But our body parts are basically the same. We all have arms, legs, feet, eyes, nose, mouth, ears, etc. and our organs are the same type, and function the same way. But our soul is what makes us different from each other and gives us our individuality and basically no two human souls are exactly alike. Our spirit, soul and body are a complete unit and can only move around as a unit or human entity. In other words, we cannot have our soul go in one direction or place and have our spirit go in another direction or

place and have our body go in yet another direction or place all at the same time. We can only move around as a spirit, soul, and body unit or entity and not separately.

022 And God had made us with a spirit, soul, and body because God had made us in his image and after his likeness. For God also has a Spirit, Soul, and Body. And this is the reason that we also have a spirit, soul, and body. God the Father represents the soul of God; and God the Lord Jesus represents the body of God; and God the Holy Spirit represents the spirit of God. And since this is the three divine, distinct and separate forms or persons of the one, true and living God; The soul of man is and was made in the express image and after the likeness of God the Father's soul: And the body of man is and was made in the express image and after the likeness of God the Lord Jesus's body: And the spirit of man is and was made in the express image and after the likeness of God the Holy Spirit's Spirit. And just like God is the three divine distinct and separate forms or persons of the one, true and living God; Man has the three distinct and separate forms of man, the spirit, the soul, and the body, that were made in the image and after the likeness of God's Spirit, Soul, and Body. The difference between God's Spirit, Soul, and body and Man's spirit, soul, and body is that God's Spirit, Soul, and Body can each move anywhere independently and at the same time; whereas man can only move around as a spirit, soul, and body unit or entity and not separately.

023 Now this should give you a clearer picture and a better understanding of who God is so that now you will be able see and understand what God's will and plan has been, is now and will be in the future as to how God is dealing with evil, sin and death. There was a time in God's past that evil, sin, and death did not exist. But then it had come into existence on its own and wasn't created by God. Some people think or have been taught

that God had created some angels or people evil and some not. This is wrong teaching or thinking. For God has never made anything or anyone evil. For its against God's nature to create anything, anyone or any of his creations with evil. God did not create evil, sin and death. Disobedience to God's law is counted as sin, and the wages of sin is death. So to disobey the laws of God is an evil act that will become or lead to disobedience and become sin and then this sin is punishable by death in accordance to God's Law.

024 God has made every creature or creation in total and complete perfection and with total and perfect righteousness. They were never made with any evil, sin, or death in them. But they were made with a free will; for God did not make robots, but God had made his created creatures as free moral agents with a free will to choose to love God or to freely reject God's love or to obey God's law or to disobey God's law. God cannot do or make any evil, sin and death; for it is not in God or in his nature. God has never had any evil, sin, or death in him and never will. For it is impossible for God to do any evil, sin, or death. For you see, God does not just tell or speak the truth, He is the Truth and because He is the Truth that's all he can speak. And this is also why God cannot lie because He is the Truth, the whole Truth and nothing but the Truth and there has never been a lie in Him, and there is no lie in Him now, and there will never, ever, be a lie in Him; and this is the very reason that it is impossible for God to lie. And God doesn't just know all things; for God is Knowledge and that's why He is all Knowing or knows all things: And God just doesn't understand all things; for God is Understanding and that's why He understands all things: And God does not and cannot make any mistakes; for God is Perfection, and because he is Perfection, anything created by God, is created and made in perfection, and without any mistakes, or errors. God is a part of his laws and all the laws of God is a part of Him. And God doesn't just obey his

laws; for God Is Obedience to all of his own laws and this is why God's Law cries out continuously, saying, obedient, righteous, true, and everlasting, living God.

025 And God doesn't just love all of his created creatures or beings with an emotional type love that we see and understand; but it's a real true and everlasting Love that we cannot fully understand or comprehend. For God doesn't just love His creation; for God is Love and in Him is no hate; but yet God hate's evil, sin, and death. Where there is evil, sin, and death there is darkness; for darkness is a part of that evil, sin, and death and that evil, sin, and death is a part of that darkness; And this is the direct opposite of who God is.

026 In other words, since there has never been and never will be any evil, sin, or death in God; there has never been and will never be any darkness in God: And this is the very reason that God is Light and the source of any and all light: And this light that shines forth from within and out of God Himself, is an everlasting and eternal light; and any darkness that would get into this everlasting and eternal light that shines forth from God will be consumed by that righteous, glorious, consuming light of God. And this why God can hate evil, sin, death, and darkness even though God is Love and there is no hate in him: For this type of hate is not an evil hate but a righteous hate. Even though God is a God of Love, He is also a God of perfect justice and in no wise can He clear the guilty. For all evil, sin, death and darkness is on or from the disobedient side of God's Law; for where there is disobedience to God's law, that is accounted as an evil act and is sin; and God's law states that the wages of sin is death; and since God will not dwell where there is sin, God will remove Himself from that sin and that sin will be removed from God. And also since God is light and Life and all light and life comes forth and from God; and since God will not dwell

where there is evil and sin; this is why that evil and sin is followed with death and darkness because God's light and life is removed thereby leaving darkness and death to evil and sin: And since God's light is an eternal light and God's Life is an eternal life; The death and darkness that follows evil and sin is an eternal death and an eternal darkness that is completely separated from God forever. For you cannot have light and darkness in the same place and at the same time.

027 Now, and as I had said before that there was a time in God's past that evil, sin, death and darkness did not exist. But then it had come into existence on its own and wasn't created by God. In other words, this whole dark universe and including planet earth did not exist originally as this dark universe with planets and galaxies void and empty of life as we see it today. For this whole universe and all of the planets, moons, and galaxies, including the earth was originally part of the eternal state of God's heaven. But it all had become desolate and void because of the first and original sin and rebellion of high archangel Lucifer and all of his angel's that he had direct control and authority over; and that was a total of one third of all of the angels of heaven that had sinned and rebelled against God and His authority and was kicked out of God's eternal heavenly place as stated in Revelation 12:7,8,9 (7) And there was war in heaven: Michael and his angels fought against the dragon, (Fallen High Angel Lucifer, whom had become Satan, the Devil and many other names), and the dragon fought and his angels, (8) And prevailed not; neither was there place found any more in heaven. (9) And the great dragon was cast out, that old serpent, called the Devil and Satan, which deceiveth the whole world: he was cast out of heaven, and his angels were cast out with him. For high archangel, Lucifer, had fallen from that high, archangelic position of power and authority and had become Satan, the Devil, and he has also been referred to as that dragon, that serpent of old. And all of the angels that were under

his, Lucifer's, power and authority had also fallen from their position of power and authority and had become demons and evil spirits.

028 But in order for you to see or understand this first sinful rebellion of Lucifer and his angels that had taken place before Adam and Eve was created; I am going to go back to a point in God's timeline of His eternal past that is just before Genesis chapter one, verse one, was even written in the heart and mind of God; For God and His heaven still existed even before the angels were made by God. And at this point in God's eternal timeline of His eternal past; there has never been any evil, sin, death or darkness anywhere in God's eternal heaven. This dark universe that we see today did not exist then. And up to this point in God's eternal timeline of His existence; God Himself has never ever seen any evil, sin, death, or darkness anywhere in His eternal heaven. For God has always known that there was always a chance that evil, sin, death and darkness could enter into his heavenly kingdom. But this evil, sin, death and darkness would never ever be made, created or be brought into existence by God Himself; for God will not and cannot make anything or any creature with any evil, sin, death, or darkness. For God is a totally righteous and living God that is Eternal Life and Eternal Light. God has never and will never create anything, any creature, or any being with any evil, sin, death, or darkness; for there are many different teachings that teach that God had created some people evil and some people without any evil. This is wrong teaching and is against the very nature of God Himself. For God will always make and create all things in total perfection and in perfect righteousness. God does not and cannot make any mistakes or errors.

029 And for whatever reason, God had decided to make all of the angels of heaven as free moral agents. In other words, God had made each angel with a free will of choice to either obey him or to disobey him; Or to

freely choose to love Him or to hate Him; etc. In other words, God did not make or create robotic angels. For God did not want any preprogrammed robots, but free moral agents or angels that would freely choose to love Him and obey Him. And God had known that by making all of these angels with a free will of their own; that there was a slight risk of any one of them choosing to hate or to disobey him. But God did not want any preprogrammed robotic angels in His heaven. An example to this would be for you to record a message on a tape recording that would repeat over and over, "I love you, I love you, etc.", and when you replayed it back to yourself, would you feel loved? The only answer is no. And this is why God didn't want any preprogrammed robotic angels in His heaven and why He had made and created them as free moral agents or angels. And even though there was this slight chance that any angel, or angels, would or could reject or rebel against Him; God had believed that since all of these angels were made with and in His perfect Love, righteousness, etc., and all that God is; Why would any of them want to reject His perfect Love?

030 Now we are back to that point in God's timeline of His eternal past; and God has, and for whatever reason, has decided to make and create all of the angels of heaven for the first time. And God did not make all of the angels with the same positions of power and authority. There were different levels or positions of power and authority from the least angels to the chief angels to the archangels. Now this is where we are at Genesis chapter one, verse one, where God is creating the heaven and this earth for the first time. For you see, that the heaven and this earth did not exist in God's heaven until He had created it for all of these angels. Before the angels were created by God in heaven, there were no positions of power and authority for any angels. So God had to rearrange and create all of these new positions of power and authority for all of these new angels: And as I had said earlier that this dark universe, this earth and all of the

other planets and galaxies throughout this dark universe that we see today did not exist at this timeline in Genesis chapter one, verse one. For all of God's eternal heaven was filled with the eternal Light of God and there was no darkness anywhere and no evil, sin, death, darkness, or hell.

031 God's heaven existed one way before the creation of the angels of heaven. But was then transformed, rearranged, renovated, to make way for all of these new angels. And the format that I had used to get an idea of how God had went about to create all of these positions of power and authority was based on the format that God had used to make Adam and Eve. In other words, God had restored this earth that was the position of the power and authority that God was going to place Adam and Eve into; and then God had created Adam and Eve and then He had placed them into that position of power and authority or into that garden of Eden on this earth; and it had taken God six days to create the position of power and authority and create Adam and Eve and then place them into that position of power and authority. And the man Adam was made in the image and after the likeness of God Himself. None of the angels wasn't made in that image or after that likeness of God but had angelic or archangelic bodies. So some angels and their positions of power and authority may have only taken one day to make; And some angels and their positions of power and authority may have only taken two days to make; And some angels and their positions of power and authority may have only taken three days to make; And some angels and their positions of power and authority may have taken four days to make; And the positions of power and authority of the archangels may have taken five days to make. So you can see that the way that God had made Adam and Eve can be used as a format as to the way God may have created all of the angels of heaven: and there are many different ways or theories as to how God had made all of the angels of heaven.

032 And since there are many different ways in which God could have or might have used to create the angels of heaven; I am not going to try to cover all of the ways in which God could have or might have used to create all of the angels of heaven. But it is a true fact that God did create all of the angels of heaven one way or the other. So I have decided to choose one possible way that God might have used to create all of the angels of heaven; because the main focus that I want to bring your attention to is not necessarily the creation of the angels but the event that had taken place after all of the angels were made. And whether the way of which I have chosen to use, as to how the angels were made, is that actual way or not that God had used, is not the main point or focus of our attention here; but is just a way to show the overall picture here that leads up to the major event that had taken place in God's heaven as to the first time sin had entered into God's heaven and how God had dealt with that sin. So eventually we will know how all of the angels were made once we get into heaven. But until then I have chosen the best possible way that God might have used to make and create all of the angels of heaven and their positions of power and authority. And this is to show you that in Genesis chapter one, verse one, is where God is creating the heaven and this earth for the first time and creating angels and their positions of power and authority and placing them into those positions of their power and authority. And this included that this earth was created by God from nothing and brought into existence for the first time and angels were placed on it. And at this time that this earth was created by God from nothing and brought into existence for the first time; this earth was not made in any darkness that we see it in today; but was created in the eternal light of God's eternal heaven for at this time of the earth's creation, there was no darkness anywhere in God's heaven; and all of the other planets, and galaxies that we see in our dark universe today was also made or created from nothing and brought into existence for the first time and in the eternal light of God's

eternal heaven. And angels, also, were originally placed on all these planets and galaxies that we see today.

033 So you see that this whole dark universe that we see today, and this earth that we are on today, was not created this way by God originally; but is in this way because of the first sinful rebellion of archangel Lucifer and all of his angels that were under his charge or authority; and also the disobedience of Adam and Eve and their fall into evil, sin, and death. For you see that Lucifer was given charge or authority over one third of the angels of heaven that was directly under his authority. Lucifer had then wanted to become god and he wanted to be worshipped by all of the angels of heaven; but he needed to remove the true and living God from his throne first, or so he must have thought he really could; but was defeated and was kicked out of heaven. And all of the angels that were under his charge or authority were also kicked out of heaven with Lucifer. Lucifer and all of his angels had originally occupied one third part of the kingdom of God's heaven. And since one third of God's angels were now evicted or expelled from heaven because of their sin; and God will not dwell where there is sin: God had remove Himself from that one third section of heaven. And since God is eternal light, eternal darkness had then filled that one third section of heaven; and since God is eternal life, eternal death had then filled that one third section of heaven; and since God is perfect order, total chaos and disorder had then filled this one third section of God's heaven and so on, and so on. In other words, all that God is was removed from that section of heaven that was occupied by Lucifer and all the angels that were directly under his charge. This is where we would be at as stated in Genesis chapter one, verse two; and the earth is without form and void and darkness is upon the face of the deep; and this is why this earth is located in this dark universe that we see today; for we, and this earth, are in that one third section of God's heaven that Lucifer and all of his angels

that were under his charge and authority was kicked out of; but this is just a quick or short version that will give you a glimpse of a much bigger picture that I am going to show you in more detail. So we are now returning back to where God has decided to create all of the angels of heaven for the first time and the timeline of where Genesis chapter one, verse one is about to be executed by God.

034 And as I had stated earlier that God's heaven had existed one way before the creation of the angels of heaven; and then God had rearranged, renovated, His heavenly kingdom to make way for all of the new angels and all of their positions of power and authority that he was about to create. And before that creation of all of the angels of heaven, God's throne is in the center most high position of his heavenly kingdom. All of God's heaven exists and extends out and away and in all and every direction, 360 degrees from God's throne forever, without end. And at this time just before God was about to make and create all of the angels of heaven; there wasn't any positions, divisions or sections in heaven for any angels yet. And just like God had created or prepared the position of power and authority first that was to be for Adam and Eve; and then He had created Adam and Eve and then God had placed them into that position. God may have created the angels and their positions just like or similar to this.

035 This was the same for how God had created all of the angels and all of their positions of their individual power and authority from the least angels, to the chief angels, to the archangels: For God had created the position and power of authority of each angel first and then He had created that angel and then God had placed that new angel into that position. But first, and before God had created any angel and its position yet; He had decided to divide and section off His heaven into three separate sections. And these sections would start at the Throne of God and would extend out

and away from the throne of God in such a way that God the Father would have a one third section of heaven that would start at His section of His throne and would now extend out and away from His throne forever; and God the Lord Jesus would also have a one third section of heaven that would start at His section of His throne and would now extend out and away from His throne forever; and also God the Holy Spirit would have a one third section of heaven that would start at His section of His throne and would now extend out and away from His throne forever. In other words, God had rerranged His one heaven, and divided into now three separate sections so that God the Father would now have a one third section of heaven that was going to be filled with one third of these new angels of heaven; And God the Lord Jesus would also now have a one third section of heaven that was going to be filled with one third of these new angels of heaven; And also God the Holy spirit would now have a one third section of heaven that was going to be filled with one third of these new angels of heaven.

036 Now to help illustrate this that will greatly show you as to how God's heaven was before, during and after God had created the angels of His heaven. I'm going to go back to that graphical outline that I had drawn on a piece of paper earlier. Where I had made this circle with the three sections on a piece of paper so that one section, or one piece of the pie was at the top; and one section or one piece of the pie was down and over to the left of that top section; and one section, or piece of the pie was down and over to the right of that top section: And in that top section of that circle I had put God the Father: And in that section of that circle that was down and over to the left, I had put God the Lord Jesus: And in that section of that circle that was down and over to the right, I had put God the Holy Spirit. This circle on my piece of paper represents the one throne of God; and inside that circle are the three sections of God's throne that represents the three div-

ine, distinct and separate positions of the individual forms or persons of the Godhead: One section for God the Father; and one section for God the Lord Jesus; and one section for God the Holy Spirit. So you see that inside of that circle is God's eternal throne. And outside of that circle is God's entire heavenly kingdom extending out and away, in all directions from His throne forever. This is basically the way that it was before God had rearranged or renovated His heaven to make way for these new angelic beings.

037 So this first step, or this first part where God is now changing, rearranging, or creating His heaven for these new angels of heaven; was to divide and section His heaven into three separate sections of heaven, with all three sections starting at the throne of God and extending out and away from each section of God's throne. So all I did on my graphical outline of the drawing of that circle on a piece of paper was to just extend those lines from inside that circle to outside and away from that circle indefinitely. So that the three sections that were inside that circle had now extended or continued outside of that circle or outside of God's throne; dividing God's one heaven now into three separate individual sections of heaven matching the three sections of God's throne. Inside of that circle is still God's throne and outside of that circle is still God's eternal heaven; but now with three separate individual sections to match or coincide with the three sections of God's throne, with one section belonging to God the Father; and one section belonging to God the Lord Jesus; and one section belonging to God the Holy Spirit. Drawing #1, on page 253, is the graphical outline of God's throne and His heaven that was around His throne that was before God had rearranged or changed His heaven and created the new angels. Drawing #2, on page 254, is another graphical outline of God's throne that is similar to drawing #1, but with the three new separate individual sections of heaven to match or coincide with the three sections of God's throne.

038 Now that God has finished rearranging and dividing His heaven into three separate individual sections; God is now about to start making and creating the first position of power and authority for that first angel and then making and creating that first angel and then placing that new angel into its new position. And like I have stated before that God could have made and created all the different kinds of angels many different ways; but I'm not going to, even try, to cover every way, that God, could of, or might have used. So I have decided to pick only one of the many ways that God might have used to make and create all of the angels of heaven. So I had picked just one of the many ways in which God might have used, but also the best one that fits closest to how this major event pans out with the scriptural events. In other words, God could have started with the making of the archangels first and then progressing down to the least angels or any of the other ways too; But I have chosen to start with God creating the least angels first and progressing up to the archangels.

039 So now God has moved out and over to the area for where this first angel is to be created and positioned. And since there are now three sections in God's heaven, there will be three first angels that will be created and place into their positions of their power and authority all at the same time. In other words, God the Father has moved over to that area that is located in His section of heaven to where His first angel and its position of power and authority is to be created and placed in heaven; and God the Lord Jesus has also moved over to that area that is located in His section of heaven to where His first angel and its position of power and authority is to be created and placed in heaven; and God the Holy Spirit has also moved over to that area that is located in His section of heaven to where His first angel and its position of power and authority is to be created and placed in heaven. So you see that God the Father, and God the Lord Jesus, and God the Holy Spirit, will each be making and creating their first

angel and its position of power and authority, all at the same time and each in their respective sections of heaven. And God has started making and creating the least angels of heaven first; and will progress up from the least angels, to the chief angels, and to the archangels.

040 Now as to the actual number of each type of angel and the total number of angels that God had actually created is really not known at this time. And we will not really know that exact number of angels that were created by God until we get into heaven. But we know that there were a bunch of angels made by God, to a number, that God could put at least one hundred thousand angels on every man, woman, and child that is alive today and also upon every man, woman, and child that has existed all the way back to and including Adam and Eve. I had "guesstimated" that there were at least three hundred trillion angels that were made by God originally. And that number may possibly be too small or too high. But that's the number that I am going to use at this time because the exact number of angels that were made or created by God is not the main focus or point of this book, but the progression of God's timeline to a major event. And now, also, since God, at this time, has started the creation of His new heaven for the new angels of heaven; we are now in Genesis chapter one, and verse one; "In the beginning God (is) creating the heaven and this earth." And at this time, if the bible were written then, that's the only verse that would be written in the whole bible. In other words, if you were to open up a bible at that time, all you would be able to read is Genesis chapter one, and verse one, that's it; there would be no verse two yet because the major event that had happened in heaven that caused verse two to be written has not happened yet.

041 And also at this time there is no darkness anywhere in God's heaven. This dark universe and this earth that we see today did not exist yet: There

was no Satan, there was no demon and evil spirits; no evil, sin, death or darkness, no hell, and mankind did not exist yet. So all of this creation of heaven and the angels of heaven were made and created in the eternal light and eternal life of God Himself. And up to this point in God's timeline of His eternal past, there has never, ever been any disobedience to God in any way, shape, or form that would lead to or result in evil, sin, death and darkness entering into God's heaven. And also, God has always known that any disobedience to His laws and commandments would be an evil act that would result in sin that would lead to eternal death and eternal darkness and separation from Him and His heaven forever. But this has never happened yet in God's heaven and up to this point in God's timeline of His eternal past. And God has never ever seen any evil, sin, death or darkness in His heaven yet and up to this point in the timeline of His eternal past; but God has always known that there was always a slight chance that it could happen. And God cannot ever create or cause any evil, sin, or death to anything or anyone, for it is against His nature.

042 Now God has started to make and create all of the least angels of heaven. And just like it had taken six days to make and create Adam and Eve and their position of power and authority; the least angels may have only taken one day to make and create each of their position of power and authority and then create that least angel and place them into that position. So it may have taken only one day for God to completely make and create the first least angel of heaven. And since it was God the Father, and God the Lord Jesus, and God the Holy Spirit that had each made their first least angel, and in their respective section of heaven, and all at the same time. That means that there were three of the least angels of heaven made and created on that first day of the creation of the new angels of heaven. And then when all of, whatever that number that was to be of all those least angels, were finished being made; God had then move up to a

greater angel with a greater position of power and authority. And this type of angel may have taken two days each to create that position of power and authority and then to create that angel and then to place that angel into that position. And the same number of angels is being made in each section of God's new heaven and at the same time. And then when all of, whatever that number that was to be of all these greater angels, were finished being made; Then again, God had then move up to an even greater angel with an even greater position of power and authority. And this type of angel may have taken three days each to create that position of power and authority and then to create that angel and then to place that angel into that position. And again, the same number of angels is being made in each section of God's new heaven and at the same time. And this is also bringing God back and closer to His throne as all of these new angels are being made and created. And as God was making and creating all of these new angels; these new angels that were already made were now praising and worshipping and singing songs of great joy which might have really tugged at the heart strings of God and may have been one of the main reasons that God wanted to make and create all of these new angels in the first place. Then again, God had then move up to an even greater angel with an even greater position of power and authority. And this type of angel may have taken four days each to create that position of power and authority and then to create that angel and then to place that angel into that position. And again, the same number of angels is being made in each section of God's new heaven and at the same time. And then when all of, whatever that number that was to be of all these greater angels, were finished being made; God had now finished making and creating all of the angels, at this time, from the least angels, to the Chief angels. And at this time in God's timeline of His eternal past; God has only three more but powerful angels that He needs to make and create in order to bring to an end to the creation of all these new angels of heaven. And these are the three main angels or Archangels of heaven that will have the greatest power and authority over all of the other angels of heaven.

043 Up to this point in God's timetable; God had finished making and creating all of the angels of heaven from the chief angels, to the least angels. There are only three more main and powerful angels, called archangels, that God wanted or needed to make and create in order to complete the total number of angels that God had determine or wanted in His heaven. And up to this point, God the Father, God the Lord Jesus, and God the Holy Spirit had each made and created all of the angels and in their respective sections of heaven independently and at the same time. But now, when it had come to the making and creating of these three main archangels, God the Father, God the Lord Jesus, and God the Holy Spirit may have worked together to make and create each archangel. And these archangels may have taken five days each to create that position of power and authority and then to create that archangel and then to place that archangel into that position.

044 Now God may have made and created Archangel Gabriel first. So God the Father, God the Lord Jesus, and God the Holy Spirit had worked together to create that position of great power and great authority for this new Archangel Gabriel. And this position of power and authority was made in the location close to and just outside the throne and section of God the Holy Spirit. And then God the Father, God the Lord Jesus, and God the Holy Spirit had then created that Archangel Gabriel and then they had placed Archangel Gabriel into that position. And then God the Father, God the Lord Jesus, and God the Holy Spirit had again worked together to create that position of great power and great authority for another new Archangel, Michael. And this position of power and authority was made in the location close to and just outside the throne and section of God the

Father. And then God the Father, God the Lord Jesus, and God the Holy Spirit had then created that Archangel Michael and then they had placed Archangel Michael into that position. And then God the Father, God the Lord Jesus, and God the Holy Spirit had again worked together to create that position of great power and great authority for another new Archangel, Lucifer. And this position of power and authority was made in the location close to and just outside the throne and section of God the Lord Jesus. And then God the Father, God the Lord Jesus, and God the Holy Spirit had then created that Archangel Lucifer and then they had placed Archangel Lucifer into that position. And now this completes all of the total number of the angels that were to be made in God's heaven. Another point that I want to make here, is that this earth was made and brought into existence from nothing for the first time and in that section of heaven and throne of God the Lord Jesus as He was making and creating all of those angels and their positions; this earth was one of those positions that was made and angels, at this time, was placed on this earth along with all of the other planets that we now see today in the dark universe. Except that this earth and all of the other planets and this dark universe didn't exist then as we see it today. This whole dark and lifeless universe that we see today was filled with the eternal light, the eternal life and living presences of God Himself; and at this time too it was also now filled with the eternal life of these newly created living angels; and the beauty and the glorious singing, praising and worshiping of all these new angels that must have been a very joyful and glorious occasion.

045 The total guesstimated number of the new angels in each section of God's heaven is one hundred trillion new angels or a grand total of three hundred trillion new angels in God's heaven. Now if you were do a ruff guesstimate of the number of years that it might have taken God to make and create all of these three hundred trillion angels; that would come close

to about or at least five hundred billion plus years. And yet bible teachers and preachers have been telling us that this earth is only about six thousand years old; that is really only about the number years of how long mankind has been on this earth and not the true age of this earth. The age of this earth from it original creation from nothing is over six hundred billion plus six thousand years old. And scientists that claim that this earth is believed to be trillions of years old are close to that correct number. But the earth is approximately six hundred billion years to one trillion years old, biblically, and this is based on the actual number of years and the way that it really had taken God to create all of the angels of heaven. It may had taken about 684,931,506,849.3151 Years to make 300 trillion angels of Heaven. (an educated guesstimation)

046 God had made and created about one hundred trillion different, and ranking angels in each section of heaven, ranking from the greatest power and authority to the least power and authority, from the archangel, to the chief angel, and from the chief angel, to the least angels of heaven. A general description of how God had positioned all His angels ranking from the greatest to the least angels is somewhat like that of a pyramid layout that had an archangel positioned close to and just outside the throne of God of that section of heaven; and close to and under that archangel was the position of power and authority of that archangel's chief angel; and then all of those positions of power and authority of all those angels that were positioned, and by ranking authority, from that chief angel to all of those least angels. And this was the same in all of the three sections of God's heaven.

047 In other words, God's heaven was laid out in such a way so that God's throne is in the center most high position of His heaven forever. And all of God's heavenly kingdom, and with these three new sections and new angels, extends out and away, in all directions from His throne for-

ever. For example; God the Holy Spirit's section of heaven is laid out so that Archangel Gabriel's position of power and authority is placed close to and just outside of the throne of God the Holy Spirit. And directly under Archangel Gabriel's position is the position of power and authority of Archangel Gabriel's Chief Angel; and under Gabriel's Chief Angel is all of the other angels in that section of heaven of God the Holy Spirit, ranking from the greatest angels to the least angels. And God the Father's section of heaven is also laid out so that Archangel Michael's position of power and authority is placed close to, and just outside of, the throne of God the Father. And directly under Archangel Michael's position is the position of power and authority of Archangel Michael's Chief Angel; and under Michael's Chief Angel is all of the other angels in that section of heaven of God the Father, ranking from the greatest angels to the least angels. And God the Lord Jesus's section of heaven is also laid out so that Archangel Lucifer's position of power, and authority, is placed close to and just outside of the throne of God the Lord Jesus. And directly under Archangel Lucifer's position is the position of power and authority of Archangel Lucifer's Chief Angel; and under Lucifer's Chief Angel is all of the other angels in that section of heaven of God the Lord Jesus, ranking from the greatest angels to the least angels. See Drawing #3 on page 255.

048 Each archangel was given charge over all of the angels that were in their section of heaven. In other words, Even though all of those angels that was in that section of heaven of God the Holy Spirit, God the Holy Spirit had given all of His angels in His section of heaven to His Archangel Gabriel. Archangel Gabriel was given total charge and responsibility over all of those angels in that section. In other words, Archangel Gabriel now had one third direct control over the angels of heaven that were directly under His charge. And, also, even though all of those angels that were in that section of heaven of God the Father; God the Father had also given

all of His angels in His section of heaven to His Archangel Michael. Archangel Michael was given total charge and responsibility over all of those angels in that section. In other words, Archangel Michael now had one third direct control over the angels of heaven that were directly under His charge. But also, Archangel Michael was also given charge over Archangel Gabriel; and this had given Archangel Michael a greater power and authority, over two thirds of all the angels of heaven; one third direct control over the angels of heaven that were directly under His charge and another one third indirect control over the angels of heaven because of his charge and authority over Archangel Gabriel and all of his angels that were under his charge. And, also, even though all of those angels that were in that section of heaven of God the Lord Jesus, God the Lord Jesus had also given all of His angels in His section of heaven to His Archangel Lucifer. Archangel Lucifer was given total charge and responsibility over all of those angels in that section of heaven. In other words, Archangel Lucifer now had one third direct control over the angels of heaven that was directly under His charge. But also, Archangel Lucifer was also given charge over Archangel Michael and Archangel Gabriel; and this had given Archangel Lucifer the greatest power and authority, over all of the angels of heaven; one third direct control over the angels of heaven that was directly under His charge and another two thirds indirect control over the angels of heaven because of his charge and authority over Archangel Michael and Archangel Gabriel and all of their angels that were under both Michael's and Gabriel's charge. And you might have seen that this may have been a way in which God might have used as a common way for a chain of command.

049 Even though it might have only taken about thirty seconds to a minute to actually write verse one of Genesis chapter one; "In the beginning God had created the heaven and the earth." The actual real time that it might

have taken God to actually perform this monumental task as generally stated in Genesis chapter one, verse one, might have been approximately five hundred billion years to one trillion years to start and finish verse one! Actually this verse, has been for years, been really overlooked by bible scholars, teachers, and preachers, etc. as to the correct time and value and the power that it had taken to accomplish this tremendous task to fulfill that True statement of Genesis chapter one, verse one. And since God had completed His monumental task of the creation of all of the angels of His heavenly kingdom, so is the completion of Genesis chapter one, and verse one. And God the Father, and God the Lord Jesus, and God the Holy Spirit had now rested or retired from the making and creating of all His new angels and His new heaven, and now He had set back and enjoyed the fruits of His labor. And it must have been a tremendously joyful and glorious occasion that might have carried on or lasted from several years to several hundreds of years, or even several thousand years: and you might have also seen that this is still adding more time, to the actual existence, and age of this earth that any and all wild guesses as to the actual age of this earth can only and will only be taimed when we see that actual age of this earth when we get to heaven. But until then, all we have is these wild guesstimations, that can only give an idea as to the existence and age of this earth that we are on today.

050 There was a certain amount of time that had existed in heaven after God had completed His creating of all of the angels and His heaven. It may have been at least several years, but it very well might have been several hundreds of years to several thousand years of time between God's completion of the angels of heaven and the time of this major event in God's heaven. Genesis chapter one, verse two has not been written yet, but at this point of time in God's eternal timeline, verse two is a dark shadow on the horizon of God's timeline of His eternal future. So now we

are at this timeline between Genesis chapter one, verse one, and Genesis chapter one, verse two. Genesis chapter one and verse one is, and at this point in God's eternal timeline of His eternal existence, is now an accomplished and completed task that is now written down in the pages of God's timeline of His eternal past. And although there was a certain amount of time that was between verse one and verse two of Genesis chapter one; this actual amount of time is not known to us at this time. But there was a certain amount of time that had existed in heaven where God and all of His angels had walked and talked with God and God had walked and talked with all of his angels in heaven, in perfect harmony and complete fellowship.

051 And all of the angels in heaven, and at this point in time, still had the total righteousness that God had made them with. And every angel was in total obedience to God and all of His laws and commandments. And up to this point in God's eternal timeline of His eternal existence, there has never, ever been any disobedience to His laws and commandments; There has never, ever been any evil, sin, death, or darkness anywhere in God's heaven yet. And as I have stated earlier that God cannot make or create anything or any creature or being with any evil, sin, death, or darkness. It is against the very nature of God and it would be impossible for God to do: For obedience to God's laws and commandments is counted as righteousness and the gift of this righteousness is eternal life in the eternal light of God. And this is the very reason that God cannot be tempted or create any evil, sin, death, and darkness; For God is obedience; God is His laws; God is righteousness; God is eternal life; God is eternal light, etc. Disobedience to God's laws and commandments is an evil act that is sin, and the wages of sin is death, and this death is an eternal death, and where there is death there is darkness, and since this death is an eternal death, this darkness is an eternal darkness. God will not dwell where there is sin; it

will be remove from Him and His heaven. All sin will be cast into a pit of eternal death and eternal darkness outside of God's eternal heaven, if that would ever happen in His heavenly kingdom.

052 There were many ways that God could have, or might have used to communicate with all of these approximately three hundred trillion angels of heaven. One way that God may have used to get His message to all of His angels in His heaven, was to speak to all of the angels of heaven at the same time. And although there were many other ways to which God may have communicated with all of his angels of His heaven; there was one main chain of command that God may have used most often. And this main chain of command may have went something like this: God would have a message that He wanted all of His angels of heaven to get or hear; so that message would be told by God to High Archangel Lucifer; and then Lucifer would then turn and tell that same message to his Chief Angel; and then Lucifer's Chief Angel would then turn and tell that same message to the angel or angels under his charge and so on and so on, "dominoing" all the way down to Lucifer's least angels: And then Archangel Lucifer would also turn and tell that same message to High Archangel Michael; and then Michael would then turn tell that same message to his Chief Angel; and then Michael's Chief Angel would then turn and tell that same message to the angel, or angels, under his charge and so on and so on, "dominoing" all the way down to Michael's least angels: And then Archangel Michael would also turn and tell that same message to High Archangel Gabriel; and then Gabriel, would then turn tell that same message to his Chief Angel: and then Gabriel's Chief Angel would then turn and tell that same message to the angel or angels under his charge and so on and so on, "dominoing" all the way down to Gabriel's least angels. This was something like that "telephone game", or test, where a teacher in a classroom would whisper a short message to the first student; and then that student

would turn and tell that same message to the student behind him and so on, and so on, until the last student would then repeat that message aloud to see if it was the same message that the teacher had started with; and ninety nine percent of the time it would be a totally different message from what the teacher had started with; But in heaven this message that God had started with is the same message exactly all the way through to the least angels and without any errors or mistakes or changes to that original message.

053 Basically, the main chain, or flow, or the position of power and authority in God's heaven, is first, God's throne, that has been in the center most high position of His heaven forever. And there is no greater position of power and complete, unanimous, righteous authority than God's Glorious Throne. The next greatest position of power and authority is Archangel Lucifer's position. Lucifer had complete power and authority over all of the angels of heaven, including, Archangels Michael, and Gabriel. In other words, Lucifer had control over all of the angels of heaven, one third direct control over the angels of heaven, that were directly under his charge; and two thirds indirect control, of the angels of heaven, because of his charge and authority over Archangels Michael and Gabriel and each of their angels. Also, Archangel Lucifer was the only angel that had the closest position to the throne of God that he was able to see a lot of the daily activity of God's throne and he also had the authority to walk amongst the stones of fire of God that was in God's throne, that most or all of the other angels didn't ever see, including Archangels Michael and Gabriel. And the next greatest position of power and authority is Archangel Michael's position. Michael had complete power and authority over two thirds of the angels of heaven including Archangel Gabriel. In other words, Michael had two thirds control over all of the angels of heaven, one third direct control over the angels of heaven that were directly under his charge and one

third indirect control of the angels of heaven because of his charge and authority over Archangel Gabriel and his angels. And the next greatest position of power and authority is Archangel Gabriel's position. Gabriel had complete power and authority over one third of the angels of heaven or one third direct control over the angels of heaven that were directly under his charge. And the next greatest position of power and authority is the three Chief angels that are positioned just one each under each archangel. So Archangel Lucifer had his Chief Angel directly under his position. And Archangel Michael had his Chief Angel directly under his position. And Archangel Gabriel had his Chief Angel directly under his position. And the rest of the angels in each section of heaven were positioned from their greatest position of power and authority from the chief angel to the least angel's position of power and authority.

054 Now you can see, or you are now able to get a better idea and a clearer understanding of how God might have created His new heaven and His new angels of heaven and how He might have laid out all the positions of power and authority ranking from God's throne, being the greatest position of power and authority, and all the way down to the least position of power and authority. And remember that God had created all of these angels with the total perfection and righteousness that God is. And because God doesn't just do things perfect; God is Perfection and that is why He can only do anything and everything in total perfection and without any mistakes or errors! It is impossible for God to make any mistakes or errors! So every angel that God had made was made in the total perfection and the total righteousness of God Himself. And also remember that I had stated earlier that God had made all of these angels with a free will of their own and that God did not make any of these angels as preprogrammed robotic angels, but were made with a free will of their own to freely choose to do or say anything that they so desired to do or say. In other

words, each angel could choose to obey or to disobey God; or to love or to hate God; or to accept or to reject God, etc. And although God had known that any angel or angels could reject and disobey him at any given moment, God may have thought that, why would any of these angels want to reject His perfect Love and everlasting life!

055 Also, God's heavenly kingdom is a spiritual place and existence; for as stated in the scriptures of the bible, all of the things that you can see with your physical eyes is temporary and the things that you cannot see with your physical eyes is forever. So you see that this earth and universe that we can see today is a temporary physical existence and did not exist anywhere in God spiritual heavenly kingdom at that time in heaven. For God's heavenly kingdom is not a physical place or existence but a complete spiritual place and existence; and there are no physical flesh and blood bodies in heaven; all of the angels that were made, were made with a celestial, spiritual type heavenly body and in this spiritual and eternal state of God's eternal heaven. And I have also stated earlier, that even though God had always known, and this may have been at the back of His mind most of the time, that disobedience and sin could enter into his heavenly kingdom, But up to this point in God's eternal timeline of His eternal existence God has never, ever seen it happen and He has never, ever had to deal with any disobedience and sin. But this is about to change and happen for the first time in all of God's eternal existence.

056 But now God had still walked with all of His angels in perfect harmony and close fellowship and perfect peace. And Archangel Lucifer was the only angel with the greatest and the highest position of power and authority above all the other angels of heaven. And as I have stated earlier, Lucifer had control over all of the angels of heaven, one third direct control over the angels of heaven that were directly under his charge, and two thirds

indirect control of the angels of heaven because of his charge and authority over Archangels Michael and Gabriel and each of their angels. Also, Archangel Lucifer was the only angel that had the closest position to the throne of God; For Lucifer was the anointed cherub that covereth the throne of God. And he was able to see a lot of the daily activity of God's throne that most or all of the other angels didn't ever see, including Archangels Michael and Gabriel. Lucifer was able, or was allowed to walk in and around and through certain parts of God's eternal throne that most or all of the other angels didn't have that authority or privilege. Lucifer walked upon the holy mountain of God. He was able and allowed to walk up and down in the midst of the stones of fire that were only located inside of God's throne. Lucifer was that most beautiful and extremely intelligent angel that God has made at this time. For every precious stone was thy covering, the Sardius, topaz, and the diamond, the beryl, the onyx, and the jasper, the sapphire, the emerald, and the carbuncle, and gold: the workmanship of thy tabrets, and of thy pipes was prepared in thee in the day that thou was created. He was the morning star and had the power over the light of heaven. He was also the choir master and had control over all of the music, melodies and singing of heaven. The only position that had greater power and authority than Archangel Lucifer's position was that position and that power of the greatest authority of heaven, was God's throne! (Ding! Ding! Ding!)

057 In other words, Lucifer was in and around God's throne on a daily basis that he was able to see the power of God in action and up close. Now even though God is no respecter of persons and He loves and cares for everyone, every angel or being all the same. But also God did not make every angel with the same position of power and authority. But God does fellowship with each of His angels differently and based on their position and of their power and of their authority that He had delegated to

them and made them with. And since Archangel Lucifer's position of power and authority was the most highest angelic position in heaven, he had the most responsibilities that came with that position that may have demanded more attention from God the Father, and God the Lord Jesus, and God the Holy Spirit: And may have been part of Lucifer's requirements that may have demanded the most or constant fellowship and attentions from God on a continuing basis; for where much is given, much is required.

058 And also, since Lucifer was up close to and around God's throne on a daily basis, he was able to see and watch or witness the constant and continuing worshipping and praising of all the angels of heaven to God the Father, and to God the Lord Jesus and to God the Holy Spirit as they would pass through and around God's throne on a daily basis. And some of the responsibilities of Lucifer were to administer and control all of the music, melodies and songs of heaven. And some of the music and melodies, and songs of praise and worship were created and administered to give special attention to Glorify, praise and worship to God the Father; and then to Glorify, praise and worship to God the Lord Jesus; and then to Glorify, praise and worship to God the Holy Spirit.

059 So you can now see that Archangel Lucifer may have developed a real close relationship to God the Father, and God the Lord Jesus and to God the Holy Spirit that he really might have thought that he had come to really know all that there was to know and understand about God and His existence. In other words, Lucifer may have developed a real close relationship and fellowship and independently with God the Father; and independently with God the Lord Jesus; and independently with God the Holy Spirit; that he might have come to a conclusion in his own heart and mind that he had really come to know and understand all that there was to know

about God's nature, and as to the way God performs and operates His responsibilities as the One and True living Godhead. And at first this was not a bad thing, from the time of Lucifer's perfect and righteous creation and up to a certain time span Lucifer and God had walked and talked and fellowshipped in perfect harmony and peace. But this is about to change and will unfold or start a major event in God's heaven for the first time!

060 So you see that Lucifer was the most beautiful and brightest angel of heaven; and the most intelligent or the smartest angel of heaven; and the highest angel with the greatest angelic position of power and authority in heaven and with the closest position to God's throne, that was that position that was close to God the Lord Jesus's throne and section of heaven. Lucifer was up close to and around God's throne on a daily basis that he was able to see and watch or witness the constant and continuing praising and worshipping by all the angels of heaven to God as they would pass through and around God's throne on a daily basis. It may have come to the point in Lucifer's heart that the brightness of his own beauty may have blurred his vision to the true vision of the truth that he was created with. And the extremely vast and high intelligence and knowledge may have puffed up his head bigger to the point that it may have also blocked some of the true and wise understandings in his heart; And the vast power and authority of his angelic position may have broadened all his vision and the thinking in his heart beyond the reach and a breach of the boundaries of Lucifer's Archangelic position of power and its high Archangelic authority that was delegated to him by God at the time of his creation.

061 In other words, and for whatever reasons that may have instigated this type of thinking, Lucifer's vision and thinking was looking into areas in his own heart as to the power and authority of God's position as God. And for a while, as Lucifer would watch all of the angels of heaven coming up

to God the Father, and then to God the Lord Jesus, and then to God the Holy Spirit and each person of the Godhead would be getting a constant and continuing flow of the angels of heaven that would be glorifying, praising and worshipping each person of the Godhead as they would flow by. And this type of adoration, glorifying, praising and worshipping to God by all of the angels of heaven was getting Lucifer's closer attention, but in a negative and jealous way. In other words, Lucifer may have at this time started to become jealous of the position and the power of God and His throne. He may have started to think in his heart that it might be possible that he could be worshipped by all of these angels of heaven instead of God. And this may have been the point of no return; and this type of thinking was about to get even worse than just thinking about it. For by this time in Lucifer's heart, he may have been thinking that, "if I could find a way to remove God from His throne, then I could ascend into heaven and exalt my own throne above the stars of God and then I would be able sit also upon the mount of the congregation, in the sides of the north and then I would ascend above the heights of the clouds; and then I would be like the most High God and then I would have all of the angels of heaven worshipping me as their god instead of the true and living God!", or so he had thought in his heart that it might be possible. But this would turn out to be a grave and deadly decision.

062 Lucifer's heart was now lifted up because of his beauty, and he had corrupted his wisdom by reason of his brightness. In other words, Lucifer was at that time the most beautiful and power angel in heaven; he may have started to think and imagine in his heart or in kind of a conceited way, that his beauty was greater than God's appearance. And the great intelligence, knowledge, wisdom, and understanding that God had made him with, has now become corrupt by the reason of the brightness of his intelligence, overshadowed with evil; for his intelligent thinking was being re-

placed with ignorant thinking; and the knowledge of God's Truth, that God had made him with, was being replaced with the darkness of lies; and the wisdom, that God had also made him with, was now also being replaced with stupidity; and God's total understanding, that God had also made him with, was now being replaced with total misunderstanding or dark understanding. For you see, if Lucifer had used this great intelligence, knowledge, wisdom, and understanding, that God had made him with, correctly; he would have never even attempted such thinking, let alone taking any action to this evil thinking. But the thinking in Lucifer's heart was that he must have really thought that there was a real possibility that God the Father, and God the Lord Jesus, and God the Holy Spirit could be destroyed and removed from His Throne so that he could then take or claim that throne as his own. But Lucifer did not really know all that there was to know about the True and Living God like he had though he did.

063 And as I have stated earlier that the main part of the attributes of God that I want to focus your attention on is that God will never die, and He cannot be destroyed. Now this main part of the attributes of God is that God WILL NEVER DIE! And God CANNOT BE DESTROYED! And, also, God is a part of His Throne and His Throne is a part of Him. In other words, God can never be separated from His Throne and God's Throne can never be separated from Him. So you can now kind-a-see that Lucifer, in all truth and honesty, really did not know God and His eternal existence and power at all; for if he had really known, that it was an impossibility for God to even die, let alone be destroyed, he would have rejected any thinking of or trying to remove and destroy God from His Throne. And another point that I would like to make on God's eternal existence is; and even though it is a total impossibility for God to be removed from His Throne, and just to show you how ludicrous, stupid, and ignorant Lucifer's thinking and decision of trying to remove God from His Throne was, and if it were

possible that Lucifer would have remove God from His Throne, that would have backfired on Lucifer, since everything exists because of God's existence and His perfect order, and if God could be removed and destroyed from his Throne; and since everything was made and exists by God including His heaven and all of the angels of His heaven, and this would include Lucifer too; God would be destroyed along with His Throne, and along with His heaven, and along with all of the angels of heaven, including Lucifer and His evil idea of taking God's Throne which would have still left him not only without a throne but he would cease to exist too. But Thanks be to God, that He will never die, and cannot be destroyed, or removed from His Throne!

064 Now as Lucifer is thinking all of this in his heart as to his planning and scheming a way of how he can overthrow and take God's Throne; He's thinking that God the Father, God the Lord Jesus, and God the Holy Spirit doesn't know as to what he is planning and scheming in his heart; And at this time none of the other angels of heaven had not known anything about Lucifer's intentions or evil plans yet. So as far as Lucifer was concerned about his evils intentions, he was the only one that had any knowledge of it yet and he had thought that it was a deep and well hidden secret deep down in his own heart hidden away from God and all of the other angels of heaven. But this type of thinking would prove to be another blind corner in the heart of Lucifer as to his understanding and the real knowledge of who God really is. For this type of Lucifer's thinking was foolish thinking; for there is nothing that is hidden from the eyes of God! There is nothing that God cannot see. God is all seeing. He knows what you are going to think in your heart before you even think it; for as a man thinketh in his heart, so is he. So you see, that even though Lucifer had thought in his own heart that he was the only one that had any knowledge of his evil intentions; God had already seen this evil intentions of Lucifer start and

develop in his heart way before Lucifer had had any knowledge of it himself. And even though God had seen this evil and sin start and develop in the heart of Lucifer, God did not let Lucifer know that he had also known about these evil and sinful intentions of Lucifer.

065 And also, this is the first time in all of God's eternal existence, and up to this point in God's timeline, there has never ever been any evil and sin in His heaven. And even though God has always known that there was always this slight chance that evil, disobedience, and sin could enter into His heavenly kingdom, He has never seen it or has never had to deal with it, until now. So the evil intentions, disobedience, and the sin that has now entered into Lucifer's heart, is the first time that God is actually seeing it happen in His heaven. And God does not like what He's seeing taken place. And even though God is a God of Love, He is also the God of perfect justice; in no wise can He clear the guilty. This sin will have to be removed and expelled from His heaven. This may have been the time in God's heaven that God the Father is about to create hell outside of the eternal existence of His heavenly kingdom for the first time. God could have already removed or expelled Lucifer from heaven, by this time, because of his sin that he had already committed in his heart; but there may have been several other reasons that God may have kept Lucifer in place, at this time temporarily, and let him continue on his own thinking, but with the ever seeing eye of God watching him very closely; to kind-of-see and watch how this sinful nature of Lucifer plays out; for you see that at this time Lucifer has only just been thinking about his evil intentions in his heart and has not yet taken any action on his own to accomplish his evil desires. And another reason that God didn't remove Lucifer and his sin yet; is that even though any disobedience to God's law is sin, and the wages of that sin is death, there is also a certain amount of time allowed to that sin to fulfill another part of God's law that there is pleasure in that sin

for a season.

066 Now Lucifer has been festering with the evil intentions in his heart, as to his lustful and evil desire of wanting the power and position of God's throne, for a short amount of time; but this desire was getting to strong to resist. And he might have thought in his heart that this task was too much of a negative risk to attempt or to try to accomplish on his own or by himself. Lucifer might have come up with what he might have thought was a brilliant and ingenious plan as to how he would attempt to over throw God the Father and God the Lord Jesus and God the Holy Spirit and His throne. And he might have actually thought that this plan was a "fool proof" plan that would never fail; but this so called "fool proof" plan of Lucifer would only prove to make him an eternal fool! For Lucifer had thought that if he could get most of or all of the angels of heaven that were directly under his charge to take his side and view of his rebellion against God and to help him overthrow God and his throne; that this would become a real possible reality of Lucifer becoming a god of heaven and over all of the angels of heaven. But by now you are beginning to see that Lucifer's great and high intelligence has been corrupted by his blind misunderstanding to the true wisdom of God and His everlasting existence.

067 But now Lucifer had started to put his evil plan into action. For he had thought that if he could get all of the angels that was in his section of heaven, that he had direct control over, to put their trust in him instead of God and to help him overthrow and remove God from His throne and that by helping him overthrow and remove God from His throne Lucifer would promise them a higher position of power and authority. So in order for Lucifer to achieve this enormous task of trying to get or convince all of these angels that was under his charge, or control, to cross over to his side and follow his plans and intentions for a new heaven and a new throne and a

new god; Lucifer had to use lying deception to trick them, he had used empty promises, without any certainty or any way to fulfill any of these promises; because God's heaven was still God's heaven at this time.

068 And one of the main promises that he had use most often on all of these angels was that they each would be given a greater position of power and authority. For example, Lucifer may have promised his position of power and authority of the highest Archangelic position in heaven to his chief angel, that was that position that was just below Lucifer's position. In other words, Lucifer may have offered his highest angelic position of heaven to his Chief angel as enticement to get him to go along with his evil and rebellious plan to over throw God and his throne. Lucifer may have told his Chief angel that if you help me remove God from his throne and heaven, so that I can make it my throne and heaven; then you could have my position as the highest and the most powerful angelic position of heaven and ruling over all of the other angels of heaven. And to Lucifer's chief angel, that had to be a tremendous and tempting offer to be able to go from being just a chief angel in only just one section of heaven to being promoted up to the most powerful angelic position over all of the other angels of heaven; or to go from being just a chief angel in heaven to the most powerful Archangel of heaven was possibly an extremely tempting offer, that this was a too good to be true, offer, and was possibly portrayed by Lucifer, as an offer, that his chief angel could not refuse! And the sad point, to this is that Lucifer's chief angel ended up going along with Lucifer and his offer and evil plan. And each angel that was under Lucifer's charge and control were given similar or like offers to entice all of them to cross over to Lucifer's evil plan and intentions to help him rebel against the True and living God. And another sad point is that Lucifer did not have that kind or that much power to be able to offer any position of heaven in heaven to anyone; for it was God's heaven, and all positions in His heaven is given

and appointed by God for His perfect purpose.

069 So now, not only has Lucifer sinned against the true and living God of heaven; but he has now and was beginning to turn all of the angels under his charge and control to turn against God through lies and deception causing each of these angels to also sin against God; which God's law would then demand death to that sin and to each angel that sinned against God; for God's law states that the wages of sin is death; and this is where Lucifer has now become, not only the source of all sin and the father of it, but he has now become the very first murder of all time! For Lucifer was made perfect at the time of his creation by God; But when Lucifer had sinned, he was not tempted into sin by anyone but he had entered into his sin on his own, thereby committing eternal suicide. And then Lucifer had tempted all of the angels that were under his charge and control, into sinning against God through lies and deception, thereby committing mass murder to one third of all the angels of heaven. And this had to break the heart of God the Father. and God the Lord Jesus. and God the Holy Spirit for the first time in all of God's eternal existence. For God had made and created all of these angels in His perfect love and perfect righteousness and they were all made as free moral agents or they were made with a free will to choose to accept or to reject God; to love or to hate God; to obey or to disobey God etc.; and since they were made with a free will, and even though God had known that they could reject or disobey Him, God really did not expect that any of them would actually choose to reject or to disobey Him; for why would any of them want to reject His perfect Love and all that God is!

070 But Lucifer had used his evil intelligence and crafty wisdom against all of these angels that was directly under his charge and control to the point that every one of those angels had chosen or crossed over to follow Luci-

fer and not the true and living God. In other words, all of these angels that were under Lucifer's charge and control should have walked by faith and trusted and believed in God the Father, and God the Lord Jesus, and God the Holy Spirit instead of even listening to Lucifer's speech or talk that was against the true and living Godhead. Regardless of anything that Lucifer was saying or promising to them, they should have immediately rejected it and trusted in the true and living God; but not one of them trusted in the true and living Godhead; for Lucifer had deceived all of those angels that were under his charge and control or one third of the angels of heaven had turned away from the true and living Godhead to put their trust and blind faith to follow Lucifer's evil and lustful intentions and plan to overthrow the true and living Godhead and His throne. And remember, while Lucifer is deceiving all of these angels of heaven that was under his control and section of heaven, Lucifer is still thinking in his heart that the Godhead still doesn't know or see what he's doing; or he thinks that God does not know or see him going from angel to angel and deceiving them and pulling them into sin against God. And Lucifer is also kind-of doing all of this deception of and to these angels in a secret or hidden campaign, and going from angel to angel, and then he might have told them to keep this a secret from all of the other angels that were under Michael and Gabriel's sections of heaven and control for a certain amount of time so as to prepare all of his angels for a surprise attack against the true and living God.

071 Now, and as I have said before, that there was an estimation of approximately three hundred trillion angels in heaven, or one hundred trillion angels in each section of heaven, totaling approximately three hundred trillion angels in God's heaven. So now in order for Lucifer to be able to deceive, convince, or sway approximately one hundred trillion of the angels of heaven over to his side of the rebellion against God, that would have taken a considerable amount of time to accomplish this secret campaign.

For example, if Lucifer would have converted one thousand angels over to his campaign against God on average per day; it would have taken him at least approximately 273,972,603 years to do this; and that is if Lucifer had went to each of those angels individually and on a one to one basis; Which would have been too long of a secret campaign to risk and keep hidden from the rest of heaven. But I think Lucifer may have used a much faster way to expedite his campaign so he can get started on the main exercise of his secret rebellion against, and the secret and surprise attack on God. So Lucifer may have converted some of the angels that was close to or near his position; and then he may have sent each of those converted angels out to convert other angels; and then those angels were also sent out to convert other angels and so on, and so on, until it domino effected to all of the angels of that section of heaven of Lucifer. And also Lucifer was still converting other angels too and then sending them out to do the same all at the same time. By doing it this way may have reduced the time frame down to a considerably narrow time of approximately ten to one hundred years. And all of this is still being done or accomplished in a type of a secret or hidden campaign against the Godhead. In other words, although Lucifer and his angels were all being engulfed into this secret campaign of Lucifer's; they were all still moving about in their daily routine as though there was nothing going on secretly; but yet they were having secret meetings that were hidden into their daily routines of heaven. So as far as Lucifer and his angels were concerned; none of the other angels that were under Archangel Michael's and Archangel Gabriel's sections of heaven had any knowledge of this hidden, and secret, campaign of Lucifer's evil intentions and rebellion against the Godhead. And Lucifer had still believed that the Godhead also didn't have any knowledge of his hidden and secret plan of attack on the Godhead.

072 But God has been seeing and watching all of this take place before

the ever and all seeing eye of God the Father, and God the Lord Jesus, and God the Holy Spirit! And also while Lucifer has been secretly working his evil campaign against the Godhead; God the Father has now already created the eternal and dark pits of death and Hell outside of His eternal heaven for the first time! And this is also being done in the secrecy of the Godhead without any of this knowledge being made known to the angels of heaven; and this would include Lucifer and his now fallen and rebellious angels. And about this time, and without Lucifer and his angel's knowledge, and also during Lucifer so called secret and hidden campaign, God the Father has called for a secret meeting between Archangels Michael and Gabriel. For you see that God is also preparing for a secret counter attack against Lucifer and all of his evil angels. In this secret meeting with God the Father, and God the Lord Jesus, and God the Holy Spirit and both Archangels Michael, and Gabriel, God the Father has given instructions to Archangel Michael to go and gather a certain amount of your most powerful angels from your section of heaven, and then you are to place them along your section of heaven where it is close to the section of Lucifer's heaven. And Michael was also instructed to place his angels in hidden points along that whole section of his heaven where it meets Lucifer's section of his heaven. And God the Father had told Michael to keep his angels hidden along the border of his section of heaven and close to Lucifer's border and section of heaven until I give you a certain command. And when you hear my command, then you and all of your angels that are along your border and section of heaven are to come out of your hiding places and fight against Lucifer and all of his angels and keep them out of your section of heaven and contain them or keep them in Lucifer's section of his heaven. And God the Father has also given the same instructions to Archangel Gabriel to go and do the same thing to his border and section of heaven where it meets Lucifer's border and section of heaven.

073 So now God has placed a gauntlet of fighting angels along both borders of Lucifer's section of his heaven; therefore trapping him and all of his now evil angels in that section of heaven. And as Lucifer and his evil angels are finishing up their converting all of the angels to cross over and follow his evil plan of attack against the Godhead, not knowing that there are now fighting angels of Archangel Michael poised and hidden along his border and section of heaven ready to attack at the command of God the Father; and, also, there are now fighting angels of Archangel Gabriel, poised, and hidden along his border and section of heaven ready to attack at the command of God the Father. So now Lucifer and all of his angels is really now contained or trapped in his section of heaven and will not be able to enter any part of Michael's or Gabriel's section of heaven. For God the Father is not going to allow or let any of Lucifer and his evil angel's sin enter into any other part of His righteous heaven. For God the Father has now contained all of that sin of Lucifer and all of his angels to remain in Lucifer's section of heaven. God didn't want any of Lucifer and his angel's sin to contaminate any other part of His heaven.

074 Now Lucifer has finished converting all of the angels in his section of heaven to trust and follow him in this secret evil plan to attack the Godhead, but is totally oblivious to the surprise counter attack that God has already put in place; for Lucifer still thinks that God doesn't know about his secret plan of attack. For you see that Lucifer thinks that the element of a surprise attack will work to his advantage. And now that he has a vast secret army of one hundred trillion fighting angels on his side and for his purpose and campaign, his plan of attack is about to be played out, or so he thinks. Lucifer's secret and surprise plan of attack is to move up to and as close to God's throne as possible and then attack and destroy God and remove him from His throne quickly before God even has a chance for a counter attack. And Lucifer may have thought in his heart that if he would

attack and destroy God the Father first and then the attack and destruction of God the Lord Jesus and God the Holy Spirit would be easier to finish off the Godhead. So now Lucifer's main and initial plan of a first strike surprise attack was to move secretly over to God the Father and attack him and His position first, and then to move to and attack both God the Lord Jesus and God the Holy Spirit at the same time. But in order for Lucifer and his angels to move over to the throne of God the Father, they would have to move from Lucifer's section of heaven and into Archangel Michael's section of heaven and then they would have to move up to and past Archangel Michael's position to get to God the Father's position and without bringing or causing any attention to this mass movement in order to then attack their first strike surprise attack. But this movement of Lucifer and his army of fighting angels will never even get out of his section of heaven. For the element of surprise will be to Lucifer and all of his fighting angels and not God.

075 So now God has been watching Lucifer and his angels getting ready to play out Lucifer's plan of attack. And this is why God has placed a gauntlet of fighting angels to both sides of Lucifer's section of heaven. For God was ready for all three ways for witch Lucifer could carry out his plan of attack. One way was for Lucifer and his fighting angels to move into and through Archangel Gabriel's section of heaven; or another way was for Lucifer and his fighting angels to move into and through Archangel Michael's section of heaven; and another way was for Lucifer and his fighting angels was to move into and through Archangel Michael's and Gabriel's sections of heaven at the same time trying to surround God's throne. But Lucifer's plan of attack was to move into and through Michael's section of heaven first in order to get to God the Father and His throne first.

076 So now as Lucifer and his fighting angels actually start their move-

ment from Lucifer's section of heaven toward Michael's section of heaven; everything at first seems to be going as planned; And since Lucifer and his angels are only moving toward Michael's section of heaven and there was no movement of Lucifer and his angels toward Gabriel's section of heaven at this time, But Gabriel and his angels were still poised and ready for any command of attack from God the Father. But now as Lucifer and his fighting angels move close to the border of his section of heaven, a powerful shout, possibly like that of a trumpet blast, and the command is given to Archangel Michael and His angels from God the Father; And much to the surprise of Lucifer and his fighting angels; they were caught off guard as Michael and his angels bolted out of their hiding places with the fierce fighting power and authority of God; And there was now war in heaven for the first time: Michael and his angels fought against Lucifer and his angels; and Lucifer and his angels fought against Michael and his angels, And Lucifer and his angels prevailed not; neither was there any place found for them any more in heaven.

077 And even though Gabriel and his fighting angels were poised and ready to fight along his section of heaven and at the border of Lucifer's section of heaven, Gabriel and his angels did not have to do any fighting, for Lucifer was now "hell bent" on trying to still go into and through Michael's section of heaven; But at that same time that God the Father had given that command to come out of his hiding places and fight, to Michael and his angels; a similar command was also given to Gabriel and his angels to come out of their hiding places also, but to stand guard at that border and along that section of Lucifer's heaven to keep all of Lucifer and his angels in his section as kind of a backup plan in case Lucifer and His angels would try to retreat from Michael's section of heaven and then try to go through Gabriel's section of heaven. But all of the fighting and the battle of Lucifer and his angels, and Michael and his angels, ended up taking

place, only, along Michael's and Lucifer's border and their sections of heaven.

078 And by this time Lucifer is really peeved off with a fierce evil anger, because he had thought that he was going to instigate a surprise attack on God the Father and His throne first, but the surprise attack was instigated on him and his angels by God first, and in his section of heaven. For you see that this battle between Michael and his angels and Lucifer and his angels was actually fought inside Lucifer's section of heaven. Lucifer and his angels was never able to cross over into Michael's section of heaven; they were not even aloud to place one foot across over and into Michael's section of heaven. And as this battle was taking place, Lucifer's army of fighting angels was getting smaller and smaller. And he was still stuck in his own section of heaven, and his whole plan is going up in smoke! And by now Lucifer is beginning to see that he really did not know as much as he thought he had known about God and His existence and power. For Lucifer and his fighting angels, this battle ended up being a suicide mission. As Michael and his angels were fighting against Lucifer and his angels, Lucifer's angels were getting the eternal life of God thrust out of them and a good portion of Lucifer's angels were immediately being cast into this new eternal place of death and hell. For the scriptures has stated that these angels of Lucifer which kept not their first estate, but they had left their own habitation and position of power and authority that God had placed them in, God has now reserved in everlasting chains under darkness unto the great day of the judgment. And another point that I want to point out is that even though all of Lucifer and his angels were fighting against Michael and all of his angels, none of Lucifer and his angels did any damage to any of Michael or his angels; there were no death or casualties of any kind to Michael and his angels; It was a total loss for Lucifer and all of his angels and a total victory for all of God and all of the other two thirds

angels of heaven.

079 And as this great battle that is being fought between Michael and his angels and Lucifer and his angels; all of Lucifer's angels have now become demons and evil spirits. A certain amount or portion of Lucifer's angels, that have now become demons and evil spirits, have already been cast into this new eternal place or the eternal pits of death and hell. In other words, a certain number or amount of Lucifer's angels that were close to him and down to a certain level were changed into demons as God had removed his eternal life and presents from them changing them from beautiful angels into hideous looking demons; And the rest of Lucifer's angels were changed into evil spirits as God had removed his eternal life and presents from them also and changing them too from their beautiful angelic appearance into their now hideous looking evil spirits. And as God had also remove his eternal life and presents from Lucifer; changing him from the most beautiful, and glorious archangel, ever made by God at the time of his creation, into the most hideous and repulsive looking creature, that anyone would only narrowly glance at his appearance quickly; and since in heaven he had the power over all of the light of heaven and was also the brightest shinning angel of heaven and was also called the morning star; he is now referred by God as that great dragon, that old serpent, called the Devil, and Satan, and is now called the prince of eternal darkness, and since he is the source of all lies he is also referred to as the father of lies. And God did not cast all of Lucifer and his angels into this new eternal pit of death and hell yet at this time for a reason.

080 When God had created and made all of the angels of heaven; they were made as free moral agents with a free will of choice to either, obey, or to disobey God, to love or to hate God, to accept or to reject God, etc.; And they were also made in the eternal state of God's heaven with spirit-

ual and celestial type heavenly bodies. They did not have these flesh and blood bodies like we have today, for there was no physical realm like this earth and universe that we have today. And when all of Lucifer and his angels had sinned in that eternal state of God's heaven, and since they already had the eternal life of God in them, they had fallen from eternal life and sinless righteousness, in God's heaven, to eternal death and sinful unrighteousness, in the pits of eternal death and hell, and outside of God's eternal state of heaven, separated from all that God is forever. In other words, when an angel that was made in the eternal state of God's heaven and was made with the eternal life of God in them with a celestial type heavenly body that is a spiritual body and not a flesh and blood physical body, and then to disobey God and his laws or commandments would be counted as sin and unrighteousness and the wages of that sin is death. And even though God is a God of love, He is also the God of perfect justice, in no wise can He just clear the guilty, that sin had to punished, and that penalty of death had to be paid. In other words, God and sin cannot dwell in the same realm of eternity and at the same time; just like you cannot have total light and total darkness in the same place and at the same time. God is eternal light and eternal life; Sin is eternal darkness and eternal death. So you see that sin is the opposite of God and God is the opposite of sin. This is the very reason that God had to remove any and all sin from his heaven.

081 When Lucifer and each angel of Lucifer was being tempted to sin, there was this narrow line that they had walked in this temptation before they had crossed over into the actual sin itself; that temptation is not any sin in itself, but is kind of a final warning to stop, don't go any farther or you will cross over to the point of no return! They should have yielded or stopped at that warning of the temptation; That was God's way of warning each of those angels to resist, stop, turn away and don't go any farther, but

without violating any of their free will; But Lucifer and all of his angels of heaven did not even yield to each of their own temptations, but gave into their temptations and freely crossed over to commit their own sin against God. And even if they did not fully understand or weigh all the consequences that came with their sin; they freely made their own decision and God will not violate their free will. But when each of those angels did sin; God had no longer seen Lucifer and all of his angels as angels, but as sin; and this sin has to be cast out from God and His heaven into eternal death and eternal darkness separated from God's eternal life and eternal light.

082 So when all of Lucifer and his angels freely crossed over and sinned against God, they had sinned in the eternal state of Gods heaven; and God's laws states that the wages of sin is death; and the other part of this same law states that there is pleasure in sin for a season; and there pleasure in sin was basically from the time that they were converted to that time that they had each fought in that battle with Michael and his angels. And since they had all sinned in the eternal state of God's heaven; They would forever be a part of their sin and their sin would forever be a part of them; there would never be a way to separate their sin from them; and even though there is another part of God's law that states that there is no remission of sin unless innocent blood be shed and applied to that sin; this law could not be used or applied to Lucifer and all of his angels; For they did not have flesh and blood bodies, therefore, that law of the remission of sin through innocent blood would not work on celestial and heavenly spiritual bodies. And since their sin had become a part of them and they had become a part of their sin; and as God had picked up their sin and cast them out of heaven, Lucifer and his entire angels, were cast out with their sin.

083 As I had said earlier that a certain amount of the angels of Lucifer,

(Now Satan), that they have now become his demons and evil spirits, were cast into hell. But God didn't cast all of Satan and his demons and evil spirits, just a certain amount of his demons and a certain amount of his evil spirits were cast into hell only at that time during the battle between Michael and Lucifer's angels. But Satan and the rest of his demons and evil spirits that wasn't cast into hell by God yet, have been temporarily left out of hell by God for a reason, but God wasn't letting them understand or know his intentions at this time. And since God hasn't cast Satan and the rest of his demons and evil spirits into hell yet, but yet they have been cast out of God's eternal state of His heaven; Satan and his demons and evil spirits are still in that section of heaven that used to be their section of heaven when Satan was Archangel Lucifer and his demons and evil spirits were his angels in God the Lord Jesus's section of heaven. (And also just to refresh another point is that this planet earth is located in this now sin contaminated section of heaven).

084 And now, since this one third section of heaven, that is God the Lord Jesus's section of heaven, has been contaminated by the sin of Lucifer and his angels; And God won't dwell where there is sin; so God had completely removed His total presents from that section of heaven. And since God is eternal light; all of that eternal light that shines forth from God was removed from that section of heaven; and a complete and total darkness had then replaced or filled that whole section of heaven. This darkness that had filled this section of heaven is nothing like the night time darkness that we see at night time today. For the darkness that we see today at night time is just a very lite shadow in comparison to this total darkness that had filled that section of heaven when God had removed His presence and eternal light from that section of heaven. This darkness was a very heavy, thick, strong, evil and violent darkness, that if it were possible, you could cut a small piece of it with a knife and hold it in your

hand; or if it were possible, that you were there alive in your flesh and blood body, that you now have today, and at that time, and you were in that darkness, your flesh and blood body would have been crushed into nonexistence. Or another example of how powerful that darkness was, and if it were possible to take all of the nuclear bombs that are on this earth today, (for this earth that was created in verse one of Genesis chapter one is now in this thick and dark section of God the Lord Jesus's section of heaven), and if they were all placed in one spot or place on this earth, and even if you were able to detonate these bombs first before they were crushed by this very powerful, violent and strong force of this darkness; the violent and strong force of this kind of darkness would have snuffed out and just absorbed all of the power of the blast of these nuclear bombs without any noticeable destruction, as though they were never detonated.

085 And again as God had removed himself and his presents from this now dark section of heaven, His eternal life was also removed and replaced by eternal death. So now this dark section of heaven is also now void of any life. And God's perfect Love was also removed from that dark and void section of heaven, replacing it with pure and total hate. And God's perfect order had also been removed from this now dark, empty and void and full of pure hate, section of heaven; and now it has been replaced with total chaos; and so on and so on. In other words, all that God is, was removed from that section of heaven; and that section of heaven had now become the very opposite image and reflection of who God is and the very image and reflection of who Satan and his demons and evil spirits have become. This dark and void section of heaven, that is now separated from the eternal state of God's heaven, has also now become the first physical realm in God's entire eternal kingdom; and has now become a second heaven to God's first heaven. And Satan and his demons and evil spirits are still in this now dark and void section of heaven that is also full of pure

hate and evil violence and a destructive chaos. Also, See Drawing #4, Page 256.

086 Everything that God had originally created and made in perfect order, in that section of heaven, has now come out of order and is now in a chaotic disorder; all of those positions of power and authority, starting from that archangelic position that Satan had held as Archangel Lucifer; is now void, desolated, and empty; and all of those positions of power and authority that Satan's demons and evil spirits had occupied as Lucifer's angels; is now also void, desolate and empty. And Satan and his demons and evils spirits, that haven't been cast into hell yet, are still in this physical, dark and void section of heaven roaming around freely trying to destroy everything in that section that had anything to do with God, and anything that was created by God; for Satan and all of his demons and evil spirits by now have developed a fierce and pure hatred toward the true and living Godhead. And Satan must have thought in his heart that since he and all of these demons and evil spirits that are still with him and are still in this dark and void section of heaven roaming freely, he might have thought that this dark and void section of heaven was where they were going to remain in for the rest of their eternity. And Satan and his demons and evil spirits were still thinking that this dark and void section of heaven that they were still roaming freely in is still their part of heaven and belongs to them.

087 But much to Satan's surprise this section of heaven still belongs to God. For this dark and void section of heaven is still one third part of the kingdom of heaven; and God is not going to have any void in His heaven. And all of those positions of power and authority that Lucifer and his angels were kicked out of will not be left void. For God has already devised a new plan to restore his heaven and to refill all those positions of power and authority. And He will restore that one third dark, void, and emp-

ty section of heaven back into His eternal state of His heavenly kingdom. But at this time God is going to leave it as this physical realm for the time being. And this is also, at this time, is where we are now at the thresh hold of Genesis chapter one, verse two where it states that this earth is now without form and void of any life, and darkness is upon this whole physical universe, even to its very depth, that used to be one third part of God the Lord Jesus's section of His eternal heaven.

088 And as I had stated earlier that Satan and his demons and evil spirits that have not been cast into hell yet are still roaming freely throughout this dark and void section of heaven. And whatever the power and force of that evil darkness, didn't damage or destroy, and along with the chaotic disorder causing its destruction, Satan and his demons and evil spirits was roaming throughout this dark and void section of heaven destroying anything and everything that was made and created by God. So every planet throughout this dark and void section of heaven, that used to be part of those positions of power and authority that Satan and his demons and evil spirits were in when they were angels in heaven, are now in a major destructive state to the point that they are without their original created form and appearance that God had made them with. For example, planets have come out of their original place and order and have been colliding with or into other planets causing a massive chain reaction of continuing destruction, and so on, and so on. And since this planet earth is in this section of heaven, this is the reason it is without its original created form that God had made it with. And Satan and his demons and evil spirits may have still been thinking that this dark and void section of heaven is still their section of heaven that they are going to spend the rest of their eternity in and that it belongs to them forever. But God is about to renovate this dark and void section of heaven despite what Satan and his demons and evil spirits think, do, or say. For this is still God's section of heaven and not Sa-

tan's or any of his demons or evil spirits; for God is not going to have any void in his heaven, it will be restored.

089 Meanwhile, God has been creating a new plan, design and method of how He is going to restore His section of heaven and to refill all those void and empty positions of power and authority that Satan and his demons and evil spirits were kicked out of. And this is where God has, and for whatever reason, decided to make and create a man in His image and after His likeness for the first time. In other words, God had made and created angels originally for all of those now void and empty positions of power and authority. But now God has decided to make all of mankind starting with the man Adam and the extension of this man Adam, a woman named Eve. And both this man Adam and his wife, a woman, named Eve was about to be created by God to refill that void and empty position of power and authority that Satan was kicked out of as high archangel Lucifer. And then all of their children or descendants that would multiply from them would be used by God to refill all of those void and empty positions of power and authority that Satan's demons and evil spirits was kicked out of as Lucifer's angels. But God was not planning on completely restoring all of this dark and void section of heaven at this time, and there is a good reason why God is not completely restoring all of this section of heaven.

090 Since God had created and made Lucifer and all of his angels as free moral agents with a free will and with the perfect righteousness of God and then they freely had chosen to cross over into rebellion and sin against God. They only had a narrow window of time to yield to that rebellion and sin in order for it to be only the temptation and not sin; and that temptation is like the final warning from God to stop and don't going any farther; resist that temptation and it will flee from you. God will not and did

not violate their free will to choose to obey or to disobey. And when they had crossed over that line of temptation and into disobedience and sin; they had also crossed over from the eternal righteousness of God to the eternal unrighteousness of sin; and from the eternal life and light of heaven, to the eternal death and darkness of hell. All of Lucifer and his angels were made with angelic and celestial type heavenly bodies; there were no flesh and blood bodies in heaven at that time. So when Lucifer and all his angels had crossed over into disobedience and sin; and since they did not have any flesh and blood bodies; they did not have any physical death, but they had went from eternal life in heaven to the eternal and spiritual death in hell. And God had seen the evil cunningness and craftiness that Lucifer had used to deceive one third of the angels of heaven into sinning against Him. That God had decided to use this evil nature of Satan and all of those demons and evil spirits to His advantage when he creates the first man Adam and his extension, a woman and wife, named Eve.

091 In other words, God has planned to create and make this first man Adam and an extension of this man, a woman and his wife, named Eve; to refill that original position of power and authority that Lucifer, now Satan, was kicked out of. And for whatever reason, God had decided to use this planet earth as a temporary place or position of their new power and authority. Now this earth may have been a part of Satan's original position of power and authority that he was kicked out of, and this may be a reason that God had chosen this planet earth instead of any of the other planets throughout this dark universe, or it may have been just the planet that God had decided to use as a temporary position of placement to test this first man's obedience first before He would put them into their permanent position of power and authority in the eternal state of God's heaven. For God had intentionally planned on making and creating this first man in this physical realm of this dark and void section of heaven that was still outside

of God's eternal state of His eternal heaven.

092 Instead of God restoring this whole dark and void section of heaven and then making and creating this first man Adam; God had planned to restore only this planet earth and bring it back to or similar to its original created form and appearance along with a certain area that surrounds this planet earth. He did not intend on restoring this whole dark and void section of heaven at this time; God had only intended to, temporarily, restore, this planet earth, and a certain area around it and to purposely leave it in the physical realm outside of the eternal state of His heavenly kingdom for a reason. God had seen the evil, sin, death and the darkness, of disobedience, enter into His heavenly kingdom for the first time through Lucifer and all of his angels; and He did not want any sin to ever enter into His heavenly kingdom again. In other words, God did not want to create this man Adam and then place him into that position of power and authority, and in the eternal state of God's heaven, that Satan was kicked out of; and then if they would disobey and sin, God would have had to kick them out of heaven too like He had done to Satan and his angels and He would still have a dark and void section of heaven. But God had come up with a greater and perfect plan to permanently restore all of those void and empty positions once and for all eternity.

093 In other words, God had decided to make and create all of mankind outside of the eternal state of His heavenly kingdom starting with just one man and one woman first. God's plan was to restore this earth from its sinful destructive state, in this physical realm outside of His eternal heavenly kingdom; restoring it to like or similar to its original created form and appearance. In other words, God was about to restore this earth and a certain area around it, and then create Adam and Eve, and all of the animal life, and the Garden of Eden to the point that this earth, Adam and Eve, the

Garden of Eden, and all animal life, will have the total and perfect appearance as though they were really created in the eternal state of God's heaven, even though they were still in this physical realm outside of God's eternal state of His heavenly kingdom. And Adam and Eve were also to be made and created with glorified physical bodies that resembled the celestial, heavenly bodies like the angels of heaven were made with; but this man Adam and his wife Eve were not going to have any angelic bodies; God had determined to create and make this man, and woman, in His image and after His likeness. The same power and authority that Satan had as Archangel Lucifer would be given to this man Adam and his extension, the woman and wife, Eve. They were originally created to eventually rule over all of the angels of heaven, just like Lucifer's Archangelic position was to rule over all of the angels of heaven, but they were first going to be made a little lower than all of the other two third angels of heaven so that God could test their obedience and allegiance to Him first.

094 In other words, God was going to make them in total obedience and with the perfect righteousness, image, and the likeness of Himself; and then He would test their obedience to His commandments and laws. And God has already seen the depth, width and length of the two paths that they could or would follow. And path one would be the path of perfect righteousness, obedience, the eternal light of God's eternal life that God is about to make them with and make them in; and path two would be the path of unrighteousness, disobedience, the eternal darkness of Sin's eternal death. God had known and had seen the full length of both paths. God would rather that the man Adam would remain on the path that He is about to create and make them in; and like the angels of heaven; God was going to make mankind as free moral agents with a free will to choose to obey, or to disobey God; to love, or to hate God; to accept or to reject God, etc.; and God was not going to violate mankind's free will also. So

you see that they only had to choose to disobey God's commandments and or laws, for they would already be made in that obedience and righteousness of God and would remain there as long as they would walk in that obedience; and they would have to choose to disobey God and His commandments and laws and they would fall into the sin of disobedience; and the wages of that sin would be death, then their glorified physical bodies would become just flesh and blood physical bodies without the glory and presents of God in them and around them.

095 And because the first part of God's law of disobedience is the wages of sin is death; but the second part of that same law is that there is pleasure in that sin for a season. Adam and Eve would remain physically alive in their flesh and blood bodies for a season; and then a physical death, the first death, would come to their physical bodies; and at that same time that the physical death comes to their physical bodies, a spiritual life or death could come to the spirit and soul of this man Adam. This spiritual death would be the second death and would be eternal death in hell separated from God and His eternal heaven and along with that same eternal death in hell with Satan and all of his demons and evil spirits: or a spiritual life of God's eternal life in His heaven that would or could be obtained through this physical death: for there is another part of God's law that states that there is no remission of sin, no forgiveness of sin, or no separation of sin unless innocent blood be shed and applied to that sin.

096 And since this man Adam and his wife Eve would be made and created with physical flesh and blood bodies giving them a physical death before the eternal spiritual death; then the law that states that the wages of sin is death could be fulfilled before the spiritual death would take place; and also the law that states that there is no remission of sin unless innocent blood be shed and applied to that sin; thereby separating man's sin

from their spirit and soul, therefore their sin could be then cast into hell only and man could then be free of his sin and then he would be free and clear to go to heaven. Through the physical death that penalty of death could be paid and sin could be remove or separated from their spirit and soul by the shedding of innocent blood and applying that innocent blood to that sin, redeeming mankind of his sin and that sin by itself would be eternally punished in hell forever and then man would be free and clear to return to God's eternal heaven. In other words, God has already prepared and preplanned a salvation plan for all of mankind, ready to put into play if this man Adam would disobey and fall into sin. And Satan and his demons and evil spirits have no knowledge of this new creation that God is about to put into play.

097 And as I have said earlier, that God has always been a part of His throne and His throne has always been a part of Him. And even though God can leave His throne and go anywhere in His heavenly kingdom and yet still be on His throne at the same time. And God is about to leave His throne and enter into this dark and void section of heaven for the first time since He had removed His total presence from it. And this is where God the Father, and God the Lord Jesus and God the Holy Spirit has now started to move from His throne and into this dark and void section of heaven. God is moving toward and to the location that this earth was originally created in, but now is in a destructive state and without its original form and appearance and void of any life. Now also, as God is moving into this dark and void section of His heaven, He is not affected by any of this thick and heavy darkness or the total chaos of all of the debris and objects flying around in this section of heaven. And, also, as God is moving into this dark and void section of heaven, Satan and his demons and his evil spirits, that have been roaming throughout this whole section of heaven all of this time, have now become disdainfully aware of this new movement by God

and into his, (Satan's heaven), for Satan may have been still thinking that this dark and void section of heaven was still his heaven and not God's heaven. And Satan may have sent a vast number of demons and evil spirits to constantly bombard and attack God as He was moving into and through this dark and void section of heaven, but with no effect; Satan still has not learned that God cannot be destroyed or killed.

098 In other words, as God is moving into and through this dark and void section of heaven, He is not effected by any of Satan and his demons and evil spirits sin and the darkness of that sin; for you see that as God is moving into and through this section of heaven; and as Satan's demons and evil spirits are trying to attack God as though they were going to try and stop God from entering this section of heaven; God was surrounded by His everlasting, eternal and consuming light: any sin that makes any attempt to try and enter that eternal light that surrounds God will be consumed by that eternal light that shines forth from God and will be immediately zapped directly to hell. So Satan could not stop God from moving through His heaven even though it was a dark and void section of heaven. God had moved to this location that this earth was originally created in but is now in a destructive state without its original form and appearance; God is now moving around this earth surveying the extreme devastation of this earth. We are now at this point in God's timeline of Genesis chapter one, verse two: And the earth is without form, and void; and darkness is upon the face of the deep. And the Spirit of God moved, (or was moving), upon the face of the waters. This verse has now been fulfilled at this time in God's timetable.

099 Now God is about to create and make this first man Adam, but He has to restore this earth first from its destructive and formless state. In other words, God has to create, or in this case, restore this position of pow-

er and authority, this earth, so that God can then create and make this first man Adam on this earth. And this is what God is about to do, is to start the restoration of this earth from its destructive state. And now we are approaching the thresh hold of Genesis chapter one, verse three: where God is about to say, Let there be light. Now remember that this dark and void section of heaven is totally and completely in the darkness of sin. There is no light from any stars or from any suns; they have not been made by God yet, for God didn't create the stars and suns until the fourth day of the restoration of this earth. And this thick, heavy and violent darkness that was throughout this whole section of heaven, including and completely surrounding and saturating this earth would have to be removed for several reasons. God has always created and made things in His heaven and in the eternal light of His heaven. And everything that has been made or created before was made new and was never restored. This is the first time God has had to restore anything back to its original creation from a destructive state. And God has never made or created anything in any darkness before. And God is not going to restore this earth in and with the presence of that darkness of sin, it is about to be removed or moved away from around this earth.

100 And also, along with that violent darkness and the chaotic disorder of this dark and void section of heaven; Satan and his demons and evil spirits are still roaming throughout this whole section of heaven destroying anything and everything that was made by God. And since God had entered this dark and void section of heaven, a vast number of Satan's demons and evil spirits have been surrounding God still trying to attack and destroy God as He has moved into, through and over to where this earth is located in this section of heaven. And as these demons and evil spirits were trying to attack God as He was moving through this dark section of heaven; and as soon as they would get even into just one ray of that light

that was coming from God that was completely surrounding Him, they would be immediately zapped to hell as lightning bolts. So this must have been a very frightening but spectacular event to see God moving through this dark section of heaven with a constant display of powerful lightning bolts shooting from all around God as He was moving though this section of heaven and over to where this earth was located.

101 So you see that God could not start restoring this earth with all of that violent darkness there that would just continually keep destroying any restoration attempt. And the second reason is that God doesn't want to restore this earth in this darkness. He has always made and created things in His eternal light. And He needed to kind-of turn on the light so that He could see what He is doing as He is restoring this earth. And also, God had to stop this chaotic and violent disorder; because God wasn't going to start this restoration project of earth with all kinds of debris and pieces of broken planets flying around and hitting this earth as He is trying to restore it. And last, but not the least, God had to push back or remove all of Satan and his demons and evil spirits from around a certain area of this earth and from this earth. For God could not have Satan and his demons and evil spirits moving around, flying around, and zipping around Him and this earth, with their fierce, hateful, destructive, and psychotic anger towards God, and this earth and its restoration. And Satan might have been trying to stop any attempt of God to restore anything in this dark and void section of God's heaven. But Satan is about to see and feel the vast power of God's powerful four little words, "Let There Be Light!", that will knock him back away from this earth.

102 And this is what God is about to speak as He was moving around this formless, void and empty of any life, earth, getting ready to start the restoration of this earth. And remember that the only light that is in this dark and

void section of heaven at this time, is the light that is shining from around, within and out of God the Father, and God the Lord Jesus, and God the Holy Spirit as He is moving around in this dark section of heaven. And this light that was around God, as He was moving around in this section of heaven, is that very light that is the Eternal Light of who God is, for God is Light! In other words, God can remove any or all other light that is in His heaven, But this Eternal Light that surrounds God Himself is just that, God's Eternal Light that can never be removed and will never go out: For God is clothed with His eternal heavenly garment of eternal light that is also eternal life. In other words, and if it were possible, and if you were in that dark section of heaven and at that time that God was moving through that section of heaven, and if you were only one foot away from God as He was passing you in that darkness, you would not have been able to see God through that one foot thick part of that darkness, even though you were that close to God as He was passing you. And even if you were just one sixteenth of an inch away from God as He passed you, you would still not be able to see Him as He passed you. So in order for you to be able to see God as He was passing you; you would of had to get into just one little ray of that Eternal Light that was around God. But your view or vision of God would have only been about One billionth of second window of time, and then you would have been zapped to hell. And this is what was happening to a vast number of Satan's demons and evil spirits.

103 So you can now see that when you read Genesis chapter one verse three: And God said, "Let there be light": and there was light: That there was a lot more to this verse than what you may have first thought or believed. And this is a temporary light that God is going to turn on or put into place to remove that violent darkness from within and around this earth and its area; And to stop and hold back that chaotic and violent disorder; And to slam back all of the evil forces of Satan and his demons and evil

spirits. And last, but not the least, it's against God's very nature of who He is, to make and create anything in any darkness let alone the restoration of this earth. And as I have said earlier that God is not going to restore this whole dark and void section of heaven at this time. He is only going to restore this earth and a certain area that surrounds this earth temporarily. God is not restoring this whole dark and void section of heaven at this time for a very good reason. Even though God is going to create this man Adam to replace or refill that position of power and authority that Satan had held when he was Archangel Lucifer and was kicked out of; God is going to make and create this man Adam outside of the eternal state of His heavenly kingdom, and in this physical section of heaven so that God can and will test this man's obedience or disobedience to Him before He would place him into that permanent position of power and authority that Satan was kicked out of.

104 In other words, God is going to make and create this man Adam and place him in this temporary position on this earth that is in this physical realm and outside of the spiritual and eternal existence of God's heaven. And God is purposely doing it this way, so that He can test this man Adam's obedience to Him; For God had made Archangel Lucifer in that position of power and authority and he had disobeyed and fell into sin, and this had happened in God's eternal state of His heavenly kingdom. And God is not going to let this evil disobedience of sin to never enter or happen in His eternal heaven again. And this is why God has decided to make this man Adam in this physical realm that is outside of His eternal spiritual heaven, so that if this man Adam walked in obedience to Him and His laws for a certain amount of time to confirm this man's obedience to Him; for God was going to use Satan to tempt this man with the sin of Satan to see if he will remain obedient to Him or sin with Satan; And if this man remained obedient; God would then put or place this man Adam into that

eternal and spiritual and permanent position of power and authority in God's eternal heaven, and then God would cast all of Satan and his demons and evil spirits into death and hell for all of eternity; and then God would restore this whole dark and void section of heaven, and including this earth, back into the eternal state of His eternal heavenly kingdom. Adam and Eve would refill that position of power and authority that Lucifer was kicked out of; and all of the positions of power and authority that Lucifer's angels were kicked out of, would then be refilled with all of the descendants of Adam and Eve. This was this first path that God had hoped that this man would stay on and follow. (If it had happened this way, we would have all been born in heaven not to know any sin).

105 The second path was that if this man Adam would walk in the evil sin of disobedience to God's commandments and laws, this sin would happen outside of God's eternal state and heavenly kingdom. And since God's law states that the wages of sin is death; that law would demand the death penalty to this man. But since God will purposely make this man with a physical flesh and blood body and with a spirit and a soul; this man would technically die two deaths; a physical death of his flesh and blood body; and a spiritual death of the spirit and soul. For Lucifer and his angels did not have any physical flesh and blood bodies, but a spiritual, celestial type heavenly bodies that only gave then one death, a spiritual and eternal death. But God had planned to use this physical death of man to redeem all of mankind of their sin: For God had seen the cunningness and craftiness of Lucifer's deception to the temptation of sin, that God had seen both complete paths that this man would or could follow. And God had known that there was an extremely high probability that this man Adam would lean more to that path of disobedience; for God is going to make this man Adam in the total obedience and righteousness of Himself; For God had seen that Lucifer was able to completely deceive all of the ap-

proximately one hundred trillion angels in his section of heaven over to the path of disobedience. So this is why God was going to use Satan to tempt Adam and his wife Eve to see if they would also follow the same path of disobedience that Lucifer's angels had chosen to follow, or remain on the path of obedience and righteousness that God is going to make them with.

106 For if this man Adam would choose or be deceived by Satan into that path of disobedience; God had already prepared a plan of salvation to redeem this man from their sin. This is why that God was going to make this man with a physical flesh and blood body and not with just a spiritual body. That if they would fall into the sin of disobedience; that law that states that the wages of sin is death, would continually demand the death penalty; well that death penalty would be paid by the physical death of his flesh and blood body; but this death penalty would not be an immediate death, but would be deferred for a certain amount of time or, in other words, this man Adam would not drop dead on the spot, but would remain alive in his sin for a season, but death would still come to this man. For even though God's law states that the wages of sin is death; there is a second part of that law that also states that there is pleasure in that sin for a season. But also, that even though this death penalty would be fulfilled and paid by this physical death; that by itself would not separate this man's sin from him, but would still be a part of him and he would still be a part of his sin. But there is another law of God that states that there is no remission of sin, no forgiveness of sin, or no separation of sin unless innocent blood be shed and applied to that sin. And this is why God is about to make and create this man Adam with a physical flesh and blood body, so that through the shedding of the innocent blood of a man, and then applying that innocent blood to the sin of this man's spirit and soul, then that sin would then be removed from all of mankind and cast into hell by itself, freeing man of his sin and clearing him to go to heaven.

107 In other words, God had seen the full length, height and width of both paths that this man would follow, even before He had created him. God had hoped that this man Adam would stay on the first path or the first agreement or testament of obedience and perfect righteousness to which God was going to make him on. But even if this man, Adam would choose to follow this second path of the sin of disobedience and unrighteousness, God will already have a backup plan or a second agreement or testament that would replace that first agreement or testament. And this would be God's salvation plan to redeem all of mankind from their sin. And this is why God is going to make this man Adam with a physical flesh and blood body, so that if this man didn't stay on the first path that God is about to make him on, God would use this backup plan to redeem all of mankind from their sin through the physical death of this flesh and blood body that would fulfill that penalty of death that the law of sin would demand; and their sin would be separated and removed from their spirit and soul and cast into hell by itself through that law that states that there is no remission of sin unless innocent blood be shed and applied to that sin. Man's sin would be removed from him and that death penalty would be paid by this salvation plan of God. And all of this knowledge is being kept hidden from Satan and all of his demons and evil spirits. And at this time Satan doesn't even know why God has entered into, and why He is moving through and over to the location of this earth.

108 And as God the Father and God the Lord Jesus and God the Holy Spirit were moving around this formless and void earth surveying the damage and destruction; God is about to speak just four little, but extremely powerful, words, Let There Be Light. For at this time there was only that light that surrounded God Himself as He was in this dark and void section of heaven. The best way I can compare this to is like when we go into the darkness of a moonless night or into a dark room, we are engulfed into

that darkness; but even though God would be in that darkness, He is still surrounded in His eternal light, we are in that darkness surrounded by that darkness. And when God was beginning to speak, Let There Be Light, it may have been God the Father and God the Lord Jesus and God the Holy Spirit speaking these words all at the same time and with the voice of a talking trumpet blast and with great thundering's and with an extremely power force that had come from God that Satan and his demons and evil spirits had never seen or expected. And as God is speaking these words; Let There Be Light!; and since God was at this location of where this earth is located in this dark and void section of heaven; This light that had surrounded God Himself had now expanded and shot forth from God Himself with an extremely powerful force and at the speed of light itself and in all directions, three hundred sixty degrees, from God himself; pushing back and or consuming all of that thick and violent darkness that had surrounded this earth; and also pushing back all of that violent chaotic disorder; and also pushing back all of Satan and His demons and evil spirits; and turning on the eternal light of God Himself around this earth and to a certain distance from this earth.

109 In other words, God had cleared this earth and a certain area that surrounded this earth and to a certain distance from this earth, of all of that thick and violent darkness; of all of that violent chaotic disorder, and of all of Satan and his demons and evil spirits; to a certain distance from this earth; and God may have placed a certain number of angels from heaven to hold back all of this; and this same boundary may have also been the location that God had separated the light from the darkness and where He had called this light day and this darkness night; for the stars and sun has not been made yet, not until the fourth day; so the light that is here at this time, is a temporary light that God is using at this time until the fourth day or He may have kept it here until He was going to create this man Adam

on the sixth day. And now that there is no darkness, and no chaotic disorder, and there is no Satan and his demons and evil spirits to get in His way; God the Father and God the Lord Jesus and God the Holy Spirit can now actually get started on the restoration of this earth from its destructive state. And we are now at the fulfillment of Genesis chapter one, verse four, and also verse five: and the evening and the morning was the first day.

110 And God had then said, Let there be a firmament, in the midst of the waters, and let it divide the waters from the waters; and God had made the firmament, and then He had divided the waters which were under the firmament from the waters which were above the firmament: and it was so. And God had called this firmament heaven. And the evening and the morning was the second day. And then God had said, Let the waters that be under the heaven be gathered together unto one place, and the dry land appeared: and it was so. And God had called this dry land Earth; and the gathering together of these waters He had called Seas: and God had seen that this was good. And then God had said, let the earth bring forth grass, the herb yielding seed, and the fruit tree yielding fruit after his kind, whose seed is in itself, upon the earth: and this was so. And so the earth had brought forth the grass, and the herb yielding seed after his kind, and the tree yielding fruit, whose seed was in itself, after his kind: and God had seen that this was good. And the evening and the morning was the third day.

111 Now God had said, let there be lights in the firmament of the heaven to divide the day from the night; and let them also be for signs, and for seasons, and for days, and for years: And let them be for lights in the firmament of the heaven to give light upon the earth, and this was so. And God had made two great lights; the greater light to rule the day, and the lesser light to rule the night; and He had made the stars also. So God had set

them in the firmament of the heaven to give light upon the earth, and to rule over the day and over the night, and to divide the light from the darkness: and God had seen that this was also good. And the evening and the morning was the fourth day. And God had then said, let the waters bring forth abundantly the moving creature that hath life, and fowl that may fly above the earth in the open firmament of heaven. And God had then created great whales, and every living creature that moveth, which the waters had brought forth abundantly, after their kind, and every winged fowl after his kind: and God had seen that this was good. Then God had blessed them, saying, be fruitful, and multiply, and fill the waters in the seas, and let the fowl multiply in the earth. And the evening and the morning was the fifth day.

112 And while God the Father and God the Lord Jesus and God the Holy Spirit was restoring this earth to like or similar to its original created form and appearance, Satan and his demons and evil spirits are still being held back by a boundary or perimeter that God had set earlier on the first day. And even though Satan and his demons and evil spirits are being held back at this great distance from the location of this earth and its restoration, he is still able to see in detail to what God is doing to this earth, and Satan may have been outraged with a fierce evil anger that God had come into his dark and void section of heaven, for Satan may have still thought that this dark section of heaven was still his heaven and not God's section of heaven, and all Satan was able to do was to just watch God performing this restoration action and wondering what and why God has entered this dark and void section of heaven and is restoring this earth; Satan still doesn't know that God is about to create and make another being or person to refill or replace that void that Satan was expelled or kicked out of, let alone being created and made in God's own image and after His likeness and as a man and not as an angel; even though Satan

was only made and created in the image and likeness of an archangel. When Satan sees God make and create this man Adam in His very own image of God Himself and after God's own likeness, Satan will then become unglued with a pure evil hatred toward this man Adam and God.

113 And God had said, Let Us now make and create this man Adam in Our own image and after Our own likeness. And the Lord God had started to form this man Adam from the dust of this earth. But I don't think that God had just pick up or used just any dirt or dust of this earth, But God may have used many different stones of this earth that existed at this time of man's creation that doesn't exist today. So God may have used several to many different stones from this earth to form this dust formed statue of a man that was to be this flesh and blood body of this man Adam. And God may have crushed these stones into a fine powder and mixing the different types of powder from the different stones that He had used as He had formed the different parts of this dust formed statue of this man Adam. And when this dust formed statue of this man Adam was finished being formed by God; Then God had breathed His breath of eternal life into this dust formed statue of this man Adam, and he had become a living soul. A more detailed picture of what had actually taken place when God had breathed into this dust formed statue of this man that was to become this man Adam, needs a more detailed explanation. For the scripture in the bible in Genesis chapter two, verse seven states that the Lord God had formed the man from the dust of the ground, and breathed into his nostrils the breath of life; and man became a living soul; which is too general of a statement and doesn't give us the clear and complete picture of this major event that God had performed to the creation of this first man Adam.

114 In other words, as God was breathing His breath of His eternal life into this dust formed statue of this man Adam; It was God the Father and God

the Lord Jesus and God the Holy Spirit all breathing into this dust formed statue of this man Adam at the same exact time. As God the Father was breathing in His breath of eternal life into this dust formed statue of this man Adam; the soul of Adam was being formed for the very first time, in the image and after the likeness of God the Father's Soul. And at the same time, as God the Lord Jesus was breathing in His breath of eternal life into this dust formed statue of this man Adam; the body of Adam was being formed for the very first time, in the image and after the likeness of God the Lord Jesus's Body. And also at the same time, as God the Holy Spirit was breathing in His breath of eternal life into this dust formed statue of this man Adam; the spirit of Adam was being formed for the very first time, in the image and after the likeness of God the Holy Spirit's Spirit.

115 So now you see that this is how man was made in the image and after the likeness of God. For the soul of Adam took on the image of God the Father; and the body of Adam took the image of God the Lord Jesus; and the spirit of the man Adam took on the image of God the Holy Spirit. And God the Father had then dwelt 100% in the soul of the man Adam; and God the Lord Jesus had then dwelt 100% in the body of the man Adam; and God the Holy Spirit had then dwelt 100% in the spirit of the man Adam. In other words; the presence of God was in, around and flowed through Adam continually to the point that even though Adam was naked, he could not see his own nakedness because he was clothed with the presence, fullness and eternal light of God Himself. (This had to be the ultimate group hug that has ever been and has not been duplicated by mankind since).

116 Now, also as God had made Adam, he was made righteous in every way and there was no sin in him at this time; God did not make him with a sinful nature; God has never made anything and will never make anything

with sin or with any sinful nature; God is totally righteousness and the source of it. And because God is righteousness, anything that is made and was made and will be made by God, is made in His perfect righteousness as it is made; and this happened to Adam as God had made the man Adam. For the very nature of God's righteousness had flowed from God to this man Adam as he was being made by God. This is why Adam was righteous when he was made. For Adam had received his righteousness from God; for it was God's righteousness and not Adam's righteousness. For Adam did not have any righteousness of his own, but received the righteousness of God, from God. For Adam had put on the righteousness of God by God. For Adam is the very image and after the likeness of God, and God is Righteousness. And Adam was that image of God's righteousness. And Adam's cloth of righteousness at that time was as white as snow. There was no sin; there was no filthy rag of unrighteousness yet; for he was in total obedience and not guilty of any point of God's law; continually fulfilling it in the presence of God. And another main point that I also want to include is that God had made this man Adam without any knowledge of the evil, sinful and rebellious attack by Satan and his evil demons and evil spirits. For God had made him to know no evil at this time.

117 In other words, God had made this man Adam in His own image and after His own likeness, that this man Adam had looked exactly like God to the point that if you were to place God the Father and God the Lord Jesus and God the Holy Spirit and this man Adam behind a curtain, and then they were all mixed up and put in a line up and then the curtain was opened, and all four were standing in a line looking exactly alike, that you would not be able to tell which one was this man Adam. For Adam had looked like God, talked like God and walked like God but yet was not God and was never made to become a god but a man with only the image and likeness of God. And this new man Adam that God had made with His

own image and after His own likeness might have really infuriated Satan with a fiery anger and hatred toward the true and living God, and now this man Adam had also enraged Satan with a jealous anger and hatred because and toward Adam's image of looking exactly like God. For remember that Satan as Lucifer when he had only the image and likeness of an Archangel and not the image and likeness of God Himself, but is now looking at this newly created man Adam with the very image and likeness of the true and living God that Satan had tried to kill and destroy but couldn't; Satan was now hell bent on trying to destroy that very image and likeness of God, this man Adam.

118 And God had planted a garden eastward in Eden, or better known as the Garden of Eden; and out of the ground, God had made to grow every tree that is pleasant to the sight and good for food; that tree of life also in the middle of the garden, and the tree of the knowledge of good and evil. And a main river head had gone out of Eden to water the garden; and then it had split or parted into four separate rivers to water this whole Garden of Eden. And then God had taken this man Adam and put him into this Garden of Eden to dress it and to keep it. And God had commanded to this man Adam, saying, that you may freely eat of every tree of this garden, except that one tree that is in the very center or middle of this garden; the tree of the knowledge of good and evil. You are not to eat of it; for in that day that you eat of it, you shall surely die! And this was that test of obedience that God was going to use to test this new man, Adam's obedience, to Him and His commandments. God had purposely made this man Adam to know no evil and he would remain that way as long as he stayed on that path of that obedience. For God had given this man Adam a direct order or commandment to not eat of that tree of the knowledge of good and evil that was in the middle of that Garden of Eden. All he had to do was to NOT eat of that tree and he would remain in

obedience to God.

119 Now it may have been while Adam was in this new Garden of Eden; that God had then said, let the earth bring forth the living creature after his kind, cattle, and creeping thing, and the beast of the earth after his kind; and it was so. And out of the ground God had made and formed every beast of the field on this earth after his kind, and cattle after his kind, and everything that creepeth upon the earth after his kind, and every fowl of the air, and then God had brought them unto Adam to see what he would call them; and whatsoever Adam had called every living creature, that was their name thereof. So Adam had given names to all of the cattle and to all the fowl of the air and to every beast of the field; but for Adam there was not found a help mate for him; but God had already planned to make this man Adam a helpmate. For God had known that it wasn't good for this man Adam to be by himself or alone; for this man could not reproduce another man by himself; and God had wanted this man to reproduce, or to multiply and replenish and to refill this earth.

120 So God is now about to start to make and create an extension of this man Adam or a help mate to complete this man. For God had made this man Adam to fulfill this position of power and authority that Satan was expelled or kicked out of; and God had wanted this man to be able to multiply and refill this earth. So God is going to make a female mate for this man Adam to complete him and to make it possible for this man Adam to multiply or reproduce after himself. So now, God was about to form and make a woman Eve; But He did not make her exactly the same way that He had made the man Adam. God will form the body of the woman Eve similar to the way that God had formed the man Adam's body, from the dust of this earth. So God had made another dust formed statue similar to Adam's, but it was not made exactly to Adam's male statue, but was

formed into a female statue of a woman to become Eve. And God did not breathe His breath of eternal life into her nostrils like He did with the man Adam; for she was to be an extension of Adam's body, and a help mate for Adam. So God had caused the man Adam to go into a deep sleep. And then God had surgically removed one of Adam's rib bone, And then God had closed up the flesh of Adam's body of where that bone was removed from and He healed the flesh closed and with no scar tissue. And then God had placed that bone, that He had removed from the man Adam, into that dust formed female statue of the woman, (Eve).

121 And now this is the reason that God had removed one of Adam's rib bone; and then He had placed it into that dust formed female statue of the woman (Eve); For the life of the body is in the blood, and the blood is manufactured or made inside of the bone or the bone marrow. This is why God had used a bone from Adam and transferred it to that dust formed statue of the woman Eve. For the life of God that was breathed into the man Adam, was in the blood of Adam. And the blood of Adam is manufactured or made in the bones of Adam. So the life of God that was in Adam, flowed through his veins and in his blood and was in the bones of the man Adam. So this same life of God and the blood of Adam were transferred from Adam to this dust formed statue of the woman Eve by that one rib bone of Adam.

122 And as God had place that rib bone of Adam into that dust formed statue of the woman (Eve); The life and blood that was in that rib bone had then flowed from that rib bone into and throughout that dust formed statue of the woman (Eve); and as the life of God had now flowed from that rib bone that had come from Adam; and since the man Adam was filled with 100% of the life and presence of God the Father and God the Lord Jesus and God the Holy Spirit; that same 100% of that life and presence of God

the Father and God the Lord Jesus and God the Holy Spirit was also in that rib bone of Adam that was now in that woman (Eve) and flowing throughout that dust formed statue of this woman(Eve), transforming and making the spirit, soul and body of that woman(Eve).

123 And so as the life of God that was in that rib bone of Adam and now in the woman (Eve); flowed from that rib bone and then that life of God split into three separate life flows and all at the same time, one of that life flow was of God the Father that flowed and formed the soul of the woman (Eve) in the image and after the likeness of Adam's soul; and that second life flow was of God the Lord Jesus that flowed and formed the body of the woman (Eve) in the image and after the likeness of Adam's body, but with a female body instead of a man or male body; and that third life flow was of God the Holy Spirit that flowed and formed the spirit in the woman(Eve) in the image and after the likeness of Adam's spirit; and then God the Father had then dwelt 100% in the soul of the woman Eve and God the Lord Jesus had then dwelt 100% in the body of the woman(Eve) and God Holy Spirit had then dwelt 100% in the spirit of the woman (Eve). The presence of God was in, around, and flowed through the woman (Eve) continually to the point that even though the woman (Eve) was naked, she could not see her own nakedness either because she was also clothed with the presence and fullness and the same righteousness of God the same way Adam was. And then God had brought this woman to the man Adam and He had given her to him as a help mate; And Adam had then said this is now bone of my bones, and flesh of my flesh: she shall be called Woman, because she was taken out of man.

124 For God had made the Woman (Eve) as an extension of the man Adam; For she was made in the image and after the likeness of the man Adam. And Adam was made in the image and after the likeness of God

the Father and God the Lord Jesus and God the Holy Spirit. For both Adam and his woman (Eve), therefore had the image and likeness of God; And before Adam and the woman (Eve) had fallen into sin, God had looked at the man Adam and his woman (Eve) as the man Adam. For the woman (Eve) was made as an extension of the man Adam, for Adam, and as a help mate so Adam would not be alone. And the body of the woman (Eve) was not her own but belonged to Adam and the body of Adam was not his own but belonged to the woman (Eve). And the main reason that the woman (Eve) was made as a helpmate for the man Adam, is because there was no way for Adam to reproduce or have any offspring; and God wanted Adam to be fruitful and multiply and refill the earth. And the woman (Eve) was made for that main purpose to be that help mate so that the man Adam would be able to reproduce so that Adam and the woman (Eve) could fulfill that command of God to be fruitful and multiply and refill the earth.

125 So God created man in His own image, and after His own likeness, in the image of God created he him, male and female created he them. And God had blessed them, and said, be fruitful, and multiply, and replenish or refill the earth, and subdue it: and have dominion over the fish of the sea, and over the fowl of the air, and over every living thing that moveth upon the earth. In other words, God had restored this earth, and He had created all life and living things or creatures on this earth, including the man Adam and his woman (Eve). And even though this earth and everything on it had belonged to God; God had given this earth and everything on it over to this man Adam and his woman (Eve) as their earth; it now had belong to this man Adam and his woman (Eve).

126 Now this had to really set coals of a fierce and fiery anger upon Satan; for he used to be the high archangel Lucifer and was made of every pre-

cious living stones with an angelic body but he was not made in the image and after the likeness of God, but yet this man Adam was made in the very image and after the likeness of God. Satan wanted to become God but he had only an angelic body that did not look like God; but God might have made man in his image and after his likeness so as to spike a jealous rage in Satan for he didn't look like God, but this man Adam had the very image and likeness of God himself and yet wasn't a god but just a man. Another point that I want to make is that while God was making the first man Adam; And even though Satan and all of his demons and evil spirits that were backed away from this earth and this section of this dark universe when God had come to restore this earth and to create the man Adam. All Satan could do was watch God restoring this earth and the making and creating of this first man Adam; for Satan was blocked and held back from being able to come any closer to this section of this dark universe and where this earth is located; for you see, before God had come back to this section of this dark universe Satan was able to move around this whole dark and void universe with ease and without any restraints until God had move from His throne and into this dark and void universe and to this planet earth that was without form and void of any life as stated in verse two of Genesis Chapter one; And when God had said let there be light as also stated in verse three of Genesis Chapter one, this is when Satan, and all of his demons, and evil spirits were slammed back to a point and distance from all directions from around this earth and he has been held back all of this time while God was restoring this earth and making and creating all life on this earth.

127 And now Adam and his woman and wife (Eve) were both in this Garden of Eden enjoying all of the benefits that this beautiful garden that God had made specifically for them and had met all of their needs perfectly. For the sunlight that had shown at this time on this garden and the man

Adam and his woman (Eve); wasn't the same sunlight that we have today; for the sunlight that we have today will give you a sunburn; but the sunlight that was there at this time that Adam and his woman (Eve) was in, was a perfect sunlight that would never burn them; they would be out in this garden all day long and in that sunlight and they would never get a sunburn. They didn't have to eat to sustain life. And any food that they did eat was completely consumed and there was no waste; or there were no restrooms at this time on earth or in this Garden of Eden. And the same was for all of the animal life too. So all of the fruit and food that they would eat would be completely consumed and they would never get full and they would never gain any weight. They ate for the pleasure of eating and enjoying the taste and flavors of the food that they ate. There were fruit trees that would bare a different fruit each month; and some trees would bare the same fruit all of the time.

128 So Adam and his woman (Eve) would be in that garden to dress it and to keep it. And they would also be constantly eating and tasting this fruit and that fruit on a daily basis. In other words, Adam would be on one side of the garden keeping the garden, and his woman (Eve) would be on the other side of the Garden and a new type of fruit would be found on a tree by Adam and then he would pick two of its fruit and then he run over to his woman with this new fruit he had picked so that they would both be able to eat it together so that they would both enjoy this new taste sensation of this new fruit together. And then the woman (Eve) would also do the same thing that Adam had done with her; she would also find a new fruit and then she would also pick two of its fruit, and then she would run over to Adam with this new fruit she had picked so that they would both be able to eat of it together so that again they would then both enjoy this new taste sensation of this new fruit together. And this may have happened, together, on a daily basis throughout the whole time that they were in that Gar-

den of Eden and before they had fallen into sin.

129 And this whole time that they were in that Garden of Eden and on this earth, God has kept Satan and his demons and evil spirits held back all of this time so that they could do nothing to this new man Adam and his woman (Eve), the Garden of Eden and this earth. And also God had wanted to see if this new man Adam and his Woman (Eve) would walk in obedience to Him on their own; and God is well pleased up to this point in time that they have been totally obedient to His commandment to not eat of that tree of the knowledge of good and evil that was in the center or middle of that garden. For the whole time that Adam and his wife (Eve) were in that garden and on this earth; and even though that tree of the knowledge of good and evil was in the center of that garden and they both may have past it many times each day; Both Adam and his wife (Eve) never gave any attention to that tree of the knowledge of good and evil. They may have just moved around that garden on a daily basis keeping and dressing that garden as if that tree of the knowledge of good and evil wasn't even there.

130 So, for a certain amount of time, God had purposely held back Satan and his demons and evil spirits so that this man Adam and his woman and wife (Eve) could and would be able to roam about in that Garden of Eden on their own without any other outside influences or temptations to interfere; So that God could and would be able to see that if this man Adam and his woman and wife (Eve) would obey His commandment and order to NOT eat of that tree of the knowledge of good and evil that was in the middle of that garden. And this was that first agreement or first testament of God's plan between God and man. And also, Satan and his demons and evil spirits may have been moving around the outside of this perimeter or boundary that had been keeping them from getting any closer to this

earth; trying and hoping to find an opening somewhere outside and along this perimeter or boundary, but without any results; for Satan may have wanted to get to this earth and destroy it and everything on it.

131 And also, as Adam and his woman (Eve) are roaming about on this earth and in that garden, they had no knowledge of this great and evil rebellion of Lucifer and his angels and their expulsion from heaven by God; and that Lucifer and his angels have then become Satan and his demons and evil spirits; and that they are being held back from this earth at a great distance. For God had made this man Adam and his woman (Eve) to know only good and they were purposely made to know no evil; for even though God had known all about the evil and sinful rebellion that had taken place in His heaven with Lucifer and his angels; God had made this man Adam and his woman (Eve) without any knowledge of this evil rebellion that had taken place in His heaven. And since one third of the angels of heaven were tempted to sin and did not yield to that temptation to disobey, but had given in to that temptation and disobedience and crossed over to sin. This is why God had put that tree of the knowledge of good and evil in that garden. To test their obedience to God; and if they remain obedient to God and His commandment and order to NOT eat of that tree of the knowledge of good and evil; they would forever live in God's eternal heaven and remain in the obedience and righteousness that God had made them with and they would never know any evil.

132 So Adam and his woman (Eve) have been roaming about in the Garden of Eden on a daily basis and that it may have been several years now since they were made by God and put into this garden on this earth. Now it's not clear to us of how long that Adam and his woman (Eve) may have been in this garden and on this earth before they had fallen into sin. But there was a certain amount of time that they were on this earth and in that

garden from the time that God had made and created them to the actual time that they had disobeyed God and had fallen into sin. And remember, that this man Adam and his woman (Eve) were purposely made on this earth outside of God's eternal state of His heavenly kingdom to test their obedience to Him; so that if they do sin, it will be sin that is committed outside of His eternal heaven. And that this one test of obedience was going to be just one main test of their obedience, but with two folds to it. The first fold of that test, was where God had put them on this earth and in that Garden of Eden and with that tree of the knowledge of good and evil being used to test their obedience; for God had made them to know only good and their eyes were closed to all understanding of evil; And the commandment and order to not eat of that tree of the knowledge of good and evil applied to both folds of that test.

133 And during that whole time of that first part or fold of that one test, the man Adam and his woman (Eve), were allowed to roam and move about on this earth and in that garden freely, by themselves, and without any other influences to get them to eat of that tree of the knowledge of good and evil. In other words, God had wanted to see if this new man Adam and his woman (Eve) would be tempted on their own to eat of that tree of the knowledge of good and evil. Well the whole time that they were on this earth, and in that Garden of Eden, and they may have passed by that tree of the knowledge of good and evil, many times each day, for all of this time in that first part or fold of this test; and they had remained obedient to that commandment and order of God.

134 And this first fold of that test of the obedience of that man Adam and his woman (Eve), may have lasted several years to where they were allowed to be on this earth, and in that garden with that tree of the knowledge of good and evil there on a daily basis; but yet the man Adam and

his woman (Eve) was never tempted to eat of that tree of the knowledge of good and evil and remained obedient to God's commandment and order to not eat of it. And since God had given that commandment and order to the man Adam and his woman (Eve) to not eat of that tree in the middle of the Garden of Eden, they may have just used a kind of blind faith to God's commandment and order and obeyed. In other words, they may have believed God at His word and didn't ask any questions or reason why and just obeyed God at His word. So this first fold of this test of obedience was completed after a certain number of years have passed that only God Himself had determined was necessary to test this man Adam and his woman's (Eve) obedience to his commandment and order.

135 And now the second part or fold to that test of Adam and his woman (Eve) was about to be put into play by God. And the second fold of that test of obedience would this time involve the use of Satan himself. For since God had seen with His own eyes as to how Satan had deceived all of one third of the angels of heaven that were under his charge and authority over to disobedience against God's law; God had wanted to use Satan to test this new man Adam and his woman's (Eve) obedience. God wanted to see if this man Adam and his woman (Eve) would be strong enough to remain in obedience to Him or would they be easily deceived just like all of Satan's angels were deceived easily by Satan's cunningness and craftiness. And God had known in his heart that there was an extremely high probability that this man Adam and or his woman (Eve) could and would also be deceived easily by Satan's cunningness and craftiness of deception to sin; and that there was only just a very small slight chance that this man Adam and his woman (Eve) would remain obedient and not give into Satan's deception to disobey and sin.

136 And during all of this time that Adam and his woman (Eve) was on this

earth and in this garden, Satan and his demons and evil spirits may have been moving around and about the outside of this perimeter that God had put into place to hold back Satan and all of his demons and evils spirits from this earth; where he was constantly trying to find a way to get through and pass this perimeter that was holding him back. For Satan may have still thought in heart that if he could get through this perimeter barrier, he would be able to kill and destroy this man Adam and his woman (Eve). For since Satan couldn't kill and destroy the true and living Godhead, he may have thought that he would then, at the very least, be able to kill and destroy the very image of God. And Satan may have also developed an extremely jealous and hateful rage toward this man Adam and his woman (Eve). But God had intended to use Satan as a final test of obedience to this man Adam and his woman (Eve); for this is the very reason that God did not cast all of Satan and his demons and evil spirits into hell immediately; for God had needed Satan to tempt this man Adam and his woman (Eve) with a temptation to disobey God's commandment and order; because it's against God's nature and law for God Himself to tempt anyone to disobedience and sin. So God is about to use Satan to perform this test for Him on this man Adam and his woman (Eve) with Satan's ability to tempt them to disobey and sin. In other words, God had made them with, the eternal test of righteousness; and Satan is going to be used, to tempt them, with the eternal test of unrighteousness. Would they obey Him or would the obey Satan? God had wanted to see if this man Adam and his woman (Eve) would remain obedient to His commandment and order, or obey Satan's command and order.

137 Now since Satan could not get through that perimeter barrier that was holding him back from coming any closer to this new earth and this new man Adam and his woman (Eve), that Satan may have presented himself to the Lord concerning this new man Adam and his woman (Eve); And the

Lord may have asked Satan, "Where have you come from Satan?"; From roaming about this dark, and void, section of heaven, but I have been blocked from around that earth. And the Lord may have said, Have you seen my new creation of this man Adam and his woman and wife (Eve) and how they have walked in total obedience to Me and my commandment and order to not eat of the tree of the knowledge of good and evil? And Satan may have said, surely they will obey you for you have put a hedge around them and blocked me from being able to get close enough to them to tempt them with a temptation to eat of that tree. So the Lord may have then said, Then I will allow for only you to come into that Garden of Eden; none of your demons or evil spirits will be allowed beyond that perimeter, only you Satan will be allowed into that Garden of Eden; You will not be allowed to violate their free will; you will only be allowed to tempt them to freely eat of that tree of the knowledge of good and evil on their own; you cannot pick that fruit from that tree and give it to them; you are only allowed to tempt them and to try and get them to freely pick the fruit and eat of that fruit of that tree on their own only and no other way. You cannot force them to eat of that tree. They have the free will to obey you and eat of that tree, or the same free will to choose to disobey you and not eat of that tree.

138 So now God had let only Satan himself to go beyond that perimeter that had been holding him back and away from this earth and this man Adam and his woman (Eve) for all of this time, which may have been several years of time. And none of Satan's demons and evil spirits was allowed to go with Satan to help him do his evil deed. Satan was not allowed to touch or do any destructive damage of any kind to this earth, to all of animal life, and to this man Adam and his woman (Eve). Basically, Satan was only allowed to persuade this man Adam and his woman (Eve) with lies and deception, similar to what he had used to persuade all of

those angels that were under his charge. In other words, Satan was not allowed to actually touch that tree of the knowledge of good and evil and pick that fruit from that tree and give it to this man Adam or his woman (Eve) to eat. He was only allowed to get them to eat of the fruit of that tree of the knowledge of good and evil on their own. He would have to get them to freely touch, pick and eat of that tree on their own. He could not threaten them or force them to eat of that tree in any way, or violate their free will. Satan could only use his cunningness and craftiness to deceive them with his lies and trickery. Also, Satan still had his eternal spiritual form and existence similar to what he had when he was an archangel in heaven with the eternal life of God, except now he has the eternal spiritual form and existence of eternal death without the eternal life and existence of God. In other words, when Satan was an archangel in heaven, he was the most beautiful angel above all of the other angels of heaven at that time, and was made of every precious living stones. Now he is the most hideous and grotesquely looking creature that exists even today.

139 And being that Satan had an eternal, nonphysical, but spiritual form of existence and this man Adam and his woman (Eve) had a glorified physical body and existence; Satan had to first overcome one main obstacle for two reasons: One was that this man Adam or his woman (Eve) had never even known that Satan and his demons and evil spirits even existed; let alone the evil rebellion and war that had taken place in heaven before God had made them. God had made them to not know anything about this evil rebellion and war that had taken place in heaven. For Satan as he appears now could not just walk up or approach this man Adam or his woman (Eve) for two reasons; For if it were possible for Satan to approach this man Adam or his woman (Eve) directly, and as he appears now, and even if they would be able to see Satan, the very appearance of Satan would immediately freak them out to where Adam and his woman

(Eve) would quickly run to God asking as to what creature is this? For Adam had named all of the animals and creatures of this earth, that God had made and had brought to Adam to name; so Satan would be another creature that they didn't recognize; and Satan would not even have a chance to have any conversation at all with them. And the second reason was that since Satan had a spiritual form of existence and Adam and his woman (Eve) had a glorified physical form of existence; Even if Satan had approached this man Adam or his woman (Eve) directly, as he appears now, face-to-face, Adam or his woman (Eve) would not have been able to see or hear this spiritual form of Satan's existence with their physical eyes and ears; They would neither be able to see him or hear anything that he would have to say to them. Or even if they could hear his voice speaking but they wasn't able to see who it was that was speaking to them, this would have also freak them out to where they wouldn't listen to him and they again would run to God with questions as to a voice talking to them that they didn't recognized or couldn't see.

140 So Satan had to find a way that he could use to approach this man Adam or his woman (Eve) so that he could be seen and heard without them freaking out and running away from him. For in order for Satan to be able to deceive and tempt them, he had to get close enough to speak with them face-to-face. Satan may have walked around on this earth and in that garden surveying the situation and looking at what was available to him that he could use to accomplish his evil plan. And by doing this, Satan may have come up with an evil and deceptive plan of seducing and possessing one of the animals or creatures that this man Adam and his woman (Eve) had both recognize and had known. And after surveying all of the animals and creatures that were on this earth and in that Garden of Eden, Satan may have decided that the serpent or snake was the creature that had a weakness in it above all of the other animals and creatures

that was on this earth and in that garden that would serve his evil purpose and plan. So Satan had move over to the serpent or snake and seduced it to the point of Satan possessing that serpent completely that now he was able to move about on this earth and into that garden freely with the physical body and appearance of that serpent that both Adam and his woman (Eve) had known and recognized. In other words, Satan could now move around and in that Garden of Eden and even go up close to Adam or his woman (Eve) face-to-face without any negative reaction or affect. For Satan would now move and talk with the same movement and with the same voice of that serpent mimicking the same movement and speaking with the same voice of that serpent to the point that this man Adam and his woman (Eve) did not notice any change in that serpent. To them it was the same serpent. This is why Satan may have watched that serpent for a while before he even went over to it to seduce and possess it. Satan may have watched that serpent's normal movements and routine and the way that serpent would speak so that he would be able to mimic the same movements and routine and speak the same way that that serpent did; thereby hiding and deceiving both Adam and his woman (Eve) as to his real identity. And this part of Satan's evil plan of seducing and possessing this serpent creature may have taken place on this earth outside of this Garden of Eden, at a great distance, and out of sight and ear shot, from both this man Adam and his Woman (Eve).

141 Satan is now ready to put the final part of his evil plan into play; and it has to go perfectly without any error, for he knows that he only has one shot or chance at this attempt to deceive and persuade both Adam and his woman (Eve) to eat of that tree of the knowledge of good and evil. For Satan had known that if he could get this man Adam and his woman (Eve) to eat of that tree of the knowledge of good and evil, that would be disobedience against God and his laws. And then this man Adam and his woman

(Eve) would both have to be kicked out of heaven just like Satan and all of his demons and evil spirits were kicked out of heaven because of their sins when they were angels in heaven, or at least that's what Satan may have thought in his heart as to what would happen. But what Satan did not really know, was that God had already had a backup plan or a second agreement ready to put into play in the event that Adam and his woman (Eve) would give into that temptation to eat of that tree of the knowledge of good and evil, breaking that first agreement that was already in place since they were made by God. And this second agreement would be able to remove or redeem all of mankind of their sin, so that their sin only, goes to hell with Satan and all of his demons and evil spirits and not all of mankind that accept this second agreement of God's backup plan.

142 And while God was allowing Satan to come to this earth and tempt Adam and his woman (Eve), and while Satan was scheming his evil plan of temptation; Adam and his woman (Eve) were still roaming around and about that Garden of Eden that they were totally unaware of what was going on behind the scenes between God and Satan and Satan's plan to tempt them and deceive them. Both Adam and his woman (Eve) were still just enjoying the beauty and the fruits of that garden like they have been doing for several years now. And as they were both keeping and dressing that garden, Adam may have been in one area of that garden and His woman (Eve) may have been in another area of that garden keeping and dressing it, and suddenly a new fruit would appear on a certain tree and Adam's woman (Eve) would see it, and she would pick two of its fruit, and then she would run over, to her man Adam and she would excitedly give one of these new fruits that she had just pick from a tree in that garden and then they would both eat of that fruit and share that moment and its new taste together. And then at another time Adam would do the same thing with his woman (Eve), a new fruit would appear on a tree in his area

that he was in and then he too would pick two of its new fruit and then he would go over to where his woman (Eve) was at and he too would excitedly give her one of these new fruits and then they both would eat and share the pleasure and joy of the taste of that new fruit's taste together. And this was basically a daily occurrence, or a daily routine and enjoyment of being in that Garden of Eden and on this earth now for several years. And remember that during all these certain number of years that Adam and his woman (Eve) was on this earth and in that Garden of Eden and even up to this point in God's timeline of eternal life; Adam and his woman (Eve) had never even considered that tree of the knowledge of good and evil to the point that it was as if it wasn't even there as they were in that garden. And they may have pasted by it many times, on a daily basis, but paid no attention to it, because God had told them not to eat of it, and they obeyed that commandment and order on their own without any temptation of their own. And God was totally pleased with this man Adam and his woman (Eve) and with their obedience to Him, that they had passed their first part of that test of their obedience to God and His commandment and order.

143 Now at this time when Adam and his woman (Eve) was in that garden and on this earth, the animals were able to communicate with Adam and his woman (Eve), and Adam and his woman (Eve), were also able to communicate with all of the animals. And this may have happened on a daily basis that there were many times when an animal would walk up to Adam or his woman (Eve) and have a conversation with them. And there were also times that Adam or his woman (Eve) would walk over to the animals and have a conversation with them too. And this is what Satan may have observed and had seen taken place that had caught his attention when he was planning and scheming his evil plan of temptation to deceived Adam and his woman (Eve). For Satan's main part to his evil

plan was that he needed to have that face-to-face ability to have a conversation with Adam or his woman (Eve) in order to deceive them and persuade them to give in to that temptation and eat of that tree of the knowledge of good and evil. For you see that since Satan could not just walk or move over to Adam or his woman (Eve) on his own appearance, for the reasons mentioned earlier, and try to have a conversation with them, this is the reason why he had decided to seduce and possess one of the animals so that he would be able to walk over to Adam or his woman (Eve) and have that conversation with them and without them having any knowledge of who it really was that they would be really talking to or with. For Satan would deceive them to his true identity by hiding himself inside that serpent through his ability to possess that serpent and then move about as though it was still that serpent completely. For Satan may have seen that serpent move over to Adam and his woman (Eve) several times and had normal conversations with them on a routine basis. This is what Satan had decided to use to his advantage. And this is why he had possessed that serpent so that he would now be able to move over to Adam or his woman (Eve) and have that very important conversation with them that was needed by Satan to persuade them to give in to the temptation and eat of that tree.

144 Also, Satan may have observed and watched both Adam and his woman (Eve) when he was scheming and planning his evil plan of temptation. He may have observed and come to a conclusion that trying to seduce and tempt both Adam and his woman (Eve) at the same time would be too high of a risk for failure. But Satan needed both Adam and his woman (Eve) to eat of that tree at the same time to fulfill and complete his evil plan of deception and temptation. Satan had then observed, and watched, both Adam and his woman (Eve) to evaluate and see which one was the weaker of the two. Satan may have seen in Adam that his convic-

tions with God were too strong to sway him away from his obedience and allegiance to God's commandments and order directly. But Adam's woman (Eve) may have appeared to be the weaker of the two, so he had decided to approach her first, independently and away from Adam. In other words, Satan had now planned on approaching Adam's woman (Eve) first, and in an area that was in that Garden of Eden where she would be by herself, and far enough away from Adam, so that he would not be able to hear any of the conversation that Satan would have with Adam's woman (Eve). For Satan had observed and he had seen both Adam and his woman (Eve) independently pick two fruits from a tree and then they would run over to the other and they would both share the new taste of that fruit together. Satan had decided to use this to his advantage. Satan was planning on walking over to Adam's woman (Eve) and have that face-to-face conversation with her, deceiving and persuading her with the temptation to eat of that tree of the knowledge of good and evil, and hoping that she would do the same as before, getting her to pick two of its evil fruit and then she would run over to her man Adam and give him one of its fruit and they would both eat and taste of this evil fruit together and this would complete and fulfill Satan's evil plan of getting both Adam and his woman (Eve) to eat of that tree and disobey God's commandment and order to not eat of that tree.

145 And now Satan was completely ready to carry out and put into play his evil plan of deception and temptation against this man Adam and his woman (Eve). For Satan has already seduced and possessed this serpent and he has been moving about this Garden of Eden and he has been moving close to Adam and his woman (Eve) several times as a way of testing their reaction to his presence as this serpent to see if they see any change of this serpent that Satan now has possessed. And since Satan did not see any reaction of Adam or his woman (Eve) as he would

move by and close to them testing their reaction, he was convinced that he now had passed himself off as that serpent that they had thought was that same serpent that God had made. So now all he had to do was to pass some time away and wait for that perfect moment to approach Adam's woman (Eve) at a time when she was in an area of that garden alone and far enough away from Adam where he would then move over to her and have that important conversation with her.

146 And this important opportunity had finally come for Satan to play out his face-to-face conversation with Adam's woman (Eve) in an area of that garden where she was alone and by herself and far enough away from Adam. So Satan had moved over and up to Adam's woman (Eve) and in such a way as to still test her reaction as he was moving as that serpent so that he would not cause her to be alarmed in any way as to his real identity. And this serpent, that Satan had now possessed, was now more subtle than any beast of the field which the Lord God had made. And Satan had said to the woman with the voice of that serpent; Wow!, this is an extremely beautiful garden!; and the woman replied and said, Yes, it is a very beautiful and lovely garden indeed. And Satan had then said with the voice of that serpent; this garden has a lot of beautiful fruit trees in it, and you can eat the fruit of all of these trees? And the woman replied and said, we may eat of all of the trees of this garden except that tree of the knowledge of good and evil that is in the middle of this garden. For God had said, you shall not eat of it, neither shall you touch it, lest you die! For in that day that you do eat of it, you shall surely die!

147 Then Satan with the voice of that serpent had said what? You shall surely die?! No, No, No, You shall not surely die! For even the very knowledge of God does truly know that in this day that you eat the fruit of this tree you will not surely die, but it's that your eyes shall be truly opened and

you will become as wise as God's wisdom and knowledge to know good and evil that God has kept from you. Does God not want you to be as wise as he is? Do you not thirst for the Knowledge and Wisdom that God has? And the woman had then started to take a different and closer look at the fruit of this tree of the knowledge of good and evil. And she began to look at this tree for the first time as good for food. And the fruit on this tree, was above all the other fruit throughout this garden, the most beautiful fruit to look at, and very pleasant to the eyes; And most of all, it had now become a very important tree to be desired to make one very wise as the wisdom of God! In other words, she may have now thought that she would become equal to God. So she was now filled with the excitement of the fruit of this tree and without thinking this through completely first, she had picked two of its evil fruits and then she had then ran over to her man Adam and she had given one of these fruits to Adam and they both had eaten these fruits together similar to like what they have been doing before on a daily basis since they have been in that garden. And Adam had taken that fruit from his woman (Eve) like he has done many times before and ate of that fruit without even knowing that that fruit was one of the fruits that had come from that tree of the knowledge of good and evil that God had forbidden them to eat of it. And suddenly they immediately had noticed a change had taken place in both of them. They could no longer see the glorified bodies that they have always had since God had made them. They could now see a naked physical flesh and blood body that they have never seen before, and they now had also become ashamed of their nakedness, and they now were, also, afraid. And they had quickly gathered up a bunch of fig leaves and they had both sewed these fig leaves together to wear as a garment or an apron to hide their nakedness and shame. And Satan had removed himself from that serpent and left that area of the garden, for he was very pleased with himself that he had accomplished his goal of seducing and tempting this man Adam and his woman (Eve) to disobey God's commandment and order to not eat of that tree of the knowledge of good and evil.

148 Now even though Adam and his woman (Eve) may have thought that God did not know that they had eaten of the fruit of that tree of the knowledge of good and evil, that actually is just the opposite. For there is nothing hidden from God. God sees and knows all things. God had seen everything that Satan had done to seduce and tempt Adam and his woman (Eve); and God had seen Adam and his woman (Eve) take the fruit of that tree of the knowledge of good and evil and both eat of it together. In other words, God was continually watching Adam and his woman (Eve) at every point and every step during their seduction and temptation by Satan. There were several reasons as to why God had to be watching them. And like I had said earlier that God had known that there was a high probability that Adam and his woman (Eve) would give into the cunningness and craftiness of Satan's ability to trick them, and seduce them, and tempt them to disobey God's commandments and order. And God was already prepared for that; for God was ready to implement a second agreement that would redeem Adam and his woman (Eve) and all of their descendants of their sin in the event that Adam and his woman (Eve) would disobey God's commandment and order and eat of the fruit of that tree of the knowledge of good and evil. And remember that God the Father had dwelt one hundred percent in the souls of Adam and his Woman (Eve); and God the Lord Jesus had dwelt one hundred percent in the bodies of Adam and his Woman (Eve); and God the Holy Spirit had dwelt one hundred percent in the spirits of Adam and his Woman (Eve), to the point that they were continually clothed with the eternal presents of God the Father and God the Lord Jesus; and God the Holy Spirit, that even though they were naked on their own, they could not see their nakedness because they were clothed with the brightness and beauty of God's con-

tinual presents that flowed in them, and through them, and around them.

149 And because Adam and his woman (Eve) were both made by God with the same righteousness that God had in Himself; this is the very reason that God can dwell in them, through them, and around them on a continual basis because they were both made without any sin. And since they were made by God, they have been surrounded by, and with this glorious presents of God, that they were clothed with this heavenly and glorious garment of the presents of God Himself. And this is why they could not see their nakedness. And this heavenly garment of God that they were clothed with is what God had to watch very closely as they were being seduced and tempted by Satan. For remember that God cannot dwell where there is sin. For you see, that God would have to remove His presents from them, at least one micron of a second, before they had actually committed their sin, for two main reasons. For if God's presents would remain in them, while they commit their sin, the very righteousness of God would consume that sin, and both Adam and his woman (Eve) would have dropped death on the spot. And the second reason is, that God, by law, could only remove up to about ninety percent of His presents and eternal life from them immediately; Even though God's law states that the wages of sin is death, there is another part of God's law that also states that there is pleasure in that sin for a season. And then when that time limit of that pleasure in sin for a season is up, the remaining ten percent of God's eternal life is also removed from man and the wages of sin is death takes place. And this is why Adam and his woman (Eve) would not die immediately and would remain alive physically for a certain number of years to fulfill that pleasure in sin for a season, and then that wages of sin is death would come to both Adam and his woman (Eve) at a time limit determined by God Himself.

150 So you can now see that even though Adam and his woman (Eve) may have thought that God didn't know or see them eat of the fruit of that tree. But God had seen, and He had known to the very split second, when they had bit into the fruit of that tree of the knowledge of good and evil. Because God had to remove ninety percent of His heavenly garment of His presence and His eternal life from them, so that they would not drop dead on the spot, and to also to fulfill both of His laws, of the pleasure of sin for a season, and the wages of sin is death. And when God had remove ninety percent of His presence from them, this is why they could now see their own nakedness for they were no longer clothed with the very presence of God and His heavenly garment. God had to remove Himself from them both, because God cannot dwell in them with their sin in them. And the very second that God had removed ninety percent of His presence and eternal life from both Adam and His woman (Eve), that had also started their time clock of that pleasure of sin for a season in both Adam and his woman (Eve): In other words, God had removed ninety percent of His eternal life and presence from them immediately one micron of a second before they had actually committed their disobedience and sin, so that they would not drop dead on the spot, and to fulfill that part of God's law, that there is pleasure in sin for a season, and so that they would remain alive physically for a certain number of years determined by God and His law, and so that God would now be able to invoke this second agreement, and allowing this first agreement to run its legal course.

151 And also remember that God had originally created and made Adam and his woman (Eve) to refill that void and empty position of power and authority that Satan had held as Archangel Lucifer, but was kicked out of that position of power and authority because of his sin and rebellion against God. And Adam and his woman (Eve) and their children or all of their descendants would have refilled all of those void and empty positions

of power and authority that all of Satan's demons and evil spirits had held as angels in heaven that were also kicked out of heaven because of their sin and rebellion with Satan against God. And now that Adam and his woman (Eve) have just disobeyed God's commandment and order, that they were not to eat of that tree of the knowledge of good and evil; that had now still left all of those void and empty positions of power and authority that Satan and his demons and evil spirits had held as angels in heaven before their sin and rebellion against God; And now Adam and his woman (Eve) and all of their descendants could not be used by God to refill all of those void and empty positions of power and authority at this time because of their disobedience, sin and unrighteousness. For Adam and his woman (Eve) were originally made with the total and complete and perfect righteous cloth that God had and made them with; but now that they had disobeyed and sinned against God and his commandment and order, their perfect righteous cloth had now become a filthy rag of unrighteousness. And their sin and filthy rag of unrighteousness would not just remain with them only; for their sin and filthy rag of unrighteousness would be passed unto all of their descendants; for by one man's sin, all have become sin. For all have sinned and come short of the Glory of God; there is none righteous, no not one.

152 Another important point that I would like to make is that God had originally made and then restored this earth to make and place Adam and his woman (Eve) on this earth. And even though this earth belongs to God, for He is the creator and owner of this earth, God had given this earth totally and completely over to Adam and his woman (Eve). God had given this earth to them free of charge; it was kind-of like a gift from God to them. They were to have dominion over all of this earth and everything that was on it. They were to subdue it and multiply, replenish or refill this earth with their descendants. In other words, Adam and his woman (Eve)

had become ownership of this earth and it was totally and completely their earth. It might have been a wedding give from God to them both. And while they had walked in obedience with God and His Laws, this earth would have remained in their possession for ever; But remember that God had told them to not eat of the fruit of that tree of the knowledge of good and evil, and Satan had come along and told them that they could eat of that tree. If they would have obeyed the true and living God and not ate of that tree, the true and living God would have remained their God forever; But since they had disobeyed the true and living God and obeyed Satan, a creature that was originally created by the true and living God; And even though Satan is not a god naturally, he had become a god in a technical since because of Adam and his woman's (Eve) obedience to him. In other words, God had told them to not eat of that tree, and Satan had come along and told them to eat of that tree; whichever one they obeyed would be God over their lives; if they would have obeyed the true and living God, He would have remained God over their lives forever; or if they would obey the lies of Satan; Satan would become a god, technically, over their lives. And this is what has happened to Adam and his woman (Eve); and since they had just obeyed the lies of Satan; that had made Satan a technical god over their lives and over all of mankind and this earth for a certain amount of time that is determined by God. In other words, this earth that was given to Adam and his woman (Eve) by God, was immediately taken from them, technically, by Satan, and He's been, the technical, and a temporary owner of it even to this very day.

153 And remember that when God had come back to this earth to restore it from a destructive state, and when God had slammed back all the forces of Satan and all of his demons and evil spirits from around this destroyed earth to a distance that was determined by God, when God had spoken that powerful phrase, "Let there be Light": Well this distance has now

changed because of Adam and his woman (Eve)'s obedience to Satan's lies. Adam and his woman (Eve) originally, was part of that family of the true and living God of Truth and righteousness; But now, they have been pulled into the family of Satan's lies and unrighteousness by a lie. And since Satan has a technical ownership in the earth for a certain timeline that is determined by the true and living God, Satan and his demons and evil spirits were now allowed, by God, to move to a much closer distance to this earth than they were originally place by God at that time of the restoration of this earth. But they were not allowed to come to this earth and physically dwell on this earth yet. So Satan now has a much closer position around this earth in all and every direction from this earth that Satan now completely surrounds this earth at a certain distance between this earth and God's heaven. And Satan has surrounded this earth as though he was trying to keep God and His angels of heaven from getting from heaven to this earth with any blessings or messages from God to mankind. And Satan has surrounded this earth as though it was a spiritual blockade between God and Mankind, and it is still there even to this very day. This is the very reason, that it had taken the Angel that God the Father had sent to Daniel, with the answer to his prayer, twenty one days to get through this spiritual blockade of Satan and all of his demons and evil spirits, to Daniel.

154 In other words, the very second that Daniel had started praying and partitioning God in prayer, Daniel's prayer had went, from the very place that he was praying from here on earth, and up and through that blockade of Satan and all of his demons and evil spirits, and straight through and into heaven and directly to the Father in heaven without any spiritual battle or hindrances of Satan or his demons or evil spirits to stop it. And even though Satan and his demons and evil spirits are powerless to stopping any prayer by man to God the Father in heaven, it's when God the Father

answer's each prayer and gives the answer to an angel, and that angel with the answer to that prayer has to go from heaven, and through this universe and through this spiritual blockade of Satan and all of his demons and evil spirits, that there is a spiritual battle of Satan and his demons and evil spirits against each angel, to try and stop that angel, from getting through to earth with that answer, blessings, or miracles to that prayer. And when Daniel had prayed, the Father in heaven immediately answered that prayer of Daniel and immediately sent an angel with the answer to his prayer, but the battle for that angel that had the answer to Daniel's prayer was so strong and intense that Archangel Michael had to come to help fight that battle so that angel was able to get through that spiritual blockade with that answer to Daniel's prayer that it had taken that angel twenty one days to get from God the Father in heaven to Daniel here on earth with the answer to his prayer.

155 So you can now see that Satan and his demons and evil spirits had become a spiritual blockade between God and mankind because of Adam and his woman's (Eve) obedience to Satan's commandment and order to eat of that tree and the disobedience to the true and living God's commandment and order to not eat of that tree; thereby, changing this Garden of Eden, and this restored earth, that was really God's Garden of Truth, into Satan's garden of lies. If Adam and his woman (Eve) would have remained obedient to the true and living God and rejected Satan's attempt to get them to eat of that tree, Satan and all of his demons and evil spirits would have been cast into hell then, and Adam and his woman (Eve) would have been brought into the eternal state of God's eternal heaven; and this whole dark universe, that we see today, would have been restored, and also brought back into God's eternal state of His heavenly kingdom, and we would have never even seen this dark universe that we can see today. We would have never known that Satan and all of his demons

and evil spirits and death and Hell ever existed. This is why God did not want Adam or his woman (Eve) to eat of that tree of the knowledge of good and evil. That is also why God had made them with only the knowledge of good and without any knowledge of the evil that had taken place in God's heaven before God had made man. But since Adam and his woman (Eve) did obey Satan's commandments and order to eat of that tree; that gave Satan a technical hold on this earth, Adam and his woman (Eve) and all of their descendants, and this is why God could not cast Satan and his demons and evil spirits into hell yet because of their technical hold on this earth and all of mankind. In other words, even though this earth was made by God and belongs to Him; God had given this earth to Adam and his woman (Eve) totally and completely, free of charge and complete ownership. This earth had become Adam and his woman (Eve)'s earth. But when they had disobeyed God's commandment and order and obeyed Satan's commandment and order, this earth was taken away from them by Satan and he has claimed this earth as his earth even to this day, and Satan has been the prince of the power of the air over this earth since then.

156 But now since Adam and his woman (Eve) have broken, breached, and disobeyed their first agreement or first testament between God and man; God was going to let this first agreement run its course by law and then a second agreement or testament between God and mankind would be put into place by God that is a much better and greater agreement than the first agreement. For you see that God had known that there was that high probability that this man Adam and his woman (Eve) would have broken or disobeyed this first agreement or testament because God had seen Satan deceive one third of the angels of heaven that was directly under his charge and control. And even though this second agreement was a much better and greater agreement than the first agreement, this

first agreement had to be put into place first and run its course completely before this second agreement could be put into place by law. Therefore by the deeds of the law there shall no flesh be justified in his sight: for by the law is the knowledge of sin; and this is why the first agreement between God and mankind had to run its course. Before Adam and Eve had fallen into disobedience, sin and unrighteousness, the law of God was still there. It's just that the law of sin and death wasn't there, because the law of obedience, righteousness, and eternal life was there praising and glorifying their obedience to God's law. And since the law of God, at this time, had seen their total obedience to Him, their obedience was counted as righteousness, and the gift of that righteousness is eternal life. So as long as they remained in obedience to God's law, they were in the law of obedience, righteousness, and eternal life.

157 But any disobedience to God's law is sin, and by God's law the wages of sin is death. So when Adam and his woman (Eve) disobeyed that commandment and order of God that they were not allowed to eat of any of that fruit of that tree of the knowledge of good and evil, their disobedience was seen by God's law of sin and death; and God's law had continually stated, "charged with disobedience to me and found guilty as charged"; And the law would continually demand that the wages of this sin is death; but that second part of that law, also states that there is pleasure in their sin for a season, and this is why that Adam and his woman (Eve) did not drop dead on the spot, but they did eventually die many years later. Wherefore, as by one man's disobedience, (Adam's), sin entered into the world and death by sin; and so death passed upon all men, for that all have sinned: For as by one man's disobedience many were made sinners; Therefore by the deeds of the law there shall no flesh be justified in his sight: for by the law is the knowledge of sin. There is nowhere or nothing in the law of God that says or states do this and you shall have

eternal life again. For the law of God will only and can only find you guilty of sin and worthy of death. It will continually demand that death penalty be paid in full.

158 In other words, in order for you to fulfill that death penalty that the law continually demands on you, is that you would have to die to fulfill that death penalty that the law demands, and be put in the grave for three days and three nights, and then be able to come back out of that grave without any of your sins. But even though you would fulfill that death penalty that the law had demanded because of your sins; that death penalty did not release you from your sins, your sins would still be a part of you and you would still be a part of your sins; and since you did not do anything to release you from your sins, you would not be able to come back out of your grave without your sins, and your sins would forever hold you in your grave for all eternity. And God is, eventually, going to cast all sin into hell, where they will remain there for all eternity. And this means that God will pick up all of your sins and cast them into hell and since you would still be a part of your sins, all of your sins would pull you to hell and your sins would hold you there in hell forever. So you can now see that not only do you need to fulfill that death penalty that the law demands, but you need to have a way for you to release and separate your sins from you so that when you do pay that penalty of death that the law of God demands, you would then be able to come back out of your grave alive and without your sins; and since your sins would then no longer be a part of you, your sins would remain in that grave and that death penalty would also be completely paid in full; and then when God picks up all of your sins in that grave, yours sins would be cast into hell by themselves without you and you would be free and clear to go to God's heaven instead of hell.

159 And as I have said, that before you would first even try to fulfill that

death penalty that the law demands, you would have to have a way to release and separate your sins from you before you would even attempt to fulfill that death penalty that the law demands. For you would have to have a way to release and separate your sins from you first, so that when you pay that death penalty and go to your grave fulfilling that death penalty that the law demands, you would also be released and separated from your sins, and then you would be able to come back out of your grave alive and without your sins. But the only major problem with this concept is that you have nothing on your own that you could use to release and separate your sins from you. For even though the law of sin and death states that the wages of sin is death; there is another part of God's law that also states that there is no remission of sin, no separation of your sin, or no forgiveness of your sins unless innocent blood be shed and applied to that sin.

160 In other words, you would have to have innocent blood to apply to your spirit and soul to release and separate your sins from you. And this cannot be just any innocent blood that you would use. Even though all animal's blood is innocent blood; it cannot be used to separate man's sins from his spirit and soul; it can only be used as a temporary covering of man's sins as a way of keeping mankind alive and placing a temporary stay of execution on all of mankind until a perfect sacrifice with the correct innocent blood that can be used to release and separate all of mankind from their sins. In other words, since it was a man that had sinned and all of mankind had become sin; then it would have to be a man that would come out of the descendants of Adam and Eve that would have to have that innocent and sinless blood that could be used to redeem all of mankind of their sins. So you can now see that we have no innocent blood that we can use on our own. We cannot even use our own sinful blood because it would not release or separate our sin from us. For this is why Jesus had said that all have sinned and come short of the glory of God,

there is none righteous, no not one. Adam's sin didn't just stay with him only; it has been passed unto all of us, even to this very day. Adam's sinful nature was passed unto Cain, Able, Seth, and all of their children that Adam and Eve had during their whole life on this earth; and then their children had passed on Adam's sinful nature to their children and so on, and so on, even to this very day.

161 So you can see that even if mankind would exist in this sinful state forever, all of mankind would continually be conceived, formed, and born into this world with a sinful and unrighteous nature. There would be no man out of the descendants of Adam and Eve that would or could be conceived, formed, and born into this world with a righteous and sinless nature that would have that innocent blood that would be needed to fulfill that law of God that there is no remission, separation and forgiveness of our sins. And this is what God had seen in advance, that there would be no man that would come out of the descendants of Adam and Eve that would or could be conceived without sin, formed without sin, and born into this world without any sin; and be able to live and walk a sinless and righteous life in total obedience to God the Father in heaven and to be tempted of every manner of sin and yet commit no sin. And since God had seen that there would be no man that could come out of the loins of Adam and Eve without that curse and sin of Adam and Eve; and God had loved all of mankind so much that God Himself was willing to become a flesh and blood, righteous and sinless man that would have that innocent blood that God would need to redeem all of mankind from their sins. For God so loved the world so much, that He was willing to give us His only begotten Son as a ransom and payment for all of the penalties and debt that the law of God demanded against all of us.

162 In other words, when Adam and Eve was just about to actually

commit their disobedience against God's commandment and order to not eat of that tree of the knowledge of good and evil, and within one split second just before they were actually about to commit their sin; God the Father not only had removed about ninety percent of His eternal life and presence from Adam and Eve, but He had also turned His face from them so that any of His righteous and glorious light that shines forth from God the Father would not shine on their sin and consume their sin as soon as it was committed, that would cause both Adam and Eve to drop dead on the spot. But also God the Lord Jesus and God the Holy Spirit had also remove ninety percent of their presence from them too at the same time that the Father had removed His presence from them. In other words, God the Father had removed ninety percent of His eternal life and presence from the souls of Adam and Eve and He had turned His face from them and committed all judgment and authority unto God the Lord Jesus who was also going to become that sinless and righteous man that would also be named Jesus the Christ or the suffering Messiah; and God the Lord Jesus had also removed ninety percent of His eternal life and presence from their physical flesh and blood bodies of both Adam and Eve and at the same time with God the Father; and this is the moment that they may have noticed that they could now see their nakedness of their flesh and blood bodies; and God the Holy Spirit had also removed ninety percent of His eternal life and presence from the spirits of both Adam and Eve, and at the same time with God the Father and God the Lord Jesus. And since the spirit of man no long had that eternal light of God the Holy Spirit, the spirit of man was now a candle unto the Lord God's eternal Light. And like a candle, once it is lit, it burns with a flickering little flame for a certain amount of time and then goes out.

163 So you see that Adam and his woman (Eve) did not really grasp or fully understand the magnitude of their situation that had taken place be-

cause of their disobedience to God's commandment to not eat of that tree. And since they no longer had that perfect righteous cloth that God had made them with, they now had a filthy rag of unrighteousness that now had all of the attributes of sin. For when you break or disobey just any point or tittle of God's law, it's as if you have broken or disobeyed all of God's laws at the same time. And some of the attributes of sin that they may have been experiencing at that moment was fear, confusion and misunderstanding. Because they had first notice that they were now naked even though they may have not had any clue as to why they were naked. They may have also experienced fear, embarrassment and may have been ashamed of their nakedness to the point that they had went around collecting fig leaves and then sewing them to gather to make aprons so as to cover up or hide their nakedness. And now they were also afraid of the presence of God that they had hid themselves amongst the trees of that garden. And they heard the voice of the Lord God walking in the garden in the cool of the day: Adam and his wife (Eve) hid themselves from the presence of the Lord God amongst the trees of the garden. This had never happened before, they were never afraid of the presence of God, let alone the very voice of God. And also, they may have always leaped up from what they were doing in that garden and they may have ran over to greet the Lord God with great joy and excitement at each moment that they would hear the voice of the Lord their God walking in the garden. But now they were both afraid and feared the Lord God that instead of running up to greet the Lord with great joy and excitement, they hid themselves amongst the trees of the garden and kept quiet out of fear.

164 And the Lord God called unto Adam, and said unto him, where art thou? Now this statement is not implying that God did not know where they were at, but is a question by God to test and see what their response was going to be because of their disobedience and sin. For God had

known exactly where they were at, for there is nothing hid from the eyes and knowledge of God. And also, since they didn't run up to greet Him with great joy and excitement like they have done before, this is the first time and reason that God had to ask that question, Where art thou?: for the normal and regular response was that God would only have to walk a few steps and they would have already been running up to greet Him with great joy and excitement. But this time God is walking in and around this garden and there is no joyous greeting at all. And since God had known exactly where they were hiding, and as God was getting closer to where both Adam and his woman (Eve) were hiding behind the trees of the garden, Adam may have come to a conclusion that they were not going to be able to hide behind these trees in this garden forever from God. So he may have stepped out of his hiding place and said, I heard your voice in the garden, but I was afraid and ashamed to come to you because I was naked. And because I was naked and ashamed, I hid myself from you. And the Lord God had said, who told you that you were naked? The only way that you would be able to even see your nakedness is, if you had eaten of the fruit of that tree of the knowledge of good and evil. Did you eat of that tree, whereof I had commanded that you should not eat? And Adam had said, the woman whom you had given to be with me, she gave me of the tree, and I did eat. She had picked two of its fruit from that tree of the knowledge of good and evil and without telling me that it was the fruit from that tree; she gave that fruit to me tricking me into eating of that fruit of that tree and I did eat. And the Lord God said unto the woman, what is this that you have done? And the woman said, the serpent had deceived and tricked me into wanting to take and eat of that tree when I was over there in that part of the garden by myself. He had tricked me into thinking that it would make me wise as you and I did pick two of its fruit and gave one to Adam and we did eat of it together. And the Lord God said unto the serpent, because you have done this, you are cursed above all cattle, and above every beast of the field; upon your belly shall you go, and dust shall you eat all the days of your life. And I will put enmity between you and the woman, and between your seed and her seed; it shall bruise your head, and you shall only bruise his heel.

165 In other words, when God was addressing that serpent, the first part, because you have done this, you are cursed above all cattle, and above every beast of the field; upon your belly shall you go, and dust shall you eat all the days of your life, was directed at that serpent, but the second part, And I will put enmity between you and the woman, and between your seed and her seed; it shall bruise your head, and you shall only bruise his heal, was directed at Satan, and his temporary power, and authority over all of mankind. This is where God has now proclaimed to Satan that out of the seed of Adam's woman (Eve) would come a savior that would destroy and take away that power of eternal death that Satan now had over all of mankind because of Adam and His woman's (Eve) disobedience and sin. This savior, that would come out of the loins or descendants of Adam and his woman (Eve), would kind-of, and in a spiritual since, stomp on Satan's head with the heal of his foot, bruising or crushing the head and authority of Satan's power of death over mankind, and this savior would end up with only a bruised heel of the foot that he used to crush Satan's head.

166 And remember that all power and authority was given by God the Father over to God the Lord Jesus. And since Adam and his woman (Eve) had fallen into disobedience and sin, God the Father had turned his face from all of mankind and committed all authority and power over to God the Lord Jesus that would also become that righteous, sinless and innocent man for man's redemption and salvation from sin; the savior that would bruise Satan's head. So it wasn't God the Father and it wasn't God the Holy Spirit that was speaking at this time; It was God the Lord Jesus that

was speaking to Adam and his woman (Eve), the serpent, and to Satan at this time and it will continue to be God the Lord Jesus that will speak to all of mankind until this man Jesus ascends to the Father and God the Holy Spirit comes to the one hundred twenty in that upper room. Then the Holy Spirit, the comforter, will come and be with mankind drawing them to feet of Jesus's salvation plan.

167 And then God had said unto the woman, I will greatly multiply your sorrow and your conception; in sorrow you shall bring forth children; and your desire shall be to your husband, and he shall rule over you. And then God had said unto Adam, because you have obeyed unto the voice of your wife (Eve), and have eaten of the tree, of which I commanded to you, saying, you shall not eat of it: cursed is the ground for your sake; in sorrow you shall eat of it all the days of your life; Thorns also and thistles shall it bring forth to you; and you shall eat the herb of the field; In the sweat of your face shall you eat bread, till you return unto the ground; for out of it you were taken: for dust you are, and unto dust shall you return. And then Adam called his wife's name Eve; because she is the mother of all living. And since it was a man that had sinned, Adam, through disobedience and unrighteousness to God's law, for as by one man's disobedience many were made sinners, so by the obedience of one shall many be made righteous. God needed only one man that would come out of the loins or descendants of Adam and Eve that would be obedient, righteous, and sinless and with innocent blood. But God had seen that all of the descendants would be conceived, formed and born into this world with the sin of Adam, for all of their descendants would be conceived with the same curse and sin of Adam and Eve. There would be none righteous, no not one; all have come short of the glory of God. And since there would be no one that would come out of the loins of Adam and Eve that could fulfill that righteous and sinless conception and to be formed in righteousness and

without sin, and to be born into this world righteous and without any sin and to be able to walk and live a righteous and sinless life and be tempted of every manner of sin and still remain obedient, righteous, and sinless; God had promised that He would take on all the sins of mankind upon himself by becoming that flesh and blood of a man, named Jesus.

168 In other words, God the lord Jesus was going to lay down that gavel of walking as God to take on the flesh and blood body of a man that would be conceived out of the loins of Adam and Eve. God the Lord Jesus was going to become that flesh and blood, obedient, righteous, sinless man with innocent blood that God needed to redeem and remove all of mankind's sins from them. For the law of disobedience, is sin; and, that law demands that the wages of that sin, is death, and that death penalty, has to be paid in full. And another part of God's law states that there is no remission of sin, no separation of sin, and no forgiveness of sin unless innocent blood be shed and applied to all of that sin. For God needed just one obedient, righteous, sinless man with innocent blood so that God could use him to pay that penalty of death that was due to all of us. And then God would be able to use this man's innocent blood to separate all of our sins from each of our spirits and souls. But this man, Jesus, would not be conceived, yet, for approximately four thousand years, for the first agreement, or Old Testament, had to run its course as a schoolmaster, to show us sin, and that we need to accept the salvation plan of God. But Adam and Eve's sin had to have a temporary covering with an innocent blood sacrifice. Because those fig leaves that they had used to make aprons to cover the nakedness of their sin could not be used even as a temporary covering for their sin, because there is no remission of sin unless innocent blood be shed and applied to that sin. So the innocent blood of animals was used as a temporary covering of their sin until that man Jesus would come.

169 In other words, for as by one man's disobedience, Adam's disobedience, many were made sinners, so by the obedience of one will many be made righteous? But since Adam's disobedience and sin would be past unto all of his descendants and none of his descendants would not be able to fulfill that obedient, righteous, sinless man with innocent blood requirement that God needed as a onetime and permanent sacrifice for all of mankind's sin; God had decided to provide himself as that man that would fulfill that requirement for our salvation and redemption. God was willing to become a flesh and blood man that would be conceived in righteousness and without any curse and sin of Adam's sin, and would be formed in righteousness and without any sin; and be born into this world righteous and without any sin; and even though it was God the Lord Jesus that would be walking, talking, acting and fulfilling that role as a totally obedient, righteous, and sinless man with innocent blood, that would be tempted in all points as we are, and yet will be without any sin, for it would be God the Lord Jesus walking as a man named Jesus and not God the Lord Jesus walking as God the Lord Jesus, for He would fulfill that requirements of an obedient, righteous, sinless man with innocent blood that no man out of the loins or descendants of Adam would be able to fulfill. And since at this time of Adam and Eve's sin, this obedient, righteous, sinless man with innocent blood, that was to be named Jesus; the Christ, Savior, and Messiah was just a promise by God that would come out of their descendants in the future and not at this immediate moment of Adam and Eve's sin. And since this innocent blood of a man would not be available for approximately four thousand years yet, the innocent blood of animals would be used as a temporary covering of mankind's sins.

170 In other words, since it was a man that had sinned and all have become sin, only the innocent blood of an obedient, righteous and sinless man could be used to remit, separate, and forgive those sins. The blood of

animals is innocent blood, but it could not be used to remit, separate, or forgive all of man's sins. But it could and would be used as a temporary covering of man's sins, and as temporary stay of the execution of that death penalty that the law of the wages of sin is death would continually demand on Adam and Eve and all of their descendants until that innocent blood of an obedient, righteous, sinless man would come and shed his innocent blood only once for all of mankind's sins. And then all the innocent blood of animals as a temporary covering would no longer be needed. And this is why all throughout the old testament that the blood sacrifices were used as a temporary covering of man's sins; and man was under the schoolmaster of the Law until Jesus would come and shed His innocent blood and die on the cross for all of mankind's sins; for Jesus is the end of the law, and the old testament, for righteousness to everyone that believeth. But after that Jesus is come we are no longer under the schoolmaster of the law, but by grace are you saved through faith and the salvation plan of Jesus, and that not of yourselves: it is the gift of God: and not of works, lest any man should boast: this is the second agreement between God and man or the new testament between God and mankind.

171 So starting with Adam and Eve and all throughout the Old Testament, all of their descendants or people of the old testament would put their trust or faith in the promise that God had made that a savior would come and redeem them from all of their sins. In other words, just like we put our faith and trust in what Jesus had already did approximately two thousand years ago that we physically did not actually see it take place, but believe and trust by faith that it did actually happen; The people of the old testament, starting with Adam and Eve, had also put their trust and faith in what Jesus was going to do that most of the people of the old testament would not live long enough to see it actually take place. In other words, the people in the Old Testament had looked forward to the cross of Jesus for their salvation,

and we look back to the cross of Jesus to our salvation. Another difference too, is that in the old testament all sin that was committed had to be covered by the temporary ceremonial blood sacrifices of the many animals that was required to cover their sin; they had to obey all of the commands, Sabbaths, rules and regulations of the laws, etc.; but today we live under the Grace of God and the shed innocent blood of Jesus and the new testament; and to a Christian that is saved by that innocent blood of Jesus, that if we sin, we can confess that sin to Jesus and have it covered by His innocent blood; for Jesus is faithful and just to forgive us of our sins.

172 In the old testament, Satan had the keys of death over all of mankind starting with Adam and Eve; and throughout the old testament Satan was continually accusing God and all of mankind of their sins; and that their sins demanded that that death penalty be paid immediately; But this is why God had used the innocent blood and the death of the different animals that would be sacrificed as a temporary covering of mankind's sin and death penalty. In other words, starting with Adam and Eve, Satan had demanded that their death penalty had to be paid in full immediately, because they had sinned and that God's law states, that the wages of sin is death. Satan may have demanded, in a mocking and sarcastic way, that their death penalty had to be paid in full immediately and that their sins had to be cast into hell immediately, in kind of a holding God's own law at God's own throat type attitude. But God had reminded Satan of the promise that He had made, that there would come a man that would come out of the seed of Eve that would pay that death penalty in full and take away all of mankind's sins. But then Satan may have retorted back at God that this man is not here at this time and that there is no payment of that death penalty right now. But then God had to show Satan that that death penalty of Adam and Eve was covered by the deaths and blood of innocent animals, which was like a temporary stay of execution on that death penalty,

and the innocent blood of that animal was also used as a temporary covering over Adam and Eve's sin until that man that would come and pay that penalty of death in full once and take away all of their sins; and the death of all of the animals and their innocent blood that would continue to be used on a daily basis throughout the old testament to continually cover all of mankind's sins and put that stay of execution on that death penalty.

173 In other words, any and all of mankind's sins that were committed during and throughout the old testament, had to be covered by the death and the shedding of the innocent blood of various animals; to keep that death penalty at bay; and the innocent blood of those animals was used as a temporary covering, and forgiveness of mankind's sins, until that permanent death payment, and the power of a man's innocent blood, that will be used to remit separate, and to completely forgive us of all of our sins. For you see, that if God did not use these blood sacrifices, of the various animals, to put a stay of execution of that death penalty, and to use the innocent blood of those animals as a temporary covering of man's sins, starting with Adam and Eve; would have reduced their life span from several hundreds of years to just a few days; for as I have said earlier, that the wages of sin is death by God's law of sin and death; and that the very reason that they did not drop dead on the spot is that the second part of God's law also states that there is pleasure in sin for a season; and if God didn't use the death and blood sacrifices of all these various animals as a temporary stay of execution of that death penalty and a covering of their sins; Adam and Eve's pleasure in sin may have been reduced to only a few days instead of several hundreds of years; And then when that pleasure in sin would have expired by God's law in just a few days after their commitment of that sin, God would have had to, by law, to remove the remaining part of His eternal life that was in Adam and Eve; and since all of God's eternal life would have been completely removed from them; Their

spirit, soul and physical flesh and blood bodies would have dropped dead on the spot. And then God would of had to pick up the sins of Adam and Eve and cast them into hell; and since there was no innocent blood to remit, separate, and forgive their sins, their sins were still a part of them and they were still a part of their sins. The souls of both Adam and Eve would have been pulled to hell with their sins; and their sins would have held them there in hell for all eternity.

174 So this is the reason, that God had to use the, temporary, death and blood sacrifices, of various animals, throughout the old testament starting with Adam and Eve's sin to all of mankind's sins as a temporary stay of the execution of that death penalty; and as a temporary covering for their sins, until that permanent, and one time death, and innocent blood sacrifice, of a righteous, and sinless man, that would come as God had promised; that would permanently pay that death penalty once and for all time; and the innocent blood that would be shed only once for all time, that would be used for the remission and the separation, and the total forgiveness of all of mankind's sins; starting with Adam and Eve's sins, and throughout all of the timeline of mankind's physical existence until the last man standing. In other words, God had gone way out of his way to save us from an eternal damnation and punishment of all of mankind's sins. For God so loved the world, that He was willing to give His only begotten Son, as a one time sacrifice for all of mankind's sins, that whosoever would believe in Him should not perish, but will have everlasting life, in God's eternal heaven. For God is not going to send His Son Jesus into the world, to condemn the world; but that the world, through His Son Jesus, might be saved from the eternal pits of hell.

175 Now God may have laid out certain rules, regulations, and commands on how Adam and Eve were to live their lives to remain obedient and

faithful to Him even though they were now living in a sinful and physical world and they were no longer allowed to enter or go into that garden of Eden; for God had driven both Adam and Eve from that garden of Eden, and God had placed at the east of the garden of Eden, Cherubim's, and a flaming sword which had turned every way, to keep Adam and Eve from getting back into that garden and eating of that tree of eternal life; For God had known that if they were allowed back into that garden and to eat of that tree of eternal life; they would live forever in their sin without no way to redeem or remove their sins from them similar to Satan and all of his demons and evil spirits sinful and rebellious nature. In other words, Satan and all of his demons and evil spirits had sinned in the eternal state of God's heaven as eternal angels of heaven; they each had the eternal life in them; and they all had angelic, celestial type spiritual bodies with eternal life; There was no physical death that could have taken place; It was a spiritual death from eternal life to eternal death with their sin, and total separation from God and his eternal heaven. There was no way to separate their sin from them; their sin, was forever a part of them, and they were forever a part of their sin; and all of those sins of Satan and his demons and evil spirits had to be removed from God's righteous and sinless heaven, and will eventually be cast into hell permanently and forever.

176 But since Adam and Eve was made outside of the eternal state of God's eternal heaven; and they were made with just physical flesh and blood human bodies that would have a physical death first before a spiritual death could even take place; and the life that was in them now was just a physical flesh and blood body life and not an eternal life; and this is why that God did not want them to get into that garden and eat of that tree of life and live forever in their sin. For you see, that Adam and Eve would live a certain amount of time, in years, and then they would eventually die; but this death would first be the death of this physical flesh and blood body.

Dust it was made from and dust it shall return too. But the spirit and soul will then either receive eternal death in hell with Satan and all of his demons and evil spirits, or receive eternal life with God in paradise. And since Adam and Eve may have been taught by God the Lord Jesus directly, on how they should live their physical life now in obedience, and by the faith in the promise that out of the seed of Eve would come that righteous, sinless, and obedient man with innocent blood, that would pay that death penalty, and take away the sins of mankind.

177 But until then Adam and Eve would have to live their physical lives following ordinances and procedures of all the animal blood sacrifices to keep all of their daily sins covered by the blood of these animal sacrifices, and the death of that animal was used by God as a stay of the execution of Adam and Eve's death penalty, and taking away any technical hold and accusations that Satan would try to use against God and his laws and Adam and Eve. For all of these death and blood sacrifices, of all of these animals was just a shadow of what the death and the shedding of his innocent blood of this righteous, sinless, and obedient man will actually do for all of mankind. For the death of those animals was only use to extend or stay that execution of man's death penalty, it did not pay that death penalty of man's sin that the law of God had demanded; for it was a man that had disobeyed God's commandment and order to not eat of that tree and sinned and not any of these animals. So the only true sacrifice that could be used by God for the total remission of sins, the total separation of man's sins, and the total forgiveness of man's sins and not just a covering or stay of execution, was the sacrifice of an innocent, righteous, sinless and obedient man with innocent blood: Since it was the disobedience of one man and all have become sin and unrighteous and death by sin; Wherefore, as by one man sin entered into the world, and death by sin; and so death passed upon all men, for that all have sinned: For as by one man's disobe-

dience, many were made sinners, so by the obedience of one shall many be made righteous. That as sin hath reigned unto death, even so might grace reign through righteousness unto eternal life by Jesus Christ our Lord. For the wages of sin is death; but the gift of God is eternal life through Jesus Christ our Lord.

178 In other words, so by the obedience of one righteous, sinless, man with innocent blood, all could be made righteous, and the gift of that righteousness is eternal life. For this is the perfect type of a man that would come out of the loins of Adam and Eve and without the curse and sin of Adam, that God could use as that one time and perfect sacrifice for all of mankind's sins. And since this man would not have any of the curse and sin of Adam and Eve; He would be conceived without sin, formed in the womb without sin, and born into this world without any sin; and He would live his life as a righteous, sinless and obedient man, and He would be tempted of every manner of sin as we are, and yet still be without any sin of His own. And this is the perfect type of man that God will be able to use to pay that death penalty in full that was due to all of mankind, and His innocent blood would also be shed to fulfill that part of God's law that there is no remission of sin, no separation of sin, and no forgiveness of sin unless innocent blood be shed and applied to that sin.

179 In other words, God was going to take all of mankind's sins; starting with Adam and Eve's sins; and all of the sins of every man woman and child of the descendants or children of Adam and Eve; even to our present day; and even to the very last man standing: and place them on this righteous, sinless and obedient man. Then God would punish all of mankind's sins on this man even to the point of this man dying and paying that death penalty that was due to all of us; and His innocent blood would be shed during this punishment of our sins. The death of this man would com-

pletely and permanently pay that death penalty in full that the law of sin and death had demanded upon each and every one of us. And the shedding of His innocent blood that He would shed during that punishment, would also fulfill that part of God's law that there is no remission of any sin, no separation of any sin, and no forgiveness of any sin unless innocent blood be shed and then applied to that sin. And the main part of why God had to use a righteous, and sinless man, is that this man had to also carry all of mankind's sins upon Himself and be put in the grave for three days and three nights with all of mankind's sins: One day and one night each for the body, spirit, and soul of mankind: Then on the third day, God the Father would look upon this man in that grave and remove all of those sins of mankind off him and set them aside in that grave for a good reason for the time being; and then since there would be no sin of His own attached to His body, spirit, and soul; There would be nothing that could hold Him in that grave, and that God the Father would be able to raised Him up to eternal life. This is what the savior that God had promise would come and redeem all of mankind from their sins would do for the complete salvation of mankind. And this is what Adam and Eve and all of their descendants of the Old Testament would put their trust and faith in that promise by God of a savior that would come and take away their sins.

180 Now Satan may have thought that when he had succeeded in getting Adam and Eve to disobey God's commandment and order to not eat of that tree and they did eat of the fruit of that tree disobeying and sinning against God; Satan may have thought that since Adam and Eve were now with a sinful nature just like he and all of his demons and evil spirits have become and they were kicked out of heaven because of their sinful nature; Adam and Eve would also be kicked out of heaven and cast into hell for all eternity or that may be what Satan may have though at first. But when God didn't remove all of his eternal life from them and they didn't receive a

spiritual and eternal death immediately, and God didn't remove Himself completely like He did when He had completely removed Himself not only from just Satan and all of his demons and evil spirits but also from that whole one third section of heaven. And even though Satan may have been boasting and making accusations to God that they were worthy of the eternal death penalty by your own law and he may have been gloating that he now had the power of death over Adam and Eve and all of their descendants; Until he had heard God make that statement to him, "And I will put enmity between thee and the woman, and between thy seed and her seed; it shall bruise thy head, thou shalt (only) bruise his heal". This statement may have knocked Satan off his high horse of a short lived glory. This promised man and savior that would come out of the seed of Eve would destroy and crush that power of death that Satan had the keys and power to, in a symbolic way, with just the heal of His foot. It would be like that if you were to stomp on a person's head with just the heel of your foot; you would end up with just a bruised heel, but he would end up with a crush and bruised head.

181 Another thing that Satan may have now been stirred with anger about, was that this man and savior that God had promised would come out of the seed of Eve, was the only detailed information that he had to go on and no exact time, date or year that this was to take place. And since Satan did not have any timeline to when this man and savior would actually come, he had set out to try and destroy any and all mankind throughout the old testament that might have anything to do with the bloodline that this man and savior might come through, and there were several times in the old testament that that bloodline was hanging on by only just one person; and that Satan had made many attempts to try and completely destroy and exterminate any and all bloodlines that this man and savior could come out of. For you see that Satan may have concluded that by killing

this promised man and savior either before he could even come on the scene and complete God's promised mission of salvation, or have Him killed after He comes on the scene; either way Satan's plan was to try and kill that promised man and savior so that He would not be able to complete that promised salvation plan of God and thinking that that would make God a liar. But God's plan of salvation is an ingenious plan far about the knowledge and complete understanding of Satan.

182 There was another strong point and accusation that Satan may have accused God of; For as the people were actually dying their physical death and throughout the old testament; Satan may have accused or proclaimed to God that even though You had promised that a man would come and be a savior for the remission of mankind's sins that would take away their sins; And Satan may have made this same statement every time that someone had died, that had died with their faith and trust in the promised salvation plan of God during the old testament timeline. And since this promised man and savior hasn't come to take away their sins yet, they cannot enter your heaven and they belong in hell with me. For all of the people of the old testament, that had put their trust and faith in that promised salvation plan of God, that did not take place yet, but had believed God at His word that it was going to take place at some point in God's timeline of their future; did not go to hell; but they could not enter God's heaven because, technically, their sins were still a part of them and they were still a part of their sins, because their death penalty, and their sins, was only temporarily covered by the death and blood sacrifices of animals; and that permanent sacrifice of a righteous, sinless, and obedient man with innocent blood that would pay that death penalty in full, and His innocent blood that would be shed that would be used for the complete remission of their sins, the complete separation of their sins, and the complete forgiveness of their sins; did not take place yet. So God had cre-

ated a separate chamber that may have been called paradise; And this chamber was still outside of God's eternal state of His heaven; and it was also outside of the pits of hell: But this chamber was close to hell, technically, because Satan was constantly accusing God that that savior did not come and pay that death penalty in full yet and their sins have not been take away from them yet, they belong to me. So that chamber of paradise was created as a temporary place for all the Old Testament believers, that was similar to God's eternal heaven, or may have been an extension of God's heaven. For you see that Satan may have thought that he was going to stop and destroy that promised man and savior, destroying God's salvation for mankind and then he would be able to claim all of those people in that chamber of paradise as his people and pull them into hell. But that plan of Satan will be completely foiled by God's promised salvation plan making an open show of him triumphing in the glory of it.

183 And Adam new his wife, Eve; and she conceived, and bare their first child Cain and said, I have gotten a man from the Lord; and she again bore his brother Abel. And Abel was a keeper of sheep, but Cain was a tiller of the ground. There are two parts here that I want to clarify. The first part is about this situation that happened between Cain and Able that had lead up to where Cain, ends up killing his own brother. And it starts out, that in a certain amount of time that had come to pass, that Cain had brought of that fruit of the ground an offering unto the Lord. And Abel, he had also brought of the firstlings of his flock and of the fat thereof. And the Lord had respect unto Abel and to his offering. But unto Cain and to his offering he had no respect. And Cain was very wroth, or angry, and his countenance fell. And then the Lord had said unto Cain, Why are you angry? And why is your countenance fallen? If thou doest well, shalt thou not be accepted? And if thou doest not well, sin lieth at the door. And unto thee shall be his desire, and thou shall rule over him. And then Cain had

talked with Abel his brother: and it came to pass, that when they were in the field where Cain had rose up against Abel his brother, and slew him. And then the Lord had said unto Cain, where is Abel thy brother? And Cain had then said I know not: Am I my brother's keeper? And God had said; what hast thou done? The voice of thy brother's blood crieth unto me from the ground! And now art thou cursed from the earth, which hath opened her mouth to receive thy brother's blood from thy hand; when thou tillest the ground, it shall not henceforth yield unto thee her strength; a fugitive and a vagabond shalt thou be in the earth. And then Cain had said unto the Lord, My punishment is greater than I can bear. Behold, thou hast driven me out this day from the face of the earth; and from thy face shall I be hid; and I shall be a fugitive and a vagabond in the earth; and it shall come to pass, that everyone that findeth me shall slay me. And then the Lord had said unto him, therefore whosoever slayeth Cain, vengeance shall be taken on him sevenfold. And the Lord had set a mark upon Cain, lest any finding him should kill him. And then Cain went out from the presence of the Lord, and dwelt in the land of Nod, on the east of Eden. And then Cain new his wife: and she conceived, and bares a son called Enoch: and Cain had built a city, and Cain had called the name of that city, after the name of his son, Enoch.

184 Now the reason, that I am taking this time, to go over this Cain and Abel situation, is that most bible critics almost always try to use this situation of Cain's offering not being respected by God and Abel's offering is respected by God; claiming that God is not a fair God. And the other part that they try to use against bible believers is when Cain went out from the presence of the Lord and then dwelt in the land of Nod; and then he knew his wife. And they always try to get you to answer their question of where did Cain get his wife. Well the answer to the situation as to why Cain's offering wasn't respected or accepted by God and Abel's offering was

respected or accepted by God can be easily explained in a more detailed explanation of the procedure that they were to follow when making their offering to God. In other words, both Cain and Abel were to each make an offering of the fruits of their labor to God. And since Cain was a tiller of the ground, he would take a certain amount of the total amount of crops that he had harvested from what had grown from the ground that he had tilled, and it would be offered up to the Lord God as an offering unto the Lord God. And also since Abel was a tender of sheep, he would also take a certain number of sheep from the total number of sheep that he had in his flock to make an offering unto the Lord God. And there was a detailed procedure that they were to each follow on how they were to make this offering unto the Lord God.

185 The procedure that both Cain and Abel were supposed to follow may have gone something like this: They each may have been required to built their alter of twelve stones and twelve sticks of equal length. And the requirement may have been, that all twelve stones were to be approximately two feet in diameter; and these twelve stones were to be placed four stones each, three layers high from the ground; In other words, they would place four of these stones together on the ground; and then place four more stones on top of those first four stones, but staggering each of these second layer stones so that they cradle in between the bottom four stones; and then place the last four stones on top of those second layer four stones, but also staggering each of these third layer stones so that they cradle in between the second layer four stones: And then they were to dig a small trench, or moat, around the base of this alter; And then they were to take four of those sticks and place them in the same direction and equally spaced across the top layer of the stones; And then again take another four sticks but placing each of these sticks at a ninety degree angle from the first four sticks and over the first layer of sticks; And then they

were to take the last four sticks and place them over the second layer of sticks and again at another ninety degree angle from the second layer sticks; Now this finished the physical building of their alter. But it is not ready to make any offering up to God yet; because that alter hasn't been purged of sin. For again God's law states that there is no remission of sin, no separation of sin, and no forgiveness of sin unless innocent blood be shed and applied to that sin. So now that last procedure and a main requirement that they each were to perform on their alter was that of an animal sacrifice and its shed blood was to be used to cleanse their alter of all sin.

186 And since Abel was a tender of sheep, he may have used a lamb that was one year old, that had no sickness or disease, wasn't maimed or deformed, and was all the same color white, perfect and spotless; He would then kill it and then place certain parts of that lamb across the top layer of those sticks of that alter; then he would take the blood of that lamb and using a hyssop stick, he would splash each and every stone and each and every stick on that alter with the blood of that lamb; then he would take the remaining blood of that lamb and pour it into that moat that surrounded the base of that alter. Then he would now pray to the Lord God asking Him to bless and purge his alter of all sin. And if everything was done exactly and according God's procedure and rules for building and cleansing an alter; Fire would come down from heaven and would consume all of the parts of that lamb, that was on the top of that alter, and all of the blood that was on all of those sticks and stones of that alter, and all of the blood that was in that moat that surrounded the base of that alter, but none of those sticks or stones was consumed; Abel's alter was now purged of all sin and is now ready for Abel to make his offering unto the Lord God. So now Abel would take that certain number, of the total number of sheep that he had in his flock, and he would prepare it and place it on that alter and offer it up to the

Lord God in prayer as an offering unto the Lord for the first fruits of his labor; and it was greatly accepted by God; for God has great respect for anyone that will follow the procedures and rules of any and every sacrificial offering made to Him.

187 But now Cain may have not followed the rules and procedures completely for building and cleansing of his alter. Cain may have built his alter with the same type and size stones and sticks just like Abel his brother did; He had placed his stones and sticks just like Abel did to his alter; But instead of purging and cleansing his alter of all sin first; He gathers that certain amount from the total amount of crops that he had harvested, and prepares it and places it directly on his alter, and then Cain offers it up to God in prayer as an offering unto the Lord for the first fruits of his labor; But his offering was rejected by God because he did not follow the procedure to purge and cleanse his alter of all sin first; for God had never even seen his offering even though Cain had placed it on the alter; all God could see was the sin that was on that alter; so to God, it was as if Cain was trying to offer and tempt the Lord God with sin. That's why it was definitely rejected and not accepted. And Cain should have repented of that disobedient and sinful offering of tempting the Lord God with sin, through his disobedience to the correct procedure of the building and cleansing of his alter, for that offering of the first fruits of his labor. Cain should have first followed that correct procedure, exactly, to the building and cleansing of his alter for any and every offering that is made unto the Lord God. And then he could have made an offering unto the Lord God for the repentence and forgiveness of this disobedience and sin; In other words, and since there is no remission of sin, no forgiveness of sin, and no separation, or cleansing of sin, unless innocent blood be shed and applied to that sin; Cain would of have had to use the innocent blood of an animal to purge his alter of sin. Cain could have went to his brother Abel, and made an agreement, with

his brother, to exchange two of his one year old lambs for a certain amount of crop that he had harvested, so that Able would then have feed for the lambs and sheep that he had remaining in his flock: and then Cain would have been able to use these two lambs to purge his alter of sin and to also cover his sin of disobedience. And since he would now have the two lambs that could have been used to make an atonement for that sin of his disobedience to that incorrect procedure of building and cleansing of his alter; he would have had to cleanse his alter first of all sin, the same way that Able had cleansed his alter of sin; and then once his alter was purged of all sin by God, the same way that Abel's alter was purged by God of all sin; Cain would of had to use the other lamb's sacrifice and innocent blood as an atonement and covering for his sin of disobedience; and once his sin issue was covered by that lamb's innocent blood; and since his alter was still cleansed of sin; Cain would now be able to make that offering of the first fruits of his labor unto the Lord God and it would have been greatly accepted. But instead of making any corrections toward the procedure and rules of purging and cleansing his alter; He gets angry with his brother Abel and at God; that God even asks him, why are you angry? For the facial expression on your face shows me that you are very angry. And the Lord had said unto Cain, Don't you think that if you would have followed the correct procedures and rules for building, cleansing and purging your alter, would not it have been accepted; instead of being rejected; And if you don't followed the correct procedures and rules for building, cleansing and purging your alter; sin lieth at the door to your heart.

188 But Cain lets his anger get the better of him, and instead of cooling off, and correcting his ways; Cain rises up against his brother Abel in anger, and kills him thinking God didn't know or see it happen. But then God brings it to Cain's attention, that his brother's blood cried unto the Lord God

from the ground. And God ends up placing a curse on him, and he is sent out from the presence of the Lord, and ended up in the land of Nod. And then the next verse says that he already has a wife, and that she gave birth to a son named Enoch; But with a little common sense and logic, this part will make more sence instead of that confusion that many people fall into when they read this section, where Cain leaves the presence of God, and then it appears that he's immediately in the land of Nod; And then he immediately has a wife that has already had Cain's first child Enoch. And this is the second part that I want to clarify that bible critics try to use as to where did Cain get his wife; and they may try to get you to believe that there were other people here on earth before, during, and after Adam and Eve's creation; So now just before Abel's death and murder by his brother Cain; there were only just four people alive on this earth; For it was Adam, Eve, Cain and Abel, that's it; one female, Eve, and three males, Adam, Cain, and Abel; And after the death of Abel, there was only three people alive on this earth; Two males, Adam and Cain, and still only one female, Eve; And then Cain was sent out from the presence of the Lord; and that had also meant that Cain was also sent out from the presence of his mother and father, Adam and Eve, because that is also where the presence of the Lord had dwelt was around Adam and Eve.

189 Many times throughout the old testament when a person or group of people, was cursed by God, it may have been for forty years or it could have been for a hundred years, or many different number of years as God had determined so; But with Cain, when he had left out from the presence of the Lord God and Adam and Eve, he did not just go directly to the land of Nod and dwelt there; and he definitely could not have found a wife there in that land of Nod immediately; because everywhere that Cain may have traveled there wasn't any other people yet; And Cain may have wondered around various parts of this earth, or basically as far as he could go, at first,

by walking from anywhere from at least forty years to one hundred years by himself before he would have been able to run across anyone; For it would have taken quite a few years for Adam and Eve to have a certain number of children and then some of their children would have children to the numbered amount that it would have taken for some of them to also move out across the land and form small villages and towns to where then Cain would be able to find a wife and have a family. For you see that since Abel was dead, and Cain was banished by God, from His presence; Adam and Eve was back to square one, just the two of them and again without any children. But then Eve conceived and gave birth to her third child Seth; and then Adam and Eve had many, many, other children of their own to the number that may have been as many as approximately one hundred and fifty children of their own. And most of the children of Adam and Eve may have followed after the teaching of God's salvation plan of redemption and many of them may have stayed close to mom and dad; but, as time had passed by, and Adam and Eve's children were multiplying, some of them may have made their decision to go their own way and moved to other areas to worship after idols and false gods; and this may have been the time that Cain was now able to meet a woman that ended up becoming his wife, and so on and so on.

190 Another important point that needs to be expressed here, is that when Eve had conceived her first child Cain; This was the very first time that the human reproductive organs, of both Adam and Eve, and its process, that was designed and made by God, was used by Adam and Eve. The only difference is that this had taken place after both Adam and Eve had already fallen into disobedience and sin. And as I have said earlier that that sin of Adam and Eve just didn't stay with them. For remember that Satan had used that serpent, as a disguise and a cover to his real identity, so that he could deceive Eve first, so that he could get her to take the evil fruit,

from that tree of the knowledge of good and evil, and then have her to run over to Adam, with that evil fruit, and then Eve was used by Satan to get Adam to eat of that fruit before he even had a chance to realize that it was the fruit from that tree of the knowledge of good and evil. For there was a main a reason that Satan needed Adam to disobey God's commandment and order to not eat of that tree and get him to eat of it and sin. For Satan needed Adam to disobey and sin. It wasn't that important if Eve would have sinned or not, but it was extremely important that Satan had to get Adam to commit that sin of disobedience against God. For Satan had considered that it was to high of a risk to go directly to Adam to try and deceive him into sinning against God; for Satan may have seen a stronger conviction of obedience in Adam than he may have seen in Eve. And this is why he may have thought that it was a safer and a better risk to use Eve indirectly to get Adam to sin against God's laws and commandments.

191 For if Satan would only get Eve to commit sin and he would fail to get Adam to sin; that sin of Eve would have only affected her and not all of or any of her children that she would ever give birth to. But by getting Adam to sin against God; Adam's sin would not just affect himself only, like Eve's sin would only affect her; But Adam's sin would affect all of his children, that would be conceive through Eve by him; and that same sin of Adam would also be passed unto all of the children that they would have directly, and to all of the grandchildren of Adam and Eve indirectly. And Adam's sin, would be continuely passed on through the sexual reproductive process, of the conception of every egg that is conceived in a woman's womb, that had started with Adam and Eve, and all the way, even to this day, and even to the last man standing. In other words, and starting with the very first conception of that egg that was in the womb of Eve, that was to become Cain; was conceived with that same curse and sin of Adam's sin. And every conception from Eve's first conception of Cain and to every

conception that had taken place after that, and even to this very day, and even to the very last conception that will take place in the future; all will be conceived with that same curse and sin of Adam's sin. Wherefore, as by one man, (Adam), sin entered into the world, and death by (Adam's) sin; and so death passed upon all men, for that all have sinned and come short of the glory of God, there is none righteous, no not one.

192 This is why Satan may have concentrated all of his efforts on mainly getting this man Adam to commit sin even though he did get Eve to commit sin too. But his main focus was getting Adam to commit sin so that this same sin of Adam will then be passed unto any and all of their descendants or all of mankind at conception. For you see, that when Adam did commit his sin against God; that perfect white cloth of righteousness that God had made him with had now been changed to a filthy rag of unrighteousness because of his sin. And Satan may have thought in his heart that by getting both Adam and Eve to commit sin against God; that would put them in the same position that Satan and all of his demons and evil spirits was in when they sinned against God as angels in heaven and was kicked out of God's heaven because of their sin; And when Adam and Eve had both committed sin against God, Satan new that all of mankind would have the same sin of Adam and since Satan was the source of all sin, Adam and Eve had now become part of the family of sin or the spiritual family of Satan and all of his demons and evil spirits, and Satan, had also become their spiritual god, and father, technically, over all of mankind and this earth because of Adam and Eve's sin. And Satan had originally thought that both Adam and Eve and all of their descendants would eventually be kicked out of heaven and cast into hell like he and all of his demons and evil spirits were already sentenced to. But God had cursed both Adam and Eve of their sin and then God had promised that a savior would come out of the seed of the woman Eve and they were only kicked out of

that garden of Eden, and that was because God didn't want them to get to that tree of eternal life so that they could not eat of it and live forever in their sin with no possible way of redeeming them of their sin through the physical death that they now have hanging over their physical life.

193 Adam had fallen from that perfect cloth of righteousness and obedience to a filthy rag of unrighteousness because of the disobedience of sin. In other words, the soul of Adam and also Eve had the perfect righteous cloth of God the Father that was removed from them just before they had committed their sin and was replaced with that filthy rag of the unrighteousness of sin; and God the Father was replaced with, technically, the father of sin, Satan: And the spirit of Adam and also Eve had the perfect righteous cloth of God the Holy Spirit that was also removed from them just before they had committed their sin and was replaced with that filthy rag of the unrighteousness of sin, and since they no longer had that eternal light of the Holy Spirit, the spirit of Adam and Eve had now become a little flickering flame of a candle unto the Lord God; And a candle only burns for a certain amount of time and then burns out: And the heavenly physical body of Adam and also Eve that they were clothed with and had the perfect righteous cloth of God the Lord Jesus that was also removed from them just before they had committed their sin and was replaced with that filthy rag of the unrighteousness of sin, and no longer had that glorious heavenly physical flesh and blood body but was also changed to just a naked physical flesh and blood body, that will die and turn back to the dust of this earth from which it had come from.

194 So now Adam's spirit, soul, flesh and blood body, had become sinful, and with a filthy rag of unrighteousness. And even though, that eternal life of God, that was originally breathed into Adam, when he was created by God, and then ninety percent of it was removed by God just before he had

sinned; and then that remaining ten percent of God's eternal life, that had remained, by God, in both Adam and Eve, to fulfill that part of God's law, that there is pleasure in sin for a season; and when that time limit, of that pleasure in sin for a season, is up or comes to an end, that is determined by God, even that remaining ten percent of God's life, will then go back or return to God from which it had come; and since Adam, Eve and all of mankind, we do not have any life of our own, the body without that life of God dies; for from the dust of this earth it was made, and dust it shall return. And the soul of mankind also dies. In other words, when that law of God, that there is pleasure in that sin for a season, has been completely fulfilled, technically and legally, God then calls that remaining ten percent of His eternal life back to himself; and since all of mankind is only alive because of that life of God, and mankind doesn't have any life of our own to replace it with; we first die the physical death of our flesh and blood body, dust it was made from and dust it shall return. And the second death takes place almost immediately after the physical death; For the soul of man without that life of God also dies a spiritual and eternal death, which is total separation from God and His eternal heaven to eternal death in hell where all sin will eventually be cast away from God's heaven. This is what would have taken place to all of mankind if God didn't provide for us a savior that will redeem us and take away our sins from us so that our sins only would be cast into hell by themselves and our souls are free and clear to go to God's heaven.

195 So the life of Adam, after he had fallen into sin, had remained based in his spirit as a flickering little flame of a candle unto the eternal light God by comparison. And this life that was in the very root of Adam's spirit, was also use to connect his soul to his spirit so that the life that was in Adam's spirit flowed from his spirit to his soul and back giving life to his soul continually; and this life flow was the only connection between Adam's soul

and his spirit: And again, this same life that was in the very root of Adam's spirit, was also used to connect his body to his spirit so that the life that was in Adam's spirit flowed from his spirit to his body and back giving life to his body continually; and again this life flow was also the only connection between Adam's spirit and his body; for the life of the body is in the blood. So you can see that when God removes the remaining life that is in the root of man's spirit that life flow connection to man's soul and his body is also cut off and leaves nothing to connect and hold the spirit, soul and body together. That is also why the body and soul both die without that life flow of God in man's spirit. This is why God had also said that we are not to fear any man that can kill only the body and not the spirit and soul; but fear God who can destroy both the body and separate the spirit from the soul and cast it into everlasting hell.

196 And the life of Adam's body was in his blood. And even though Adam's blood was sinful; that life of God that was still in Adam's spirit, soul and body was sinless, for it was still that same breath of God that He had originally breathed into Adam at Adam's creation. And that life of God was only still in mankind to fulfill that law that there is pleasure in sin for a season, so that the other part of God's law that the wages of sin is death can then be fulfilled. And since Adam's blood was sinful or it carried that curse and sin of Adam's sin in it; And this is how his sin was transmitted or passed unto all of us. It has been Adam's blood line of his sin that was and is still passed unto all of us at conception even to this very day. In other words, before Adam had fallen into sin, he had sinless and innocent blood because of the righteousness and obedience that God had made him with. But after he had fallen into the unrighteousness of sin; Adam's blood had become sinful. Every cell of Adam's blood carried in it the curse and sin of Adam's sin. And since Adam and Eve didn't have any children of their own until after they had sinned and was expelled from that garden of

Eden by God; Every human egg that was conceived in the womb of Eve, starting with the first conception of Cain in the womb of Eve, that was conceived by Adam with that life of God that was in Adam and with at least one blood cell of Adam's sinful blood.

197 In other words, the human egg, that was made in the ovaries of Eve's reproductive organs, was just a human egg, it was neither a righteous egg nor an unrighteous egg, and neither did that human egg have any life in it and neither was that human egg dead, it was just a sinless human egg. And when that human egg that was made in the ovary of Eve, that was to become Cain; that human egg did not receive its life and its blood from Eve. As Adam's sperm cells were made in his reproductive organs, the life and the blood that was in Adam, was also transferred to each of his sperm cells; for the life of the body is in the blood. So as each of Adam's sperm cells were being made in his reproductive organs, each of his sperm cells were made with at least one blood cell from Adam's blood that also had that life of Adam in it; and that life of Adam was the original life of God that He had breathed into Adam at his creation. So technically, that life that was transferred to each of Adam's sperm cells was actually the life of God and not Adam's life. And even though that life of God that was still in sinful Adam and Eve, that life of God was still a righteous and sinless life. But the curse and sin of Adam's sin was in his blood, and since Adam's blood was transferred to each of his sperms cells as they were being made in his reproductive organs, and that curse and sin of Adam's sin was also transferred to each of his sperm cells.

198 Now when Adam and Eve had decided to have sexual relations for the first time to conceive their first child Cain; This is when Adam had transferred his sperm cells into Eve and close to her uterus, through sexual intercourse; and since these sperm cells are alive with the life from its

host, Adam, and the life of God; they can now move on their own and through the uterus of Eve and into her fallopian tubes in just as little as a few hours; and when they had come to that human egg that was to become Cain; all of Adam's sperm cells had then, by design, tried to penetrate the outer layer or shell of that egg, but as soon as only one of Adam's sperm cells had penetrated, and burrowed into that human egg, the outer layer, or shell of that egg, had immediately changed, to stop any other sperm cells from getting into that egg; and that sperm cell that had burrowed itself into that human egg that was going to be Cain had now become a permanent part of that egg and that egg had become a permanent part of that sperm cell. Life did not begin here at conception; Life continues here at conception. For the life that was in Adam was transferred to his sperm cells and that same life of Adam that was in that sperm cell that burrowed into that egg, had now become the life of that egg; In other words, the life of Adam was transferred to that human egg, that was in Eve, through his sperm cells. And as soon as that sperm cell had burrowed into that sinless egg, and since that sperm cell, that had come from Adam, had carried with it the curse and sin of Adam's sin in that single blood cell, the curse and sin of Adam's sin was also carried and transferred to that egg at the same time. So not only did that egg, that was to become Cain, received the life of Adam, but also that curse and sin of Adam's sin and that filthy rag of unrighteousness.

199 So the life of God, and the curse and sin of Adam's sin, was passed into that egg, that was to become Cain at conception. And the very second that that life of God, that had entered into that egg of Cain, had also started that candle unto the Lord, of that pleasure in sin for a season. So Cain was conceived with the curse and sin of Adam, and he also received Adam's filthy rag of unrighteousness. So Cain was conceived in sin, formed in sin, and was born into this world with the curse and sin of Adam's sin. And this

sin that Cain had received at conception, is the sin that damns us all to hell. For it's not any sin that Cain had did on his own after he was born into this world, but it's the sin that was passed unto him at conception, from Adam, before he had even started forming in his mother's womb, Eve. For any sin, that Cain had did after he was already born into this world, was just adding more sin to the sinful nature that was already there at conception. And this is why Jesus had said Wherefore, as by one man, sin entered into the world, and death by sin; and so death passed upon all men, for that all have sinned and come short of the glory of God, there is none righteous, no not one. So all of the children that Eve was conceived by Adam with, had all received their life and the curse and sin of Adam the same way that Cain had received his. And all of Adam and Eve's children had conceived their children in the same way, and so on and so on and even to this very day; that life of God and that curse and sin of Adam's sin is still being passed unto every child at conception even to this very day and even to the last human conception that will take place in the future. So you can see that Adam's sin just didn't affect him only, but was also passed unto all of his descendants, even to today and even to the last man standing.

200 Another serious point that I want to make here, is that nowhere in the design of the human reproductive organs, that was designed by God to reproduce another human being, starting at conception, and continuing from conception and forming in the womb of a woman and until it is birthed into this world as an infant or baby human being, that will continue to grow older from that baby into a child, and into an adult human being and will continue to grow older and older until they die of natural causes, and that is if nothing stops our life, anywhere along this timeline, of human life. Both the reproductive organs of Adam and Eve were purposely designed by God so that they would be able to reproduce and multiply and replenish

this earth with all of their descendants; for God had commanded them to be fruitful and multiply and replenish or refill this earth with all of your descendants; and nowhere in this design of the human reproductive organs and for any reason did God make or promote a homosexual lifestyle. This is definitely a bogus life style that was trumped up and promoted by Satan as a way of mocking God and this reproductive process that God had designed for mankind to be able to multiply and replenish or refill this earth with all of mankind. For remember that this earth was originally created for the first time and was filled with Satan's angels when he was Archangel Lucifer before he had sinned and rebelled against God. And Satan may have developed a strong disdain for this male and female reproductive process of Adam and Eve that this may have been one of the reasons that Satan may have started and promoted this useless and senseless life style of his homosexual lifestyle campaign against God's sexual reproductive process. For there is no biological reason for a homosexual lifestyle to exist, and it's against the natural design and purpose of the human sexual reproductive organs. And there is also no reason and purpose for this manmade process of abortion that murders the baby human being in the womb before it is born into this world, to be promoted and performed for any reason. For God did not design the reproductive process with a natural abortive process to stop this human development once it has started. So this manmade abortion process had basically come from the evil mind of Satan to steal, kill and destroy anything against God and mankind.

201 Now remember that when God had restored this earth from a destructive state to like or similar to its original created form and appearance, it was cleansed from all of the sin, lies and unrighteousness of Satan and all of his demons and evil spirits. And it was restored back to God's perfect truth, and righteousness. In other words, after God had restored this earth, and created Adam and Eve, and created that Garden of Eden, this was

God's garden of Truth. The Earth, Adam and Eve and that garden of Eden was God's garden of total Truth, for there was no lies of Satan mixed in with God's Truth at this time yet. But then also remember that God had let Satan come into His garden of Truth with his lies, for Satan is the source of all lies and the father of it; And Satan was allowed to tempt Adam and Eve to disobey and sin against God, but he was not allowed to violate in any way Adam and Eve's free will. Satan could not do anything to force them or move them in any way that would violate their free will. He was allowed only to, basically, through persuasion to get them to disobey and sin. And this is exactly what Satan had done to get Adam and Eve to freely choose to disobey God and obey him; for he had used trickery, deception and a lie to get them to freely disobey the true and living God and to obey the false and deadly god of sin and death, Satan.

202 So now God had let a lie come into His garden of Truth, and Adam and Eve had freely accepted that lie as though it was true. And since Adam and Eve had put their trust and faith in Satan's lie, God's garden of truth had now become Satan's garden of lies. And the true and living God of Adam and Eve had been replaced with the false and deadly god of sin and death, Satan. For now Satan had become the god, technically, over this earth and Adam and Eve and all of their descendants; for Satan is only a god, technically, because of Adam and Eve's obedience to him instead of the true and living God. For Satan is not a god at all; because he doesn't meet the qualification and attributes of what it takes to be a god. For the attributes of a true and living God is: That you were never born or created by anyone or anything; Satan was created by the true and living God; And you cannot be destroyed and you will never die; And the true and living God has already destroyed Satan and he was kicked out of heaven and has already been sentenced to eternal death in hell forever separated from the true and living God and His eternal heaven: So Satan

is only a god technically and only for a season and then his reign as a god will be over and then he will be cast into the pits of hell forever.

203 The God of Truth was the true and living God over His garden of truth; but now it had been flipped over to a garden of lies; and a false god of sin and death, and the god and source of all lies, Satan, was now god over his garden of lies;. And he has been there even to this very day. And since God had a garden of truth, and a lie had come into that garden of truth, and Adam and Eve had freely accepted that lie as truth, by faith, and receiving eternal sin and death; So God the Lord Jesus was going to come into Satan's garden of lies with His Truth, and also without violating anyone's free will, He will persuade them with the truth and to get them to freely accept His Truth as the real and only Truth and receive the righteousness of eternal life. And anyone who freely accepts this truth that God the Lord Jesus will offer, He will flip their eternal sin and death existence back to God's eternal life and righteousness; and this is what Satan has been against ever since God had promised that a savior would come and take away all of man's sins.

204 And since God had promise that a righteous, sinless, and obedient man with innocent blood would come out of the seed of Adam and Eve's descendants that would take away all of mankind's sins, the savior and salvation of mankind; Satan may have again thought in his heart that by killing off the blood line that this promised savior would come out of, that that would destroy God's salvation plan to take away all of mankind's sin and Satan may have also thought that this would also make God a liar too. But God's plan is more secure and set in motion more than Satan can even begin to try and out smart or exalt his knowledge against the real knowledge of God. For God has the advantage here, He knows exactly as to when, where, and through whom this man and savior will be conceived,

formed and born into this world through. But Satan has only the knowledge of that promise, that a man and savior will come out of the seed of the woman, Eve, that will crush Satan's power and authority of sin and death that Satan had over Adam and Eve and all of their descendants. And this power and authority that Satan had over all of mankind was a power and authority that he did not want to lose in any way shape or form.

205 So Satan's main goal and focus throughout the old testament, and since he did not know the exact time as to when, and where and through whom this promised man and savior would come into this world through; Satan may have concentrated most of his efforts on trying to kill off the blood line that this man and savior would come through, such as the high priest bloodline; and Satan would also have innocent newborn babies murdered in his insane and evil effort and attempt to try and kill off this promised savior to the point that he was so infatuated with trying to find any and every way that he could, to kill either the blood line and or any newborn baby that he thought might be the savior. And there were several times in the Old Testament that this bloodline that this savior was going to come into this world through was hanging on by only just one man, that if Satan had known this, he would have directly targeted that man to have him killed immediately. But God is in total control of His plan of salvation for mankind and is in control of Satan too. For God may have put in Satan's heart a desire to want to kill this man and savior that ended up becoming Satan's passion and main focus throughout the old testament timeline that he would not quit until this promised savior was dead.

206 But much to Satan's blindness and misunderstanding of how God's plan of salvation was really going to be played out; for had Satan known that his evil plan of trying to kill off that man and savior was actually helping God fulfill his plan of salvation for mankind, that by not killing this promised

man and savior would have destroyed God's plan. For you see that God's law states that the wages of sin is death, and that law continually demands that that death penalty be paid in full; And this is one of the main things that this man and savior was going to do, is to pay that death penalty in full for all of us; And this is what God was going to use Satan for; for Satan had become so strongly and blindly involved in trying to kill off this promised savior that when this man and savior Jesus did come on the scene, Satan had tried to kill him while he was just an infant baby Jesus when Satan had king Herod murder a multitude of infants and children up to two years old in an insane and evil attempt to kill him. And all throughout Jesus's life, Satan was constantly trying and plotting against him to find some way to have him put to death; And when Satan had finally had his evil, lying, and mockery of a trial, that ended up putting this man Jesus to death on a wooden cross, that all of Satan and his demons and evil spirits had gathered around, that cross, and they had celebrated what they had though was a great victory, for Satan had though, that since he had finally killed off this man and savior, that God had promised would come and take away all of the sins of mankind, that he had defeated God's plan, and also making God a liar.

207 But by the hand of Satan, that law that the wages of sin is death was paid in full by Jesus's death on the cross; and also the innocent blood that was shed by Jesus by the severe beatings and lash whipping's and the nailing him to the cross and the crown of sharp thorns that was forced upon his head, had shed his innocent blood, thereby also fulfilling that other part of God's law that there is no remission of sin unless innocent blood be shed and applied to that sin. So Satan's victory celebration was short lived; for God had made an open show of Satan and triumphing over in it and God had received all the real Praise, Glory, and Worship that belongs' to Him! For you see that all of mankind was worthy of that death

penalty because we all had that curse and sin, that was passed unto all of us at conception from Adam's sin. But this man and savior Jesus did not have that curse and sin of Adam's sin because he was not conceived by any man, but directly by God the Holy Spirit. So that curse and sin of Adam's sin did not get passed unto Jesus at his conception but was conceived in righteousness and without any sin because he was conceived by God the Holy Spirit. So when this man Jesus was put to death on the cross and died, he was the first man that was righteous and without any sin and not worthy of any death penalty. But yet even though Jesus himself did not have any sin of his own; he was willing to go to that cross and die with all of the sins of mankind upon Himself, and all of mankind's sins were punished on Jesus while He was on that cross even to the point of dying and paying that death penalty that was due to all of us.

208 In other words, since it was a man that had sinned, Adam, and his sin and filthy rag of unrighteousness was passed unto all of his descendants through the continual bloodline of Adam. Basically, Adam's sinful blood has been passed unto all of his descendants, even to this day, and even to the last man standing or the last man or person that would be conceived, formed and born into this world. We all have that sinful and unrighteous blood of Adam in all of us, for all have sinned and come short of the glory of God, there is none righteous in the sight of God's judgment, no not one. For God had only needed one man that would be conceived somewhere out of the loins or descendants of Adam, that would be conceived in righteousness and without any curse and sin of Adam's sin, formed in righteousness in the womb of a woman and without that curse and sin of Adam's sin; and born into this world totally sinless and with a perfect cloth of righteousness and thereby having innocent blood. This is the exact type of a man that God would need to redeem all of mankind from their sins. In order for God to be able to use any man as a savior for all of mankind's

sins; This man had to be conceived, formed, and born into this world somewhere out of the descendants of Adam and Eve. And this man, had to be conceived in righteousness and without any sin thereby giving and having innocent blood. And this man would also live his life starting as an infant baby and growing into a child and growing into an adult man that would live his whole life in total obedience to God the Father in heaven, and being tempted of every manner of sin as we are, but yet, he remains sinless; In other words, this man would be conceived without sin, formed in the womb of a woman without sin, and born into this world without sin, and live his whole life, being tempted of every manner of sin as we are tempted of sin, but yet he resists every temptation to sin, by walking in total obedience to God the Father, and his word, and his commandments.

209 But you can now see that there was no man that would be able to come out of any of the descendants of Adam and Eve that would be able to fulfill that role, and all of its requirements, that was needed by God, to be used by God as a savior and redeemer for all of mankind's sins. And even though God is a God of pure Love; God is also a God of perfect justice, and in no wise can He just clear the guilty and their sins, and then just let them come into His heaven along with their sins. That would be impossible for God to have both sin and righteousness in his heaven at the same time; for you cannot have both light and darkness in the same place and at the same time. It will either be totally all darkness or totally all light. And also light is greater than darkness; for you can see that when we go into a room that is dark as night, we just flip a switch and turn on the light and that darkness is gone. But now most people will think that when that switch is turned back off, and darkness fills that room again, that that was that same darkness that was there before they had turned on that light switch in the first place. But that is wrong thinking; for that darkness that was there before that light was turned on in the first place, is not that same

darkness that refills that room when that light is turned off. For that darkness that was there before that light switch was turned on, was consumed by that light the very second that that light was turned on. And all of that time while that light is on, darkness is continually trying to regain or refill that room with its darkness, but it is continually being consumed by that light during the whole duration that that light remains on in that room. And when that light is turned off, new darkness will regain and refill that room because there wasn't any more light to consume that darkness. And this new darkness, that refills that room, is not the same darkness that was there before that light was turned on.

210 And this is the same reason that God cannot let the darkness of any sin come into his heaven. For God's heaven is an Eternal light that will never be turned off. And hell is an eternal darkness that will never have any light; for the only reason that there is only total darkness in hell is because God's eternal light will never be present there. And this is why God had to create this dark, void and empty place called hell. For God had to have a place to put or cast all of that darkness of evil, sin and death. If any of that darkness of sin, would get into just one small ray of that eternal light that shines from God and his heaven, it would be completely consumed by that eternal light of God, and would be immediately zapped to hell into eternal darkness and death, forever separated from God and His eternal heaven. This is also why that no man has been able to see God the Father in heaven face-to-face and then be able to come back and tell anyone, for the very second that any sinful man would get into just one small ray of that eternal light, would be immediately consumed by that light of God and zapped to hell and would not be able to return and do anything let alone tell anyone. So you can now see that even though God is a God of love, God is also a God of perfect justice, in no wise can He just clear the guilty. For by God's own law, that sin has to be punished and that

death penalty has to be paid in full. God doesn't just obey his own laws, for God is obedience and it is impossible for Him to disobey any of His laws for any reason. So God can only operate in total obedience to His own laws. And this is why God had to have a man that was a righteous, sinless, an obedient man and with innocent blood that would be able to completely fulfill all of God's own laws and at the same time separate man's sin from his spirit and soul legally so that all of mankind's sin can then be cast into hell separately and by themselves, so that their sin, only, goes to hell and not the spirit and souls of Adam and Eve or any of their descendants.

211 But since Adam and Eve or any of their descendants would not be able to provide that man that would meet all of the legal requirements that God needed to have in order to be able to use him as a savior and redeemer for all of mankind's sin: At first it may have look hopeless and that all of mankind would also be cast into hell along with all of Satan and all of his demons and evil spirits. But the will of God the Father is that none of Adam and Eve or any of his descendants should perish, but would come to repentance and eternal life through His salvation plan. And just like Abraham was willing to sacrifice his only begotten son to God, in obedience, but was stopped by God, for Abraham had such faith in God that even if Abraham would have killed his own son, that Abraham may have believed that God could raise him up to life again. Another point too, is that as both Abraham and his son, Isaac, were walking up the mountain, and upon the back of Isaac was the wood of the burnt offering, and Abraham was carrying the fire, and a knife in his hands, and Isaac had said to his father Abraham, I see that we have only the fire, and the wood, for the burnt offering: but where is the lamb for the burnt offering? And Abraham had said, my son, God will provide Himself, a(s) (a) lamb for a burnt offering. And since Abraham was willing to offer his only begotten son as a sacrifice unto God; God the Father was also willing to offer His only begotten son as a sacri-

fice unto all of mankind. For God the Father so loved the world, that he was willing to give his only begotten Son, that whosoever believeth in him should not perish, but have everlasting life: Amen and give God the Father all of the Glory!

212 And since there was no man that would be able to completely fulfill all of those requirements that was needed by God so that God could use that man as a sacrifice for all of mankind's sin to completely take away their sins; God himself had decided to become that man that would completely fulfill every one of those requirements, and be legally qualified, to fulfill that role as the sacrificial lamb of God, savior, and redeemer, and to take away all of the sins of mankind; And as it states in John 1:1 In the beginning was the Word, and the Word was with God, and the Word was God. And then in John 1:14 And the Word was made flesh, and dwelt among us full of grace and truth; And since Jesus is the author and finisher of our faith, and faith is the substance of things hoped for, and the evidence of things not (yet) seen, and this same faith cometh by hearing and hearing by the word. The bible is the word of the Lord Jesus; for Jesus is the author and finisher of our faith; and also Jesus is the very substance of things hoped for, and the evidence of things not (yet) seen, and this same Jesus cometh by hearing and hearing by the word or the bible. So in the beginning was the Lord Jesus, and the Lord Jesus was with God the Father and God the Holy Spirit: And the Lord Jesus was God the Lord Jesus. And this same God the Lord Jesus was made into that flesh and blood of a man named Jesus the Christ and Messiah. And in Philippians 2:5-11 Let this mind be in you, which was also in Christ Jesus: Who, being in the form of God, thought it not robbery to be equal with God: But made himself of no reputation, and took upon him the form of a servant, and was made in the likeness of men: And being found in fashion as a man, and became obedient unto death, even the death of the cross. Wherefore God also hath highly

exalted him, and given him a name which is above every name: That at the name of Jesus every knee should bow, of things in heaven, and of things in earth, and of things under the earth; And that every tongue should confess that Jesus Christ is Lord, to the glory of God the Father.

213 So, in other words, it was God the Lord Jesus that had temporarily decided to lay down his gavel as God so that He can be made into a flesh and blood body, spirit and soul of a man that was to be named Jesus. And since it was God the Lord Jesus that had become that flesh and blood man Jesus, that this may have been the reason as to why Joseph was told in a dream that he was to call this baby that Mary was conceived with, Jesus. It wasn't God the Father, and it wasn't God the Holy Spirit that had become a flesh and blood man. It was God the Lord Jesus that had laid down His gavel of walking as God the Lord Jesus to become an ordinary flesh and blood man, to walk, talk, act and to live the life of a flesh and blood man with a spirit and a soul and a physical flesh and blood body of a man similar to the descendants of Adam and Eve. He would also come into this world the same way that all of Adam and Eve's descendants was conceived, formed and born into this world. God the lord Jesus would live and walk his life as this ordinary flesh and blood of a man named Jesus. And even though it was completely God the Lord Jesus walking as a man, He did not walk in any way as himself, God the Lord Jesus, because He did not come as a man to walk as God but to walk, talk, act and to live the life of a righteous, sinless, man with innocent blood in total obedience to God the Father in heaven, fulfilling that perfect role of a man that God could use as that perfect and blameless sacrifice for the remission of all of mankind's sin. For by the disobedience and sin of one man, all have become disobedient and sin; so then by the obedience and righteousness of one man, all can be made obedient and righteous.

214 In other words, If I was going to play or act the part, in a play, of Abraham Lincoln, I would not come on stage in my own appearance, dressed as myself and then to walk and talk as I would normally walk and talk as myself, because this would only be me playing, or acting out the part of myself, and not that part of Abraham Lincoln: And if people that had come to see a play of Abraham Lincoln would most likely walk out in disgust and disappointment. So in order for me to play, act and to fulfill that role of Abraham Lincoln; I would have to lay down that gavel of Me walking and talking as myself and to completely walk, talk, dress and look as though Abraham Lincoln had come back from the dead and is alive and living again on stage and nobody would even know that it was me actually just playing that part of Abraham Lincoln. And this is what God was willing to do for us: to lay down that gavel of God the Lord Jesus walking, talking as Himself as God the Lord Jesus and to completely walk, talk, dress and to look as though He was just an ordinary man just like any other man that was conceived, formed, and born into this world as a descendant of Adam and Eve.

215 God was going to play out this perfect role of a righteous and sinless man with innocent blood that starts at conception, and continues through the formation of himself in the womb of a woman name Mary. That is then birthed into this world in the same way that all of the descendants of Adam and Eve had been birthed into this world. But this baby Jesus that God the Lord Jesus is playing that part and role of a perfect, righteous, and sinless man with innocent blood is the only baby that will be born into this world without any curse and sin of Adam's sin; For He would be conceived by the righteous and sinless blood of God the Holy Spirit, and not by the sinful blood of Adam's blood. And not only is this man Jesus, that God the Lord Jesus is playing that part and role of that righteous, sinless, and obedient man with innocent blood, going to be born into this world without any sin;

but He will live His whole life being tempted of every manner of sin as we all are, but yet He will not yield or do any sin of His own; He will remain sinless and righteous and in total obedience to God the Father in heaven and all of His laws. This man Jesus will be the perfect, righteous, sinless, an obedient man with innocent blood, that Adam should have remained. And this is the perfect type of a man, that would come out of the descendants of Adam and Eve, that God the Father would be able to use, to put all of the sins of Adam and Eve and their descendants upon Him so that God will be able punish those sins to the point that He will shed his innocent blood and die, paying that death penalty that was due to all of us, and the shedding of his innocent blood that was needed to separate our sin from our spirit and souls, so that our sins can be sent to hell by themselves without our sins pulling us to hell. Then we will be totally free and clear to go to God's heaven.

216 And now, since God the Lord Jesus was going to become that flesh and blood of a man that was going to be named Jesus that would have a spirit, soul, and body just like any other man that was conceived, formed and born into this world out of the descendants of Adam and Eve; God the Lord Jesus was going to have Himself conceived in the human egg of a woman to fulfill that requirement that a righteous man had to be conceived, formed and born into this world the same way that all men have been conceived, formed and born into this world since Adam and Eve's first child Cain. This is where God will break that continuous stream of Adam's sinful nature being passed on through his sinful blood at conception. For God the Lord Jesus is not going to be conceived in the human egg of a woman with any of Adam's sinful blood and life, but with the righteous and sinless blood of God the Holy Spirit. And remember that I had showed you earlier that that human egg that is made in the ovaries of the human female reproductive organs, by itself, is neither alive nor dead and it is nei-

ther a righteous nor an unrighteous egg. It's just a plain human egg. It's when that egg, that is fertilized with the life of sinful blood, that that human egg becomes a sinful human egg that will then be formed into another human baby that will be formed in sin and will be born into this world as a human baby that will still have that sinful nature that it was conceived with. And also, if that human egg is fertilized with the life of sinless blood, then that human egg becomes a sinless and righteous human egg, that will then be formed into another human baby that will be formed without any sin and will be born into this world as a human baby that will still have that sinless and righteous nature that it was conceived with. And this is how God the Lord Jesus was going to be conceived, formed and born into this world without any curse and sin of Adam's sin.

217 And since Adam's disobedience and sin, was passed unto all of mankind through his blood at conception, and all of mankind, or Adam's descendants, had become disobedient and sin: and since there would be no man, that would be able to come somewhere out of the descendants of Adam and Eve, that would be able to fulfill that legal requirement of a man that would be conceived, formed, and born into this world righteous, sinless and a man that would have innocent blood and to able to live his life in total obedience to God the Father in heaven. This is where God himself would become that spirit, soul, and flesh and blood body of a man named Jesus that would completely fulfill all of those legal requirements of a righteous, sinless man with innocent blood that would live his life in total obedience to God the Father in heaven. God the Lord Jesus would also be conceived, formed, and born into this world of a woman, righteous and sinless and out of the descendants of Adam and Eve. In other words, since God could not use any of Adam and Eve's descendants as a sacrificial offering or savior to take away all of mankind's sins because of Adam's sin was in every one of his descendants; for by one man's disobe-

dience to sin and unrighteousness, all of his descendants had received that same disobedient to sin and unrighteousness; So the same would be that if one of his descendants was sinless and obedient to righteousness, Adam and Eve and their descendants could be made sinless and obedient to righteousness through this one man's righteous, sinless and obedient life; And this is exactly what God the Lord Jesus was going to do. He was going to have himself, conceived in the human egg of woman, that was a descendant of Adam and Eve, thereby conceiving himself as a man named Jesus, with a spirit, soul, and physical flesh and blood body of a man and descendant of that woman, thereby fulfilling that legal requirement as a descendant of Adam and Eve and a legal part of the human race of mankind.

218 So now, and out of all of the vast number of people that would be the total number of the descendants of Adam and Eve, God had chosen a young virgin woman named Mary to have himself, God the Lord Jesus, conceived into one of her human eggs. Now God had needed a virgin woman that did not have any sexual relation with any man. And at that time that Mary was chosen, ninety nine percent of the women were virgins; there was, really, no real significance as to why God had chosen Mary, and not any of the other virgin women. But the main reason, was that he only needed just one woman, to have himself conceived in her, to accomplish his plan, and not any other number of women. And for whatever reason as to why he had decided to choose Mary is his decision and nobody else's. But now the main possible reason that God may have chosen Mary was the physical blood line that he wanted to be conceived into as a physical flesh and blood descendant of Adam and Eve. Another important point that I want to make clear here, that even though that it was God the Lord Jesus, that was going to become that flesh and blood man named Jesus, that was going to be conceived, formed and born into this world through

Mary; Mary was not going to be giving birth to God in any way shape or form; She was going to be giving birth to a physical flesh and blood man named Jesus; and Mary will become the physical mother of that physical flesh and blood of a man named Jesus, that God the Lord Jesus was playing and fulfilling that role through, But she is not and can never be the mother of God; for God himself has never been born or created by anything or anyone. And Mary was conceived into this world with the same sinful blood line of Adam's sinful blood, as we all are. And as Jesus had stated, that all have sinned and come short of the glory of God, there is none righteous, no not one. There is nowhere in that statement that says except Mary. And just because Mary had given birth to this man named Jesus, that was actually God the Lord Jesus in the form of a flesh and blood body of a man named Jesus, did not make her holy or something to be worshipped greater than Jesus that she had given birthed to, as some religions want to make or lead you to believe.

219 God did not make Mary special in any way shape or form. She was just an ordinary virgin woman that God had found favor with to use in his salvation plan, as a way for God himself to come into this world of mankind, and take on the form of a man to walk, talk and to live an ordinary life as a descendant of Adam and Eve and the first righteous, sinless, man with innocent blood, since Adam and Eve's fall into sin; and to walk and live his life, being tempted to every manner of sin, but yet he will still remain obedient and sinless to God the Father in heaven. Mary was just a doorway for God the Lord Jesus to come into this physical world of mankind and place himself as that perfect righteous, sinless man with innocent blood for our salvation. For God had to temporarily lay down his gavel as God the Lord Jesus so that he could take on the form of a man to fulfill that role of a man completely, and not as God the Lord Jesus in any way shape or form. For example, as God the Lord Jesus was playing that part

and role of that man Jesus where he was being tempted by Satan in the desert, and Satan had said, that if thou be the Son of God, command this stone that it be made bread. And Jesus answered him, saying, it is written, that man shall not live by bread alone, but by every word that proceedeth out of the mouth of God. For if God the Lord Jesus, walking as that man Jesus, would have did what Satan had asked him to do, and turned that stone into bread; one, that would have put Jesus walking in obedience to Satan, instead of obedience to God the Father in heaven; And two, only God would have that power, to be able to turn that stone into bread, and that would void and nullify God the Lord Jesus walking as a man and become God walking as God, and that would have then put an end to a righteous, sinless, and obedient man, with innocent blood, that was needed by God to redeem all of mankind and to take away their sins. But thanks be to God that this didn't happen.

220 And as I had said earlier that Mary was conceived into this world with the same sinful blood line of Adam's sinful blood as we all are. And even though Mary had the same curse and sin of Adam's sin in her spirit, soul and flesh and blood body, God the Lord Jesus was still conceived in her without any of her sin, and God the Lord Jesus was still formed in her womb without any of her sin and born into this world without her sin. And again I remind you that that human egg that is made in the ovary of the human female reproductive organs, by itself, is neither alive nor dead, and it is neither a righteous nor an unrighteous egg. It's just a plain human egg. So when that human egg that was in Mary that was conceived with that first blood cell and the life of God the Holy Spirit, and with God the Lord Jesus that was now going to be that physical flesh and blood man named Jesus, and since the blood from the Holy Spirit is sinless and righteous, that egg in Mary had also become a sinless and righteous egg. And this is the first time that any of Adam and Eve's descendants has ever been con-

ceived without that curse and sin of Adam's sin. For you can now see that in order to break that continuous sin and unrighteous conception of Adam's sin at every conception, was for God to have himself conceived as a man in the womb of a woman, named Mary, with his perfect, sinless and righteous nature and not Adam's sinful and unrighteous nature. And since that human egg, that was in Mary was fertilized with the sinless and righteous blood of God the Holy Spirit, then that human egg becomes a sinless and righteous human egg, that will then be formed into that human baby, named Jesus, that will be formed without any sin and will be born into this world as a human baby Jesus that will still have that sinless and righteous nature that he was conceived with.

221 So even though Jesus was conceived, formed and born into this world through Mary, He did not receive any of Adam's sin and neither did he receive any of Mary's sin. For the first blood cell and the life of that human egg doesn't come from the woman, but from the man. And in Mary's situation, this first blood cell didn't come from her or a man, but from God himself. For when Mary was conceived by God the Holy Spirit, that sinless and righteous egg of Jesus had started its growing and forming process into baby Jesus. And there was an organ in the womb of Mary that is called the placenta. And Mary's blood vessels were connected to just one side of that placenta so that the blood in Mary flowed from Mary to that placenta and then back to Mary. And baby Jesus's blood vessels were also connected to the other side of that placenta so that the blood in baby Jesus had flowed from baby Jesus to that placenta and then back to baby Jesus again. There was no blood connection between Mary's blood and baby Jesus's blood. And as Mary's blood flows to that placenta and back to Mary again, Mary's blood stored up food in that placenta; And as baby Jesus's blood flowed to that placenta and back to baby Jesus again, baby Jesus's blood picked up that food and feeds off it. So now you can truly

see how Jesus was conceived sinless and in total righteousness, and was formed, and had grown in that womb of Mary into baby Jesus without any of her sin, and that's why Jesus was born into this world sinless and righteous even though Mary had the curse and sin of Adam's sin in her.

222 And not only was Jesus just born into this world sinless and righteous and with innocent blood, but he had lived his life sinless and righteous and in total obedience to God the Father in heaven, that he was even tempted to every manner of sin and yet he resisted every temptation that he did not do any sin of his own during his total time that he was alive on this earth. Jesus didn't even tell or speak even one lie, He spoke only the Truth. And remember that during this whole time that this man Jesus was alive here on this earth; it was still God the Lord Jesus playing out that role of that righteous, and sinless man with innocent blood that was in total obedient to God the Father in heaven. And as righteous, and sinless as Jesus was, he could have done His own will; but He even died to His own will completely, and did only God the Father's will; for as He had seen God the Father do, He did; and as He had heard God the Father speak, He spoke. And when Jesus was baptized by John the Baptist in the river Jordan, and when Jesus had come back up and out of the water, the Spirit of God, the Holy Spirit, had come down from heaven above and landed on Jesus in the form of a dove, and then a voice from heaven had proclaimed; This is my beloved Son in whom I am well pleased. Now Jesus is the only man that God the Father has ever said that to since Adam and Eve had fallen into sin.

223 So even though it was a physical flesh and blood man named Jesus; it was God the Lord Jesus in the form of a man; walking, talking and living a life as a man that was in total obedient to the will of God the Father. And this is why Jesus had said that if you have seen me, you have seen my

Father in heaven; and if you have heard me speak, you have also heard my Father speak; and this is why Jesus had also said that I am in the Father, and the Father is also in me, I and my father are one and the same. And this is a true statement; for Jesus had completely died to his own will and the will of God the Father had been completely and totally the will of that man Jesus; For if you would have seen Jesus then, you would have been looking at the very image of the will of God the Father instead of just that man Jesus. And also, after Jesus had received the power of God the Holy Spirit after being baptized by John the Baptist in the river Jordan, the power of the Holy Spirit had then become a part of the spirit of that man Jesus, and, all of the miracles, and healing's, were performed by God the Holy Spirit and according to the will of the Father. So basically, as that flesh and blood body of a man named Jesus was walking, talking and living his life on a daily basis, it was as though it was God the Lord Jesus, And God the Father, And God the Holy Spirit all walking in that man Jesus and all at the same time, God in the flesh.

224 Now Jesus did not really start his ministry until he was about thirty years old. And most of that life of Jesus up to about thirty years old is left blank and not much was written or said about his life as a child, except that when Jesus was born as baby Jesus in Bethlehem and when Jesus was a boy about twelve years old and ended up finding him in the temple talking and teaching scripture with the elders of the church. And there may have been good reason as to why these years may have been intentionally left blank, and nothing was written, or spoken about it. For you remember that it was God the Lord Jesus that had become that whole life of this man Jesus from conception, and during his formation and growing inside the womb of Mary, and during his birth into this world as a human flesh and blood baby Jesus, and during those times that he had grown from a baby Jesus to a toddler, to a young boy, and into an older boy, and into his

teens, and then into a young man, and then he had grown into an older man becoming about thirty years of age. For you see that God the Lord Jesus was acting out, playing that role, and part, of a righteous, and sinless man with innocent blood, in every detail to the point that it had to be fulfilled in every detail that this man Jesus had appeared to be just an ordinary man that was just living his life just like all the other people or distant descendants of Adam and Eve had lived their lives.

225 And the other part as to why those younger years may have been left blank and not much was said or written about him, is that God may have hid this savior Jesus from Satan during those younger years so that he would be able to reached the age of about thirty without any trouble from Satan. For most of the Jewish leaders have been looking for a messiah to come and rule over Israel and all of the Jewish people, but they were looking for a great and mighty warrior type, and a big and mighty man of great stature and strength to come as a Messiah and to rule as a king; but they had miss read and greatly misunderstood what the scripture had really said and implied, because this Jesus the Christ and Messiah had really come as a meek and lowly servant and as a suffering savior for all of mankind. For even though Satan had made that attempt on baby Jesus's life when he had King Herod kill all the male baby boys from two years old and under in Bethlehem, Satan really didn't know for sure if that had even really killed that newborn baby boy, King of the Jews. So Satan may have been watching and listening to what people were saying and doing to try and see if there was anything more said about this King of the Jews or the Christ or Messiah during this whole time that Jesus was growing from a baby Jesus into a thirty year old man. So God had kind of kept Jesus hidden in plain sight from Satan as a meek and lowly man and of no great importance. Jesus did not even have the stature or strength of a man to even qualify for the training as a roman soldier let alone having any appearance

of ever becoming a King of anything or anyone. But let this be a lesson to you, don't ever doubt God and think that He doesn't know what he is doing, for I guarantee you, that God knows exactly what He's doing at all times. For it's not that God doesn't know what he is doing, but it's that you will not know what God is doing; and may even appear confusing and senseless; and to coin a phrase here, is that those who think they know, (try to) spoil it for those who really do (know).

226 And as I had said earlier that the true and living God was Adam and Eve's God from the time that they were created by the true and living God, and up to the very second that they both had obeyed Satan's command, instead of the true and living God's commandment. So between this narrow time frame of Adam and Eve's living existence with the true and living Godhead, God the Father was their living and spiritual Father. But after they had disobeyed the true and living God and obeyed Satan, that is not a god in any way shape or form, but had become a god, technically, over Adam and Eve and all of their descendants and this earth because of their allegiance of obedience to him instead of the true and living God. So Adam and Eve's spiritual God the Father of Truth had been switched to their new spiritual and technical false god, Satan, the father of lies. Adam and Eve was transferred from the family of the true and living Godhead, to the family of a false and deadly, technical god, Satan. And every one of Adam and Eve's descendants would now be conceived in sin, formed in sin, and born with sin, into this same family of Satan. All of these descendants would be born from below from their spiritual father Satan, the father of lies, evil, sin and eternal death. None of these descendants of Adam and Eve would ever be able to claim the true and living God the Father in heaven as their Father, or at least until this man Jesus was conceived with righteousness, formed with righteousness, and born with righteousness, into this world as that first man that had broken that allegiance of obedi-

ence to Satan through Adam's cursed and sinful blood of Adam's sinful allegiance of obedience to Satan's commandment against God's commandment.

227 God's family is the family of the sinless, and the eternal life of obedience and righteousness. Satan's family is the family of the sinful, and the eternal death of disobedience and unrighteousness. And since, "we all", as descendants of Adam and Eve, have been conceived with sin, and formed in sin, and born into this world with this same sin and curse of Adam's sin; we are all born into this world physically and spiritually into Satan's family of the sinful, and the eternal death of disobedience and unrighteousness. Our spiritual father, by the technicality of Adam's sin being passed unto all of us at conception, is Satan; because we are all born into Satan's family of lies, evil, sin and eternal death. We are all sons and daughters of our spiritual father Satan, and that's why we are all born from below, Satan's hell and not from above, God's heaven. And this may have been Satan's boast, and claim against God, that all of mankind belong with him, in hell, for all eternity and that you can't allow them into your heaven, like you had did to me and all of my angels because of sin. For Satan's thinking, in his heart again, may have thought that there was no way that God would be able to clear their guilt and penalty of all of mankind's sin, and that they were all guilty of sin and worthy of eternal death in hell with him.

228 But much to Satan's surprise and disappointment, God himself had become that flesh and blood man that would break that continual sinful conception that has been passed onto all of Adam and Eve's descendants by Adam's sinful blood line. For this man Jesus was not going to be conceived by the blood of any sinful man, breaking that blood line of Adam's sinful conception of Adam's sin and curse. In other words, this man Jesus would not be conceived by Adam's sinful bloodline, but by the sinless and

righteous bloodline of God the Holy Spirit. And this is the first and only flesh and blood man that has been and would ever be conceived without the curse and sin of Adam's sin. And since this man Jesus was conceived without any sin, and formed in the womb of a sinful woman without any sin, and then born into this world without any sin, He was born from above and into the family of the true and living God of the sinless, and the eternal life of obedience and righteousness. Jesus was not part of the family of Satan. Jesus's spiritual Father was, truly, God the Father in heaven. That is why Jesus could really and truly say that the Father in heaven was truly His Father. Satan had no hold or claim on or against this man Jesus, for there was no sin in this man Jesus that Satan could use against him. Jesus was the son of man, but not as a son of Satan, for He was the son of God, the only son of man that was able to truly claim himself as also the son of God, and to be able to truly claim God the Father as his Father in heaven. Jesus was a son of mankind because he was born as a flesh and blood man that had come into this world out of the descendants of Adam and Eve.

229 In other words, I am a flesh and blood man born into this world as a descendant of Adam and Eve; That makes me a son of mankind; and since I was conceived, formed and born into this world with the same curse and sin of Adam's sin, I was also born spiritually into the family of Satan, that had, technically, made me a son of Satan's spiritual family of lies, evil, sin and eternal death: So the very second that I was born into this world, I had become a physical flesh and blood son of mankind and a spiritual son of the family of Satan. Well, Jesus was also a flesh and blood man born into this world as a descendant of Adam and Eve; That had made Jesus a son of mankind also; But since He was conceived, formed and born into this world without that curse and sin of Adam's sin or any sin, He was conceived without any sin; He was also born spiritually into the

family of the true and living God in heaven, that had made that man Jesus a son of the spiritual family of the true and living God of eternal truth, righteousness, and eternal life. So the very second that Jesus was born into this world, He had become a physical flesh and blood son of mankind and a spiritual Son of the family of God. And since Jesus is the only man that was born from above, He was the only begotten Son of God the Father to which He is well pleased with. For you can now see that even though Jesus was born into this world as an ordinary flesh and blood man, Satan could not claim him as part of his evil family of sin and eternal death; because there was no sin in this man Jesus that Satan could use against him and claim that he is worthy of eternal death because of sin; for since there was no sin in this man Jesus that Satan could use, this was the first man that was born out of the descendants of Adam and Eve that was not worthy of any death penalty; for God's law only makes that statement, that the wages of sin is death, to only those who are guilty and have sin. That law did not have any claim against this man Jesus, for God's law also states that where there is obedience to God's law, that is accounted as righteousness, and the gift of that righteousness is eternal life; So the complete law of God states that although the wages of sin is death, the gift of righteousness is eternal life!; which will become our gift of righteousness and eternal life through our Lord and savior Jesus Christ.

230 And since this man Jesus is the only man, that had come out of the descendants of Adam and Eve, that was born from above, and was this perfect righteous, sinless and obedient man with innocent blood that God could now use as that sacrificial Lamb of God that would take away all of the sins of mankind. For God so loved the world, that he was willing to give his only begotten Son, that whosoever believeth in him should not perish, but have everlasting life. For God sent not his Son into the world to condemn the world; but that the world through him might be saved. He that

believeth on him is not condemned: but he that believeth not is condemned already, because he hath not believed in the name of the only begotten Son of God, Jesus, the Christ, and the Messiah, and the sacrificial Lamb of God. As it states above, God the Father did not send his only begotten Son into this world to condemn the world of sin; but that the world through him might be saved from the eternal punishment of sin in hell. In other words, Jesus did not come into this world to get married and have a family as some people or religions want to lead you to believe. For God the Lord Jesus did not lay down His gavel as God to take on the form of a flesh and blood man to live a complete life of an ordinary man for the purpose to get married and have a family, God did not become a man for that reason. God the Lord Jesus had only taken on the form of an ordinary flesh and blood man so that all of mankind would be able to have all of their sins taken away.

231 All of mankind, had needed this type of a righteous, sinless, obedient man that had innocent blood that would have to come out of the descendants of Adam and Eve so that God would be able to use him as a sacrificial lamb. And since no man that would ever come out of the descendants of Adam and Eve, on their own; would never be able to provide or completely fulfill that role of that type of a man that God had needed for the redemption of all of mankind's sins; God himself had decided to become that man that would completely fulfill that role as that perfect type of a flesh and blood man that God would be able to use to take away all of mankind's sins. So God the Lord Jesus was willing to lay down His gavel as the true and living God of heaven; and was willing to take on the form of an ordinary flesh and blood man to completely fulfill that role of a righteous, sinless, and obedient man with innocent blood, and to fulfill that legal part that this man had to be, or come out of the descendants as one of the descendants of Adam and Eve; and God the Lord Jesus, as and in the form

of this flesh and blood man, was willing to have all the sins of mankind placed upon him; and then He was willing to suffer the pain and anguish and the punishment of everyone of all those sins of mankind, even to the point of him dying on a cross, the complete death of a man, and to pay that death penalty that all of those sins of mankind were guilty of; and having his innocent blood shed while on that cross; thereby paying that death penalty in full, that the law of God had demanded against all of the descendants of Adam and Eve. And since his innocent and sinless blood would be shed while on that cross, this would also fulfill that second part of God's law, that there is no remission of sin, no separation of sin, no forgiveness of sin unless innocent blood be shed and applied to that sin. So this is that reason that God had become a flesh and blood man so that he would be able to take away and completely remove all of mankind's sin from each and every one of all of the descendants of, and, including Adam and Eve. And there was no reason for God to become a man, to have a family as some people want you to believe or teach.

232 And, as I had said before, that God had restored this earth and made Adam and Eve and the garden of Eden in total righteousness and Truth; The earth, Adam and Eve, and that garden of Eden was God's complete garden of Truth. But God had let the Father of lies, Satan, come into His garden of Truth to preach his lies to Adam and Eve to test and see if they would remain in obedience to the true and Living God of heaven. Satan was only allowed to come into God's garden of Truth to preach his lies to Adam and Eve, and they freely accepted, and obeyed Satan's commanding lies, by faith, as though it was true. And God's garden of Truth had then been flipped into Satan's garden of lies. So now God is going to let the Father of truth, (in) Jesus, come into Satan's garden of lies and to preach His Truth of His redemption and salvation plan unto eternal life, that all mankind will have to do, is to only believe, and accept it by faith. And this

may have been one of the main reasons that Jesus had started His ministry preaching the Truth of God the Father, through Jesus, that the kingdom of heaven is now at hand.

233 And when Jesus was baptized in the river Jordan, this was basically the starting point of His ministry and the preaching of His truth and salvation plan in Satan's garden of lies. And before Jesus had come on the scene, the Scribes and Pharisees would read, or quote the Holy Scripture, in the Temple, and also in the public square, or arena; but not with the power, and authority of God the Holy Spirit, but with their own might, and blind understanding. So when Jesus had started making his ministry and appearance known throughout the whole land and with the power and authority of God the Holy Spirit, and with powerful miracles, healings, and the dead being raised again; that this must have really started to make the Scribes and the Pharisees look like complete fools to all of the people, that it may have stirred up a fierce and jealous rage deep in their hearts; that this had progressively grown into a jealous plot to try and find a way to have him put to death, for they may have also thought in their hearts that it was better that one man should be put to death instead of the many that could die, because of him. And, somewhere, throughout the years, the Scribes and Pharisees, had lost their true vision, and understanding of the scriptures, and had become arrogant, and blind to the real truth, and their real purpose, as religious leaders of God's people. For if they had really, and truly known and understood the scriptures, they would have seen who Jesus really was, and they would have never rejected him. And since the Scribes and the Pharisees were blind to who this man Jesus really was, Satan may have also used this to his advantage; because Satan was still on that same path and motive of trying to kill off this savior thinking that that will destroy God's plan, and this man Jesus was getting more and more of Satan's attention, each day, that his popularity was gaining mo-

mentum.

234 And remember that God may have been leading Satan to believe that by having this savior killed, that that would destroy and stop God's Salvation plan for all of mankind. And also, every time the Scribes and Pharisees would try and get Jesus to make a mistake with the scripture of God, thinking that they would be able to trip Him up, by getting Him to give a wrong answer to everyone of their scripturally based questions, but ended up backfiring on themselves; for Jesus had answered every one of their questions with such a precise, and direct aim, that it was more of a direct hit back at them, than their attack was at Him. In other words, these Scribes and Pharisees were the religious leaders of their time, and were fully versed on the knowledge, of the scriptures, and of the laws, and the Sabbaths and all of the things that pertained to the exercise and obedience to it. And most of these Scribes, and Pharisees, had even puffed themselves up above all of the ordinary people, of their time, that they may have even looked down on them as sinners; and they may have looked at themselves, as righteous, and sinless men of God; But they had really made themselves out to be blind fools in the sight of God.

235 So when this man Jesus had come on the scene, and as an ordinary man, that He could easily hide Himself in amongst the ordinary people, and not as religious leader like the Scribes and Pharisees, but yet, not only did Jesus teach and preach and proclaimed the scriptures with power and authority and precise accuracy, but He had the power to heal the sick, make the lame walk, and give sight to the blind, and feed a multitude of five thousand with only two fish and five loaves of bread, and even had the power to raise the dead; but none of these Scribes or Pharisees or any of these religious leaders were able to do any of the things that this ordinary man Jesus was doing, to the point that most of the ordinary people were

flocking to this man Jesus instead of these religious leaders. And this may have sparked a bit of jealously in most of those religious leaders; that since they couldn't find any fault in Him, and trying to trip Him up scripturally had backfired on themselves and had only turned the people to this man Jesus; that the religious leaders may have decided to come up with a way to have this man Jesus be put to death as a way to get rid of Him.

236 So these Scribes and Pharisees may have become so angered, and frustrated with this man Jesus, that that may have even attracted the attention of Satan himself. And Satan may have helped these religious leaders, Scribes, and Pharisees, to promote an evil plot and plan to have this man Jesus put to death, for Satan has been wanting this promised savior of mankind destroyed from the time that God had announced that out of the seed of the woman Eve or that somewhere in one of her descendants would come a man and a savior that would not only take away all of the sins of mankind, but he would also crush and destroy the head of Satan's power over the death of all of mankind. For Satan did not want any power that he had remaining in him taken away or destroyed. And remember that Satan was able to deceive and get one third of all of the angels of heaven that was under his charge and authority to disobey, sin and rebel against the true and living God of heaven. And he had also deceived all of mankind by getting both Adam and Eve to disobey and sin against the true and living God. That Satan may have thought in his heart that he was very clever and had puffed himself up with pride that he was able to deceive one of the disciples of this man Jesus and used him to betray his own master, Jesus. That Jesus was turned over to a mock trial that was basically a corrupt trial to railroad Jesus into a death sentence: the scribes and Pharisees and most of the religious leaders didn't have any religious or local laws of their own that would demand a death penalty; but the Roman courts had laws that would demand a death penalty; And this is where the

Jewish religious leaders had then handed this man Jesus over to the Roman authorities and courts so that they could find Him guilty of any kind of a crime that would require a death penalty.

237 And as these religious leaders, Scribes and Pharisees, and the Roman authorities and courts, were starting their mockery of a trial, that was only going to railroad this man into a dishonest and corrupt verdict of a trumped up crime that would demand a death penalty; for that's all these religious leaders, Scribes and Pharisees was wanting in the first place, was that this man Jesus be put to death to get Him out of the way, so that these religious leaders Scribes and Pharisees can get back to their normal routine of puffing themselves up above all of these lowly sinners. But God was going to use this mockery of a trial to fulfill his Salvation plan for all of mankind. For most of the time that Jesus was preaching and teaching and performing miracles and healing people, etc.; the Scribes and Pharisee were constantly trying to find some fault of any kind that they could use to have Him arrested, but have failed at every attempt. But what they really didn't see because of their religious blindness of the real and true meaning and understanding of the scriptures is that God the Father in heaven was in complete control of what exact time that they would even be allowed to arrest Jesus and start their corrupt and mockery of a trial. And also, God the Father may have placed all of the sins of mankind upon this man Jesus at that moment that He was arrested in that garden of Gethsemane. In other words, that was all of the sins that were committed by Adam and Eve, and all of the sins of all of their descendants and including that sin and curse of Adam's sin that we all receive when we were conceived in our mother's womb; all sins committed by mankind from Adam and Eve, and to that very moment that God had placed mankind's sins upon Jesus; and from that moment to this very day that we are alive right now; and to the very end of that last man that is conceived in the womb of a woman.

238 Now remember that this man Jesus did not have any sins of His own upon His spirit, soul, and body. He was sinless, and there was no law of God that had demanded that the wages of sin is death, because there was no sin in Him to impute that law; and because there was no sin in Him, is because there was no disobedience by Him to God's law; He was totally obedient to God's laws. And God's laws states, that where there is obedient to Me and My laws, that is accounted as righteousness, and the gift of that righteousness is, Eternal Life. And this is the eternal life that we all receive through Jesus. But when God the Father had put all of the sins of mankind upon His only begotten Son, Jesus; He had become a sinful man for our salvation. And immediately after God the Father had put all of mankind's sins upon Jesus, He had become sin, because of our sins that were placed upon Him, for He had no sins of His own to make Him sinful. And, also, the very second that all of mankind's sins were place upon Jesus, and even though Jesus Himself did not have any sins of His own on Him, the law of God had immediately seen all of those sins as disobedience to God and all of His laws and immediately demanded that the wages of all those sins is death; that death penalty that was due to all of us was now transferred to this man Jesus; and this man Jesus had now bore the full weight of all of mankind's sins, starting with all of Adam and Eve's sins, and every descendant that Adam and Eve will ever have, and even to this very day, and even to the very last man standing.

239 And, also, remember that it was God the Lord Jesus that had become that flesh and blood of man, Jesus, for our sakes for the full purpose of becoming that flesh and blood man so that God the Father would have an innocent and righteous man with sinless blood to be able to place all of our sins upon him for our salvation. And also remember that since it was God the Lord Jesus that had become that flesh and blood of a man, Jesus, and God the Lord Jesus has never ever had any sin of His own in Him, and will

never ever have any sin of His own in Him, but was also willing to become a flesh and blood man to purposely carry all of the weight of mankind's sins upon Himself, and for the first time in all of His eternal existence, He was willing to experience sin and the sting of its death. There is only one reason why a true and living God, who has never ever had any sin of His own, would even want to become a man that was purposely going to be used to put all of mankind's sin on this man, that has never had any sin, that would then become sin for mankind's salvation and take on the full force of God's judgment and punishment of that sin, even to the point of dying a full physical death in our place for all of us; and John 3:16-17 clearly shows us why; For God, the Father, so loved the world, that he was willing to give his only begotten Son, that whosoever believeth in him should not perish, but have everlasting life. For God, the Father sent not his Son into the world to condemn the world; but that the world through him might be saved from an eternal death in hell. For the Father's will is that none should perish, but all should come to repentance unto eternal life.

240 So now as Jesus was arrested, and because of false accusations by the Jewish religious leaders, and at the same time of His arrest, God the Father may have placed all of the sins of mankind upon His only begotten Son. And the main part, or point of this false arrest, and the false accusations, and trumped up charges, against this innocent man Jesus, and this mockery of a trial, was not about justice or having a real guilty person arrested on a real charge of a crime with true eye witness accounts and testimonies to convict a guilty person of his crime through a fair and just court trial; But instead, this was an elaborate way of having an innocent man, that was not guilty of any crime, or any wrong, or any fault, against anyone, or anything; assassinated or murdered by using a corrupt and unfair court system and proceedings by crooked and dishonest people to have

Him railroaded through this corrupt court system and proceedings, using trumped up charges, that would demand a death penalty, false and lying witnesses, false testimonies, and entrapment into a guilty verdict. But on the other hand both God and Satan were each using this to their advantage. But God had the upper hand here; For God was able to see what Satan was always thinking in his heart and what his evil plans and intentions were going to be. But Satan was always trying to outsmart God and may have continually tried to find and kill this promised savior of a man that would come out of the seed of Eve as promised by God back there when God had promised this to Eve as they were being expelled from that Garden of Eden.

241 The very second that Adam and Eve had fallen into sin, God had known the exact hour and time limit as to when this man Jesus was going to come on the scene. God has already seen in advance, everything that this promised savior and man Jesus was going to come and do and accomplish before He had even promised to Eve that a savior would come somewhere out of her seed. But Satan did not have any clue of who this man, and savior would be and when He would come on the scene. So Satan was continually trying throughout the old testament time period to try and kill off any of the bloodline, or descendants, that he may have thought was either the savior himself or that this savior might come out of. And when the baby Jesus was born in Bethlehem, and even though Satan may have not really known as to which baby might be this newborn Messiah and possible savior, or King of the Jews, but the possible location was in Bethlehem. So Satan had stirred up King Herod's heart with a jealous rage of a newborn baby that was going to be King of all the Jewish people. And King Herod's anger was magnified even greater when he tried to use the wise men to help him find this newborn child King, and they were supposed to return to him and tell him where this newborn baby

King of the Jews was at, but when these wise men did find baby Jesus, they returned to their homeland by another route instead of having to pass again through King Herod's kingdom or territory. And this had infuriated King Herod that since He was unable to find just this one little baby, He had decided or reasoned that he would have all the children that were in Bethlehem, and in all of the coastlands too, from two years of age and under, slain, thinking that that would definitely kill and get rid of that newborn King threat against him and his kingdom.

242 And since there was, basically, nothing else mentioned about a newborn King of the Jews, anymore; and since all those children were killed off by King Herod's murderous order, for many years, that even Satan may have thought that this baby King of Jews, and or Messiah, was also killed. But that may have been one of the main reasons as to why there is not much written or said about the life of Jesus from when He was a baby until He had come on the scene after being baptized by John the Baptist in the river Jordan. There was a small situation, when Jesus was age twelve, where he was left behind in Jerusalem, after celebrating the yearly feast of the Passover, and Mary and Joseph were already traveling back home when they had realized that Jesus was not with them, that Mary and Joseph had then returned back to Jerusalem, and they had searched for him for three days in Jerusalem, and finely found Him in the Temple. Now even though this is mentioned in the bible, it wasn't that big of deal or situation that had drawn worldwide attention that even Satan may have not even heard anything about this situation. It was just a small family situation that at that time was not that significant of an event, because this little boy, Jesus, was just that, a regular twelve year old boy in a small town and of no importance or fame yet. And this situation may have been made known and even was put in writing only after the fact that Jesus had grown up into the man Jesus that had then become famous throughout the whole land.

243 But anyway, Jesus has already been arrested by the religious leaders and Roman authorities. And God the Father has put all of the sins of mankind upon His only begotten son; and Jesus may have become sin at this point. And the punishment phase of God's magnificent salvation plan is already beginning to be played out by God's use of Satan's thinking that by finding and killing off this promised savior that that would destroy God's plan and promise and making God a liar. But God has been letting Satan think this type of thinking; for this motive and thinking of Satan was actually working with God's plan of salvation and the actual purpose of this man and Savior Jesus. So when Jesus was taken and beaten, He was beaten, severely enough, that there wasn't just bruising; but He was beaten to the point that He was shedding His innocent blood severely, and they had made a mocking crown of thorns, and they had forced it upon His head causing Him to shed more of His innocent blood. And then Jesus was taken and He was given, thirty nine severe lashings, of a Roman whip. A Roman whip wasn't just a leather whip; but a whip, that was designed with several strong leather tips at the whipping end of the whip, that also had chard's of sharp stones, glass and metal, that was designed to, cut deep and also rip away chunks of flesh to each lashing. So when Jesus was given thirty nine lashings of that Roman whip, His back was so severely wounded, that not only did He shed His innocent blood, but His back was so severely torn up, that it was possible to see part of His ribs and backbone. And then they ended up having Jesus carry His own cross, on His badly wounded, and lash whipped back, that most men would have died by this time. And then they had nailed Jesus to His cross through His hands and feet, again causing Jesus to shed more of His innocent blood. And after Jesus had died on the cross; He again had shed more of His innocent blood by that soldier piercing Jesus's side with a spear.

244 So when Jesus was being punished, having no fault and not guilty of

any crime, it wasn't actually Jesus that was being punished, but it was God the Father punishing all of those sins, of mankind, that was on this man Jesus. And as all these sins, of mankind, were being punished on this man Jesus, He was still able to carry our sins to the cross with Him without giving in or giving up even to the point of even willing to stay and completely endure all that punishment even to the point of dying on the cross. Now the punishment part of our sins was completed, when Jesus had died on that cross. And also, Jesus had completely fulfilled that requirement of the law, that the wages of sin is death. Jesus's death on that cross was the complete payment in full of that death penalty that that law, of the wages of sin is death had continually demanded on everyone of mankind's sins, that were now, all on Jesus at the time that He had died, that physical death of that flesh and blood of a man Jesus. And the other part of God's law that this man Jesus had also completely fulfilled, is that law that there is no remission of sin, no separation of sin, and no forgiveness of sin unless innocent blood be shed and applied to that sin. Well, Jesus's innocent blood was shed ,while he was beaten severely by the soldiers; by that mockery of a crown of thorns, that the soldiers had made and then they had jammed it onto His head; and by the thirty nine whip lashings on His back, and when he was forced to carry His own cross on His already lashed whipped back; and when Jesus was pierced by the nails through His hands and through His feet, as he was nailed to a cross; and when Jesus was pierced through His side by a spear of a soldier that was checking to see if He was already dead, and since the soldier had seen that He was already dead by the blood and water that had come out of his spear piercing of Jesus's side, they didn't need to break His legs, fulfilling the prophesy that not a bone in His body will be broken. Jesus had fulfilled that first part of that law, by the shedding of His innocent blood; and the second part of this law will be fulfilled and applied later.

245 Now that Jesus had completed and fulfilled that punishment phase and part of our salvation plan; and that death penalty was completely paid in full, to fulfill that demand of the law of God, that the wages of sin is death; and the shedding of His innocent and sinless blood had fulfilled that first part of God's law that there is no remission of sin unless innocent blood be shed and applied to that sin. His innocent blood was shed, but the application of His innocent blood will come later. But now, as Jesus was taken off the cross and buried in a grave, and was buried in that grave for three days and for three nights; Jesus still had upon Him all of the sins of mankind. So when Jesus was taken of that cross and put in the grave, He had carried all of mankind's sins, all of our sins to that grave with Him. And the reason that He will be in that grave for three days and three nights, is that since man has a spirit, soul, and body; all of mankind's sins was completely saturated on his spirit, soul, and body. So when God the Father had placed all of mankind's sin on this man Jesus, He had placed all of the sins of the spirit of mankind on the spirit of Jesus; and He had placed all of the sins of the soul of mankind on the soul of Jesus; and He had placed all of the sins of the body of mankind on the body of Jesus. And this is why Jesus had to carry all of our sins upon His Spirit, Soul, and Body, to the grave, and be in that grave one day, and one night, for the spirit of all of mankind's sins, and one day, and one night, for soul of all of mankind's sins, and one day, and one night, for the body of all of mankind's sins. Jesus was not a part of mankind's sins, and neither were all of mankind's sins a part of Jesus; They were just placed on, and not in, the Spirit, Soul, and Body of Jesus, so that He was allowed to carry all of mankind's sins through the punishment phase, to the cross, during and enduring that time on the cross even to the point of His death on the cross, and to the grave for three days and three nights.

246 The death of this man Jesus on the cross was both a physical, and a

spiritual event. Even though, in the physical part of this event, it may have seemed, that a relatively small group of corrupt religious leaders, had used the legal system of the Roman authorities to have an innocent man, not guilty of any fault or crime, murdered or assassinated through the use of a trumped up charge of a crime that entrapped Him into a guilty verdict and conviction that conveniently had demanded a sentence of death by crucifixtion. This was only a physical part of a major spiritual event. For in the spiritual realm or world, there was a spiritual battle taking place before, during and after this man Jesus's ministry, false arrest, corrupt trial, entrapped guilty verdict and conviction, the sentence of death by crucifixtion on a cross, and His death on the cross. This was an extremely satisfying time and a joyful period to Satan and his demons an evil spirits. For remember that Satan has been looking for this promised man and savior that God had promised to Eve back there when Adam and Eve was being expelled from the garden of Eden. And ever since God had made that promise that a man would come somewhere out of one of Eve's descendants that would take away all of the sins of mankind and He would also crush and take away that power of death that Satan had over all of mankind. Satan did not want that power of death, the keys of death over all of mankind taken away from him.

247 So Satan has been trying to find and kill off this promised man and savior throughout the Old Testament time period. And when this man Jesus had appeared on the scene, starting with His baptism in the river Jordan by John the Baptist, this may have immediately caught the eye of Satan, and when this man Jesus was speaking and performing healing miracles, Satan may have immediately started concentrating his focus and attention on this man Jesus; And even when Satan was tempting this man Jesus, where Jesus, after being baptized by John the Baptist, was led into the wilderness by the Holy Spirit to be tempted of Satan, Satan did not

even know for sure that if this was that promise man and savior, that at the same time that Satan was trying to tempt this man to sin, he was also testing this man, Jesus, to see if he was this Son of God and savior. For, Satan, would first prompt Him, by saying, "IF THOU BE THE SON OF GOD!, command that theses stones to be made bread; for if Satan had really known that this man Jesus was this promise man and savior, he would have just made the statement, "command that these stones to be made bread". For this question and statement of Satan was a two fold trick question and statement. For if Jesus would have actually commanded that those stones of Satan to be made into bread, instead of answering Satan with scripture," It is written, Man shall not live by bread alone, but by every word that proceedeth out of the mouth of God"; One, that would have definitely confirmed that He was the Son of God and the promised Savior, and Two, He would have automatically disqualified Himself as fulfilling that role of God walking, talking and living an ordinary life of man: because only God can change stones into bread and not a man, for that would change God walking and talking as a man to God walking and talking as God. So Satan was trying to get Jesus to confirm His identity and to nullify that savior part of His mission so that mankind's sins would remain.

248 And since these religious leaders, scribes, and Pharisees, that were there, at that time that Jesus had started His ministry, had somehow, become arrogant, and may have seen themselves as righteous, religious leaders, that have become blind spiritually, and they had puffed themselves up more with false beliefs and misunderstandings of the scriptures, instead of the real and true understandings of what the scriptures had really meant and implied. Most of these religious leaders were actually moved more by Satan than by the true and living God. For if they had truly known and understood the scriptures as Abraham, Moses and Isaiah had, they

would have never rejected or crucified this man Jesus. But these religious leaders, Scribes, and Pharisees were being used by Satan and they didn't even know it. And they may have thought in their hearts that by killing this man Jesus that they were doing God's service. But it was Satan's service that they were actually doing instead of God's. For Satan was hell bent on having this man and savior Jesus killed off; still thinking that this was going to destroy God's plan of salvation for all of mankind's sins, and it would also stop, that part, to take away his power of death over all of mankind. So when this man Jesus did actually die that death on the cross, this was a tremendously joyous occasion for Satan, that Satan and most of his demons and evil spirits, if not all, were there at that cross celebrating the death of God's promised Savior, and they may have been mocking God at the same time. But this joyous occasion of Satan and all of his demons and evil spirits, will be a short lived glory three days later.

249 Throughout the Old Testament time line, Satan was too busy trying to find and kill this promised Savior, that when he actually did find and kill Him; and that by killing this man Jesus, Satan had failed to see and understand that by killing this man Jesus was actually helping God with His salvation plan. For God had needed this man Jesus to actually die a complete physical death with all of the sins of mankind on Him to fulfill and pay in full that death penalty that was demanded by that law that the wages of sin is death. For since this man Jesus was without any sin of His own, and was totally righteous and already had eternal life in him, there was nothing on God's end that He was able to do to cause this righteous man's death: For He, (Jesus), was not worthy of death. And this is where God had use Satan's blind misunderstanding of His salvation plan; For Satan may have continually thought that every man that was conceived out of the descendants of Adam and Eve was conceived with the curse and sin of Adam's sin, and worthy of death. But this man Jesus was the first man that was

not conceived with Adam's sin and was conceived with the righteousness of the Holy Spirit. There was no disobedience to any of God's law, there was no sin to demand a death penalty, He was not worthy of any death, so this was also the first man that was killed by Satan that was not worthy of any death penalty, even though He carried all of mankind's sins upon Himself. He still did not have any sins of His own.

250 And this is where Satan may have misunderstood or he did not look close enough to see that that sin that was on Jesus, was not His own sin, even though the curse and sin of Adam's sin was on Jesus, along with all of the other sins of mankind, Jesus did not receive any curse and sin of Adam's sin at His conception in the womb of Mary. Jesus was conceived by the Holy Spirit, and since the Holy Spirit did not have any sin, Jesus was conceived with the same righteousness and sinless nature of the Holy Spirit. But when God the Father had placed all of the sins of mankind on the spirit, soul, and body of this man Jesus, that curse and sin of Adam's sin was the main sin that was place on Jesus because it's the main sin that everyone of Adam's descendants had received at conception or was passed unto each descendant through conception. For it is this sin, of Adam's sin, that we all had received the very second that we were conceived in our mother's womb, that had dammed all of us to hell. And all of the other sins that we received on our own, or do after we were already born into this world, is just more sin that we add to a sinful nature that was already there at conception.

251 But Satan may have been blinded by that sin of Adam's sin that was only on this man Jesus and not a part of this man Jesus; for Jesus did not have any sin of His own in Him. But since Satan may have been conditioned or used to seeing, or he may have just assumed that every man, born out of the loins of Adam had that same curse and sin of Adam's sin

on all of mankind since Adam and Eve had fallen into sin. And he may have over looked that this sin of Adam's sin was only on Him and not in Him or a part of His spirit, soul, and body. For Jesus did not have any sin of His own, and that curse and sin of Adam's sin was not His sin, but was man's sins that was purposely placed on Him for the only reason so that He could legally carry all of mankind's sin on himself so that God the Father would have a man to legally be able to place all of mankind's sin on, so that He could legally punish all of mankind's sins on this man Jesus, so that God the Father could legally fulfill that requirement that that sin of mankind had to be punished, and having this man Jesus pay in full that death penalty that was due to all of mankind's sins, by having this man Jesus die a complete physical death on that cross. And it was Satan's use of his corrupt religious leaders and their use of the Roman authorities and courts to have this man Jesus entrapped into a guilty verdict that would demand a death sentence, which was nothing more than murder, by using a corrupt legal system of a court to have this man Jesus assassinated; This way, all of those religious leaders will still appear to be righteous and holy to all of the people in their community again, or at least that is what they may have thought.

252 In other words, God the Lord Jesus had temporarily laid down his gavel as walking, and ruling as God so that He could become a flesh and blood man, name Jesus, that would come out of the descendants of Adam and Eve, by having Himself conceived, formed and born into this world in and from a woman named Mary, to completely fulfill that role of that righteous, sinless, and obedient man with innocent blood, and to be tempted of every manner of sin as we are, and remained sinless and in total obedience to God the Father in heaven, that He was well pleased with; And so that God the Father would then have that perfect man, that He would now be able to use to place all of the sins of mankind upon, so that, He would

then be able to punish all of mankind's sins on this man Jesus so that the legal requirement of the punishment of all of mankind's sins would be completely fulfilled; And that this man Jesus, even though he was not worthy of any death penalty Himself, for there was no disobedience to God's law, for obedience to God's law is counted as righteousness, and the gift of that righteousness is Eternal life with God in heaven; He was willing to lay down His eternal life, and with all of the sins of mankind upon Him, so that that death penalty that would have been due to Adam and Eve and to all of their descendants, would be completely paid in full by the death of only one man, this man Jesus.

253 Another major point that I would like to clarify or make here, is that while Jesus was on His cross suffering and dying, He had made that final statement, "It is finished", and then Jesus had bowed his head and gave up the ghost. This is where Jesus had laid down His life at that exact moment of time. Everything had to be completely accomplished perfectly, even the exact timing of His death. For remember, that this was God the Lord Jesus fulfilling that complete and perfect role of that perfect man, for God the Lord Jesus cannot be destroyed and He can never die. So God the lord Jesus had to lay down that life of Himself that was in that man Jesus, so that that man Jesus would die that physical death of an ordinary man dying. But also, When Jesus had made that powerful statement, "It is finished"; there were two major things that were finished that may have been what Jesus was referring to as He had made that statement. The first and obvious one, was that complete salvation plan of God for the remission, separation, and complete forgiveness of all of mankind's sins. And the second one, was that Jesus had now filled that void and empty position of power and authority that Satan had held when he was archangel Lucifer and was expelled or kicked out of heaven, because of his sin and rebellion; and Adam and Eve were also made to refill that same po-

sition of power and authority that Lucifer was kicked out of; and all of the descendants of Adam and Eve would have refilled all of those void and empty positions of power and authority that Lucifer's angel's had held and were also kicked out of heaven; but Adam and Eve had sinned before they were even placed into it, leaving all of those positions of power and authority that Lucifer and all of his angel's had held, still in that void and empty state. Well now, Jesus had completely passed that sin temptation test that Adam and Eve had failed. So now Jesus had filled that void and empty position of power and authority that Lucifer was kicked out of, and Adam and Eve did not fill because of their sinful default; And all of those positions of power and authority that Lucifer's angels had held and was kicked out of, will now be filled by all of the descendants of Adam and Eve that accept this salvation plan that Jesus had died for. In other words, all of the descendants of Adam and Eve that accept Jesus as their Lord and Savior and have all of their sins removed by the washing of His innocent blood will be used by God to refill all of those void and empty positions of power and authority of Lucifer's angels. This is what was also completely finished by Jesus dying on the cross.

254 God the Father was able to use His only begotten Son Jesus, whom He had sent into this world for this main purpose of placing all of mankind's sins on His Son Jesus, so that Jesus would then be able to carry all of these sins of mankind upon Himself, so that God the Father could then completely punish all of mankind's sins, to the point that His innocent blood was severely shed during this punishment phase, and then by having His Son Jesus willing to endure the complete time it had taken to punish all of mankind's sin, even to the point of His only begotten Son Jesus dying a complete physical death, of that death sentence, on the cross. And then His Son Jesus was taken down off the cross after He had died that death sentence on that cross. And then He was put in His own

new grave carrying all of mankind's sins with Him, being buried in His grave with all of mankind's sins, for three days, and three nights. One day, and one night, for the sins of the man's soul; and one day and one night for man's spirit; and one day, and one night, for man's body; so all of mankind's sins were completely punished on God's only Son, Jesus, fulfilling that requirement that all sin had to be punished. And Jesus's innocent blood was shed during that punishment phase of all of mankind's sins. And Jesus had also fulfilled that death penalty of His own death on that cross that He was willing to accomplish even though He was not worthy of any death penalty of Himself, but was still willing to lay down His own life to completely pay that death penalty that was due to all of us, to fulfill that law that the wages of sin is death. This is the true Love of God for all of mankind that Jesus was willing to go through all of this suffering so that all of our sins could be removed from us so that we are then free and clear to go and enter into God's eternal heavenly kingdom.

255 And Jesus's innocent blood, that was shed during that punishment phase, had completely fulfilled that first part of God's law that there is no remission of sin, no separation of sin, and no forgiveness of sin unless innocent blood be shed and applied to that sin. The second part of that law where this innocent blood of Jesus will be applied to mankind's sins that will cut that stronghold that sin had on each of mankind's spirit and soul. But this will be accomplished and applied later. After Jesus was in His grave for three complete days and nights, which may have been another requirement that had to be fulfilled. And then on the third morning, God the Father had then looked upon His Son Jesus in His grave. He had seen all of the sins of mankind upon His Son Jesus's Spirit, Soul, and Body. And since all of the legal requirements of mankind's sins had been completely fulfilled and paid in full while upon Jesus, there wasn't any further need, for mankind's sins to remain upon the Spirit, Soul and body of His Son Jesus;

So God the Father had completely removed all of mankind's sins from off of His Son Jesus, for all of these sins were just mankind's sins and none of them had belong to or was not any part of this man Jesus's Spirit, Soul, and Body. God the Father had then set all of mankind's sins aside in that grave of Jesus until that time to apply His innocent blood to all of those sins is fulfilled. And then as God the Father had looked back upon the Spirit, Soul, and Body of His Son, Jesus, He did not see any sin in His Spirit, Soul, and Body or any sin that belonged to Jesus. There was no sin that could hold him in that grave and there was no sin of His own that could pull Him to hell. God the Father was then able to raise His Son Jesus back to Eternal life and He has been alive ever since, even to this very day. And all of mankind's sins had remained in that grave of Jesus and was not cast into hell yet, to offer a Grace period for man's salvation.

256 And one of the first things that Jesus had did after He had risen from His grave is that He had went into the Holy Holy place in the temple with His innocent blood, and even with that Veil or curtain that was torn from top to the bottom, He still went in and offered His innocent blood as that one time and complete innocent blood sacrifice of a man that was needed by God for the remission, for the separation, and for the forgiveness of all of mankind's sins, starting with Adam's sin. In other words, the innocent blood of this man Jesus was that blood that was needed by God that would be used to do away with man's sins, for the remission, separation, and forgiveness of man's sins. And this had also ended all of those animal blood sacrifices of the Old Testament that was only used as a temporary covering of man's sin and did not do away with their sins, but was used as a temporary stay of the execution of that death penalty that was constantly being demanded, by that law of sin and death. For the innocent blood of all of those animals that was shed year after year throughout the old testament was just a shadow of what the innocent blood of this man Jesus, that

was shed and offered only once, would permanently take away all of man's sins. So when Jesus was punished, with the shedding of His innocent blood, and nailed to a cross, to the point of his death on the cross, ended all of those animal blood sacrifices, and was also the end of the Old Testament; for Christ is the end of the law for righteousness to everyone that believeth.

257 Now we know that what things so ever the law saith, it saith to them who are under the law: that every mouth may be stopped, and the entire world may become guilty before God. Therefore by the deeds of the law there shall no flesh be justified in his sight: for by the law is the knowledge of sin. Wherefore, as by one man sin entered into the world, and death by sin; and so death passed upon all men, for that all have sinned and come short of the glory of God, there is none righteous, no not one: (For until the law sin was in the world: but sin is not imputed when there is no law). Nevertheless death reigned from Adam to Moses, even over them that had not sinned after the similitude of Adam's transgression, who is the figure of him that was to come. But not as the offence, so also is the free gift. For if through the offence of one, many be dead, How much more is the grace of God, and the gift by grace, which is by one man, Jesus Christ, hath abounded unto many. And not as it was by one that sinned, so is the gift: for the judgment was by one to condemnation, but the free gift is of many offences unto justification. For if by one man's offence death reined by one; how much more are they, which receive abundance of grace, and of the gift of righteousness, shall rein in life by one, Jesus Christ. Therefore as by the offence of one, judgment came upon all men to condemnation; even so by the righteousness of one, the free gift came upon all men unto justification of life. For as by one man's disobedience many were made sinners, so by the obedience of one, shall many be made righteous. Moreover the law entered, that the offence might abound. But where sin a-

bounded, grace did much more abound: That as sin hath reigned unto death, even so might grace reign through righteousness unto eternal life by Jesus Christ our Lord. For the wages of sin is death; but the gift of God is eternal life through Jesus Christ our Lord.

258 Now when Jesus had entered into that Holy Holy place of that temple to offer His onetime offering of His innocent blood for the atonement for all of mankind's sins, He did this even with that Veil or curtain completely torn from top to bottom. But, in order for you to be able to see the significance of this one time offering that Jesus had did in that temple and with that Veil or curtain torn from top to bottom, you need to have an understanding of the three main parts, areas, or sections of that temple and the significance of each area or part of that temple. That temple had one area that was basically called the outer court, that the children of Israel would be able to come and worship God. But if any of the children of Israel had committed or had any outstanding sin issues they were not allowed into that outer court to worship God, they were to first call for the High Priest to come outside of that temple and plead for an atonement for that sin issue, then that High Priest would tell them to go and get a certain animal that he could use as an atonement to cover that type of sin. Then they would come back with that type of animal that the High Priest would then be able to use as a sacrifice for the atonement of that type of sin. And then the High Priest would perform that animal sacrifice outside of that temple, having that person that committed or had a sin issue to place His hands on the head of that animal, and then the High Priest would then kill that animal and then he would take the blood of that animal sacrifice and would offer it to God for an atonement or covering of that persons sin. Once this type of animal sacrifice is performed by the High Priest on anyone that had any sin issue, then their sin issue is covered by that blood sacrifice and they are now free and clear to enter that outer court again and worship God.

259 There was a Veil or curtain that had completely surrounded that whole temple. This Veil or curtain, is the outside wall of the temple. So when you would enter into that temple from the outside world, this is the first curtain or Veil that you would have to pass through to enter that temple. And then once you have entered that temple and through that outside Veil or curtain or outside wall of the temple, you would then be inside of the outer court of that temple. And since there was only basically three people that were allowed to go into any other parts or areas of that temple, which were the High Priest and his two helpers that was as far as you were allowed to go. But once you have entered into that temple, and you were standing inside of that outer court area of that temple, you would have immediately seen another curtain or Veil, that was higher than the outer curtain or Veil of that temple. And you would have also been able to see another curtain or Veil that was inside of that curtain or Veil that was even higher that the other two curtains or Veil. So as you are still standing in that outer court of the inside of that temple, that first curtain or Veil that you would see immediately, was that wall of a curtain or Veil that separated the outer court from that Holy place of that temple. And that curtain or Veil, that had surrounded that Holy place, was located in the center of that outer court area of the inside of that temple that you would be able to walk completely around, and outside of that Holy place, inside of that outer court area of that temple. And like I had said earlier that only the High Priest and his two helpers were aloud in that Holy place of that temple, and the children of Israel was not allowed in that Holy place of that temple.

260 So now, if you were one of the children of Israel and you had any sin issues, you were not allowed to go into that outer court of that temple until you have had that sin issue covered by an animal blood sacrifice by the High Priest; That if you were to walk into that outer court of that temple with a sin issue that was not cover by an animal sacrifice by the High Priest,

you may have been stricken with a serious disease or sickness or even immediate death. And also, even the children of Israel that did not have any sin issues and were free and clear to enter into that outer court of the inside of that temple, they were not allowed to enter that Holy place of that temple; That if anyone of the children of Israel that was already in the outer court of that temple had continued and entered into that Holy place of that temple, and even though that person didn't have any sin issues and was able to freely enter that outer court of that temple, he was not free and clear to be able to enter that Holy place of that temple; for the very second that if any of the children of Israel would dare to enter that Holy place of that temple, except for the High Priest and his two helpers, that itself would be a disobedient act that would become sin and may have immediately caused them to drop dead on the spot, for the shadow of God's presence was in that Holy place.

261 And the final place or area of that temple was the Holy Holy place; that was located in the center of that Holy place. This Holy Holy place was the smallest area, and had the highest and thickest curtain or Veil of the temple. This curtain or Veil of this Holy Holy place may have been made of a special type of material that was to be completely woven as one continuous curtain and made thick enough so that light would not be able to pass through it. There could not be any small holes, tares, rips, or seams in this curtain at all. It had to made as one continuous thick fabric that would meet all of the dimensions of the height and the length of this curtain or Veil so that when it was hung, and put in its place, around this Holy Holy place, it would be the highest curtain or Veil of that temple and it would also wrap around that Holy Holy place several times around, and it would drape down on the ground so that the inside part of that curtain or Veil, would drape over, and toward the center of that Holy Holy place, and the outside part of that curtain or Veil would drape out and away from that Holy

Holy place and into that Holy place; so that no light of this world would not be able to pass through that curtain or Veil and into that Holy Holy place, and that no light from God would pass through that curtain or Veil and into this world from that Holy Holy place. For this is the place where the Ark of the Covenant and the Ten Commandments of God was placed and where God had dwelt.

262 This Holy Holy place of the temple was also where God had dwelt as a pillar of fire by night and a pillar of a cloud by day. And the only person that was aloud in this Holy Holy part, area or place of the temple was the High Priest. Even the High Priest's helpers were not allowed to enter into this Holy Holy place of the temple during the time that God had dwelt there or even when God wasn't there. And even when the high priest would plan to enter into that Holy Holy place each year with that sacrifice and blood atonement for all of the children of Israel, which was a shadow of what Jesus would do, with His own Blood, the High Priest would have to make sure that he had completely covered any and every sin issues of himself before he even attempted to enter that Holy Holy place of that temple with the presence of God dwelling in that Holy Holy place. For if that High Priest would enter into that Holy Holy place, having any uncover sin issues, and entering into that glorious presence and righteousness of God, that would be in that Holy Holy place, that Priest's sin would immediately be consumed by the righteousness of God and he would drop dead on the spot. And the second problem that this would cause, is that the High Priest's helpers would not be able to go into that Holy Holy place and bring out his body for one main reason, they were not allowed in there, and if they would dare to enter that Holy Holy place, even if they didn't have any sin issues, that would still be disobedience, and would become sin, and they would drop dead on the spot, also, because of that sin of disobedience.

263 So to keep this type of a situation of where a High Priest may drop dead because of some uncovered sin in that Holy Holy place, the High Priest would wear a robe that may have had bells on the bottom of his robe, and he would also have a heavy long rope tied to his waist, so that as this High Priest would enter, this Holy Holy place, and as he would walk, around, and around, through the several layers of this thick curtain or Veil; he would keep those bells on his robe ringing so that his helpers outside, in that Holy place, would know that he was still alive and well; and once he had reached the inside of the Holy Holy place, the High Priest may have ended the bell ringing with a coded ringing signal, similar to a Morris code type of a signal to let his helpers know that he had entered into the Holy Holy place without any problems. For if the High Priest's helpers would have heard the ringing bells stop ringing at any given moment, and there was no coded signal, to tell them that he had entered ok; his two helpers would then assume that he had dropped dead, and then they would be able to pull the High Priest's dead body out by just pulling on that rope that was outside of that Holy Holy place and having the other end tied around the High Priest's waist.

264 And when Moses and the children of Israel were wondering in the desert for forty years, that temple, with its three sections of curtains or Veils and all of the necessary equipment and hardware that it had taken to make and assemble and erect that temple, and also had to be taken down, and packed up, so that it would move with them as they had moved to a different location. And everytime that they would arrive at a new location, they would have to unpack and reassemble and erect that temple again. And after that temple was finished being reassembled and erected, Moses would first have to cleanse and purge every part, object, and curtains or Veil throughout all three sections of that temple. And especially the section of that Holy Holy place. It had to be assembled, erected, and

put up perfectly. That big, heavy, thick curtain or Veil of that Holy Holy place had to be thoroughly inspected for any rips, tares, blemishes or stains, etc., before it was put up and hung in its place. For if there were any of these defects, that curtain or Veil would have to be completely replaced with a new one. For God will only dwell in that Holy Holy place without sin. For if there would be anything not right with that curtain or Veil, or anything in that Holy Holy place or any uncovered sin in that whole temple, God would not come down as a pillar of fire by night or a pillar of a cloud by day and dwell in that temple until it is completely cleansed and purged of all sin. For everything of that temple had to be completely cleansed and purged of sin with the innocent blood of an animal sacrifice, and in most cases, a one year old lamb, that did not have any sickness or diseases, and was completely the color of white only, and could not be deformed or maimed in any way. Then that animal would be killed in that sacrifice and its blood would then be used to splash every part, object, curtains or Veil of that temple, purging that whole temple of all sin.

265 So you now have a better understanding of the significance of the three areas or sections of that temple. And the main section or area of that temple, was that Holy Holy place, and the big heavy thick curtain or Veil that was hung and surrounded and divided that Holy Holy place or area from the Holy place or area of that temple. That curtain or vial of that Holy Holy place was the only wall of separation, that had separated the righteous and eternal light of God Himself, and the sinful light of this world from colliding against each other. And above the height or top of that curtain or Veil, is where God had also separated Himself from this world and His righteousness, by using a pillar of fire by night and by the use of a pillar of a cloud by day. But yet, when Jesus had risen from His grave on the third morning, by God the Father; one of the very first things that He had did, was to take His innocent blood, that He had shed during that punishment

phase of that trial, and He had walked over and into that temple, and even with that big heavy thick curtain or vial still in that torn from top to bottom condition, and with that Holy Holy Place now wide open, and no longer is there any separation between God and mankind by a curtain or Veil. Jesus had offered His innocent Human blood, not any animal's blood, but the righteous, obedient, sinless, human blood of Himself, and as our one and eternal Highest above all High Priests, as an atonement for all of mankind's sins.

266 For all of those High Priests of the old testament, had entered into that Holy Holy place every year, with the innocent blood of animal's blood that was only a temporary covering of mankind's sins and did not separate, remit, of completely forgive man's sins; but was only a stay of the execution of that death penalty that was due to all of mankind. For the unrighteous and sinful blood of one man, Adam, had baptized all of mankind with this same unrighteous sinful Blood. So then, it is the same, that the righteous, sinless blood of one man, Jesus, (or the second Adam), all can be baptized with this same righteous, sinless blood. And this righteous and sinless blood of Jesus is the only human blood sacrifice that is only needed to be offered once and not every year as the Old Testament High Priests had to do with only animal's blood. For this human blood of Jesus, is the blood that completely separates, provides complete remission, and completely forgives our sins. This is that Savior that God had promised, to Adam and Eve, that would come and take away all of the sins of mankind.

267 Then after Jesus had offered His innocent blood in that Holy Holy place of that temple, He had then descended into hell and walked over to Satan and had taken that remaining power and authority of death that Satan had over mankind since Adam and Eve had fallen into sin, by taking the keys of death away from Satan. For as much then as the children are

partakers of flesh and blood, Jesus also, himself, likewise, took part of the same; that through death he might destroy him that had the power of death that is, the devil; Thereby giving to Jesus that power of death so that Jesus now had all the keys of eternal death and eternal life; And Jesus had also preached to all of those that were in hell, but not to their salvation, but to confirm His truth, concerning all truth, that was preached to them, when they were alive on earth. In other words, Jesus had preached basically the same message of His truth unto His salvation plan confirming this same message that was preached to them while they were alive on earth by the preachers, prophets and ministers of His truth. And He had also lead captivity captive and had taken them to heaven with Him.

268 In other words, there was still that temporary place where all of the Old Testament Believers, Saints, and Christians had gone to when they had died. And this was that place that was basically called Paradise, which was a temporary place that God had to make for all of the people that had died during that Old Testament period. All of those people of the Old Testament still had to die that physical death eventually, even if they were covered by the innocent blood of animal's blood. And all of these people of the Old Testament were still baptized by the unrighteous and sinful blood of Adam's blood at their conception in their mother's womb. And since the curse and sin of Adam's sin was still a part of them and they were still a part of Adam's sin, and along with all of their own sins that they had committed on their own during their life span on earth; none of them were free and clear of their sins to be able to enter into God's heaven. For as each of these Old Testament people would die their physical death, they would each die with all of their sins still a part of them. God could not let any of these Old Testament people into His heaven with their sins still attached to them; for no sin will be allowed into His heaven. All of their sins must be completely removed and separated from their spirit and souls first, before

they will ever be allowed into God's heaven. And this is what God the Father was going to do with this promise Savior, to take away all of mankind's sins.

269 But yet not all of these old testament people, descendants of, and including Adam and Eve, were not qualified to be cast into hell either. And just like today, we put our trust, hope and faith into the salvation plan of God, of everything that Jesus had already did for our salvation, approximately two thousand years ago. All of those people of the old testament time period had also put their trust, hope and faith into the same salvation plan of God of everything that Jesus was going to do for their salvation, as much as approximately four thousand years before Jesus had actually came and accomplished God's complete salvation plan for all mankind. So all of those people of that Old Testament time period were also to accept that salvation plan of God by putting their trust, hope and faith into that promise of God that a savior would come out of the seed of Abraham and He would completely remove and separate all of mankind's sins from them. All of those old testament people that did accept this salvation plan and promised Savior of God by faith, hope and trust, that this savior would come and take away all of their sins, would have all of their sins removed from them, when Jesus would come as promised. And He would accomplish everything, that was needed, to have their entire sins remove from them.

270 So all of these old testament people that did basically accept this promised salvation plan of God by complete trust, hope, and faith, that a savior was going to come and take away their sins, and even though they had lived their life span here on this earth believing and trusting in that promised salvation plan of God, And even though they had all of their sins covered by the innocent blood of all of those animal blood sacrifices, that

was only a covering of their sins and did not remove or take away any of their sins, They had still died with all of their sins still attached to them, and they were still a part of their sins and their sins were still a part of them. And all of their sins will be, future tense, removed when this promised Savior, Jesus Christ, the Messiah, would actually come and accomplish this complete salvation plan to completely remove, and separate all of their sins at that time. But since they had still died with all of their sins, technically, still attached to them, they were not qualified to enter into God's heavenly kingdom yet, because their sins would not be removed from them yet, because God's law states that there is no remission of sin unless innocent blood be shed and applied to that sin. This is what Jesus would accomplish, as promised by God. But the promise was given, approximately, four thousand years before Jesus had actually come and accomplished that promised salvation, plan to actually remove and take away all of the sins of mankind.

271 So all of these old testament Believers, Saints, and Christians that had accepted that promised salvation plan of God by faith, and even though all of their sins would be removed from them when Jesus would actually come and accomplish this salvation plan to take away all of mankind's sins. They still had died that physical death of this physical life here on earth with their sins still attached to them. And since God cannot and will not let any sin into His heavenly kingdom, all of these Believers, Saints, and Christians of the Old Testament time period were, technically, disqualified to enter into God's heaven, because of their sins. But, also, and since all of their sins would actually be removed and separated from them and cast into hell by themselves, as promised by God, they were not qualified to be cast into hell either. So this is where God had to make a temporary place or chamber that may have been called Paradise as Stated by Jesus when He was on the cross between the two thieves, and Jesus had told

the one thief that "Today you shall be with me in Paradise". So basically, this place or chamber, called paradise, was a separate place, that God had to make, that was outside of His eternal heaven, and also outside of the eternal pits, of eternal hell. It was a temporary place that God may have placed close to hell because of Satan's accusations that they were worthy of death and hell; and they all still had sin; And Satan may have been constantly claiming and accusing God that all of those believers, Saints and Christians in that paradise chamber had belonged to him because they all still had all of their sins and that promised Savior had not come to take away their sins.

272 This place or chamber, called Paradise, was not a place of any torment or punishment, but was a temporary external extension of God's heaven. It was not a place of Purgatory, as some religions want to teach you. It was an outside extension of God's internal Paradise of heaven. And even though this place or chamber called Paradise may have been close to, but outside of hell, Satan or any of his demons or any of his evil spirits was not allowed inside of this place or chamber of Paradise. And may have been guarded and secured by angels of God to keep Satan from even getting close to the area of where this chamber or place of paradise is located. And this is where Jesus may have went and stayed as the spirit and soul of that man Jesus while His flesh and blood body was in His grave for three days and three nights; For Jesus had told that thief while He was on that cross that, today you shall be with me in paradise. So the spirit and soul of that thief was in this place or chamber called Paradise, and along with Jesus and all of the other Old Testament Saints, Christians, and Believers and while all of their flesh and blood bodies were still in their graves or where ever they had died that physical death. So this place called Paradise was this place to which all of the Old Testament Saints, Believers, and Christians, starting with Adam and Eve, and all the way

throughout this Old Testament time period, and until Jesus had risen from His grave and descended back into this place or chamber of Paradise to lead all of those Saints, Believers, and Christians, and for the first time since Adam and Eve had sinned and was expelled from heaven, Jesus had lead them from this temporary place, or chamber, of Paradise and into His eternal heaven, leading the captivity and bondage of their sins to the captivity of that righteousness and eternal life of Jesus Christ.

273 In other words, All of those old testament Believers, Saints, and Christians that were in this place or chamber of Paradise because all of their sins were, technically, still a part of them and they all were still a part of their sins until Jesus had come and died to fulfill that death penalty and to use his innocent blood as that one time perfect atonement, that would, and did completely remove, take away, separate, and forgave, and was for the complete remission for all of mankind's sins. And at that same time that God the Father had completely removed all of those sins that were on Jesus when He was in His grave, God the Father had then separated all of those sins that had belonged to all of those Believers, Saints, and Christians that were in that place or chamber of Paradise, and then He had pick them up and out of that grave of His Son Jesus and cast all of them into hell by themselves. And all of those Old Testament Believers, Saints, and Christians, were now separated from all of their sins. And they were all free and clear to go to God's heaven. This is one of the main reasons why Jesus, then, had to descend down to the seat of Satan to take the keys of the death that Satan had over all of mankind since Adam and Eve had chosen to obey Satan instead of God Himself; and to preach to all those that were in hell, that they were in there because they had all rejected the promise that Jesus had come and already accomplished so that they were all without excuses. And then Jesus had then walked over from hell and into Paradise and Jesus may have proclaimed with great joy to all of

those Old Testament Believers, Saints, and Christians, that were in this chamber of Paradise, "Come and follow me to my Father's, and now your Father's heavenly Kingdom. And then this is where Jesus had lead captivity captive for Himself; for they were all in the captivity of sin, but Jesus had made them all free from their sins and captive to the righteousness and eternal life of their Lord and Savior Jesus Christ. Jesus had lead all of these Old Testament Believers, Saints, and Christians to heaven with Him, and that place or chamber of Paradise was no longer needed; for all of the believers of this new testament time period will go directly to the Father's heavenly Kingdom as they each die their physical death of this life here on earth.

274 But all of those people of the old testament time period that did not accept but rejected this salvation plan of God, and when they did die the first physical death of their life here on earth, they still had all of their sins attached to them at the time of this physical death, and they had also died a second, spiritual death that is total separation from God and His heaven. Their sins were picked up by God and cast into hell and all of their sins had then pulled them to hell where their sins will hold them in hell for all eternity. This is that eternal death and separation, in hell, from God's eternal life in heaven. And since they had rejected God's salvation plan to have their sins removed by Jesus, when He would come, and since their sins would not be removed by Jesus, from them, by their own refusal and rejection of that promised salvation plan of God when they were alive, this is the reason why God had to cast them into hell at the time of their death. For all of these people of the old testament that had rejected that promised salvation plan of God and was cast into hell, had rejected God's salvation plan because of their unbelief. During their life on this earth, they were preach to, ministered to, and the prophets had spoken the truth concerning God's salvation plan of a savior that would come and take away their

sins, so that they would not go to hell, and would be able to go to heaven; but they had continually throughout their whole life had rejected and hardened their hearts toward and against this truth and died with their sins still a part of them and they were still a part of their sins, and their sins had pulled them to hell when God had picked up all of their sins and He had cast them into hell.

275 And this is the reason that Jesus had descended into hell to preach His truth that was preached to them while they were alive on this earth, to show all of those people of the old testament time period, that were already in hell, that Jesus was this promised Savior that had come as promised by God that they all had refused and rejected and were continually warned about of this place called hell, to confirm and justify that they are without any excuse for them to be in hell. For by refusing and rejecting that salvation plan of God, that was preached to them at least once and are without excuse, they had made their own choice to go to hell, for God will not violate your free will of your decision or choice. For just like people today, that don't even believe that there is a God, a heaven, or a hell, there were people during that Old Testament time period, that didn't believe, that this promised Savior, Jesus, the Christ. and the Messiah would come and take away all of their sins so that they would be able to go to God's heaven and not be cast into hell with their sins. So this was one of the reasons that Jesus had descended into hell, and not to be tormented as all of those souls that were already in hell as some people, today, try to teach, but to preach and show all of those that were in hell, were in hell because they had freely rejected this promised Savior that would come and take away their sins; And Jesus had preached to them that He was that promised savior that did come as promised and it was not a lie; but was a true promise as it was preached to all of them during their life span here on earth through and by all of God's ministers, preacher's and prophets, and all

they had to do was to just believe and accept this promised savior into their hearts by faith, but they freely rejected it because of unbelief.

276 Jesus had made many different appearances throughout the area within about fifty days after He had risen from His grave and before He had ascended into heaven; For Jesus has told his disciples to remain in Jerusalem until they were all baptized with the power of the Holy Ghost. And on the day of Pentecost there were about one hundred twenty in that upper room when the Holy Spirit had come upon all of those in that upper room like a mighty rushing wind, and they were all filled with the Holy Spirit, and they each had spoken in a different language that was not their own language. The Holy Spirit did not come until Jesus had ascended into heaven and He had sit on High and to the right of God the Father. And then Jesus had asked the Father to send the Holy Spirit, the Comforter, as Jesus had told his disciples He would. And then the Holy Spirit had made His first presence in that upper room, and the Holy Spirit has continued His presence and the ministry of God the Father and God the Lord and Savior Jesus Christ ever since, even to this very day. The Holy Spirit's ministry and goal is to fulfill the Father's will that none should perish and all should come unto repentance to eternal life through our Lord and Savior Jesus Christ. And the Holy Spirit has been bringing every man, woman, and child, under conviction of their sins, since Jesus had risen from His grave with His innocent blood. And at the same time, Jesus has been spiritually standing, and knocking on the door to everyone's heart, since He has risen from His grave, so that He can come into their spirit and soul with His innocent blood, to baptize their spirit and soul with His innocent blood, to complete His salvation plan in you by fulfilling that part of God's law that there is no remission of sin, no separation of sin, and no forgiveness of sin, unless the innocent blood of a sinless man is shed and applied to that sin, to break that hold and bond of all of their sins, that were attached to their

spirit and soul. For by one man's sin, Adam's sin, all were baptized by the sinful blood of Adam's blood and all were made disobedient, sinful and unrighteous, and the wages of that sin is eternal death. But the same is also true, that by one man's obedience, Jesus's obedience, all can be baptized by the sinless blood of Jesus's blood, and all can be made obedient, sinless, and righteous; and the Gift of that righteousness of Jesus Christ, is Eternal Life.

277 In other words, Jesus had accomplished everything that was needed to legally remove and separate all of our sins from the spirits and souls of mankind, so that all of our sins can still be picked up by God the Father and cast into hell by themselves and we will not be pulled to hell by our sins. For that innocent blood of Jesus is the only innocent blood that was needed, and the only innocent blood that can be used to completely separate and remove all of your sins from your spirit and soul, breaking that stronghold or bond that your sins had upon your spirit, soul and body. But the first important thing that Jesus had accomplished for all of mankind is that He had paid that death penalty of Himself dying on that cross with all of mankind's sins upon himself. And the very reason that Jesus was that perfect man that was able to carry all of mankind's sins upon Himself is because Jesus did not have any sin of His own in His Spirit, Soul, and Body. He was a totally obedient, sinless and righteous man that had come out of the seed of Abraham. And because Jesus did not have any disobedience to God's law, there was no sin in Him, and because there was no sin in Him, the law of the wages of sin is death found Him not guilty of any sin but found Him obedient and righteous, and the gift of that righteousness is eternal life. So Jesus Himself was not worthy of any death penalty, but instead He had already had eternal life and technically could have never tasted any death and could have went straight to heaven directly without ever dying even a physical death.

278 And this was that perfect righteous, sinless. and obedient man that God had needed to come out of the seed of Abraham so that He could be used to place all of mankind's sins upon Him, and have all of mankind's sins completely and legally punished on this man Jesus, and having His innocent and sinless blood shed during that punishment phase, to fulfill that part of God's law that there is no remission, separation, or forgiveness of sin, unless innocent blood be shed; And, by having all of mankind's sins upon Jesus, He had become our sins temporarily, even though He still did not have any sin of His own; by dying a complete physical death on that cross, to pay that death penalty, that was due to all of mankind, even though Jesus Himself was not worthy of any death penalty. In other words, Jesus had taken upon Himself all of the sins of mankind and carried them on Himself through that severe punishment phase that had caused Him to shed His Innocent blood severely, even to the point of having to die a physical death, even though this man Jesus was not worthy of any death penalty; but was willing to temporarily lay down His eternal life and tasted a physical death with our sins still on Him so that He would completely fulfill that death penalty that was due to all of us, that He had paid in Full, instead of each of us paying it in full individually. And this is the part that we would have not been able to do on an individual basis. Jesus had then carried all of mankind's sins to His grave, and was buried with all of our sins, completely, for three days and three nights. And then on the third morning God the Father had removed all of those sins of mankind from off of Jesus; and this is why Jesus could be raised back to eternal life is because He did not have any sins of His own, whereas we all would have remained in that grave forever and when God the Father would have picked up all of our sins like he did when He had removed all of mankind's sins from Jesus, God the Father would have picked up all of your sins and cast them into hell, and all of your sins would have pulled you to hell with them, and they would have forever held you there in eternal death and hell.

279 This is why God the Father could only use this perfect man Jesus to completely punish all of mankind's sins legally; and at, and during this punishment phase, also, intentionally having most, if not all, of His innocent blood shed to legally fulfill that part of God's law that there is no remission, no separation, and no forgiveness of sin unless the innocent blood of a righteous, sinless and obedient man be shed; and to completely and legally pay in full, that demand of God's law, that the wages of sin is death, by having Jesus die a physical death, with all of mankind's sins on Him, making Him sin for us, in our place, and Jesus was willing to carry all of our sins attached to Him, even though, He was not worthy of any death penalty; because He had no sin of His own; and He was willing to go through a complete physical death on that cross; and into a grave for three days and three nights with all of mankind's sins still attached to Him. And then having all of mankind's sins removed from Him by God the Father, and setting them aside in that grave of Jesus, until all of mankind's salvation is completed, legally. And then God the Father was able to raise this perfect man, Jesus, back to His eternal life, which He already had before He was even falsely arrested; that He was willing to temporarily lay down, and set aside for three day and three nights, fully knowing that He was going to get His eternal life back again after tasting the death of all of mankind's sins for three days and three nights. And Jesus had known that by doing all of this, would completely accomplish everything that was needed, to legally remove and separate all of mankind's sin from them, so that God the Father would then be able to pick up man's sins, by themselves, and cast them into hell separately, by cutting that binding stronghold that sin had on mankind, with that innocent blood of Jesus, freeing all of mankind from that law of sin and eternal death in hell, to the law of the righteousness of Jesus Christ and His Gift of eternal life with Him and His Father, and now your Father in heaven. For the law of the Spirit of life in Christ Jesus hath made me free from the law of sin and death. For, by the Law,

the wages of sin is death; but through Faith, the gift of God is eternal life through Jesus Christ our Lord.

280 And since that death penalty, that was due to each of us by God's law of sin and death, was completely paid in full by Jesus's death on the cross, with our sins attached to Him, technically, we no longer have that demand of, a death penalty, hanging over us by God's law. But this is only contingent on the acceptance of this complete salvation plan that Jesus had accomplished for us. For Jesus had accomplished ninety nine point nine percent of everything that was needed to legally separate, remove and free us from our sins. And this final part of God's salvation plan, that actually is that important part that breaks that binding hold that your sins have on you, is where Jesus has to come into your spirit and soul and apply His innocent blood, baptizing your spirit and soul with His innocent blood to complete and fulfill that part of God's law, and salvation plan, legally, that there is no remission, no separation, and no forgiveness of your sins unless that innocent blood of Jesus, that was shed, is applied to your sins. For the innocent blood of Jesus was shed to fulfill the first part of God's law for the remission of sins, But this second part of that law of God, for the remission of sins, is where Jesus has to come into your spirit and soul, and apply His innocent blood to your sins to break that binding hold of your sins, so that they will not pull you to hell when God the Father reaches down into that grave of Jesus and then picks up all of your sins, and cast them into eternal death and hell. But Jesus will not come into your spirit and soul by force to apply His innocent blood to all of your sins. He will only come in by faith. For by Grace, (For by Jesus), are you saved, from an eternal death in hell, through faith (Jesus), and not by works, unless anyone should boast. Jesus cannot, and will not, violate your free will. Jesus will stand at the door to your heart knocking and waiting for you to give him permission to come in.

281 And like I had said earlier that Jesus had accomplished everything that was needed, by God's law legally; the punishment of our sins was punished, that death penalty was paid in full, and His innocent blood was shed. But even though all of this was completed by Jesus, there is still one more important, and I mean, very, and extremely important part of God's salvation plan, that still remains to be completed, and accomplished by Jesus. For, even though, Jesus's innocent blood was shed during that punishment phase, it was shed intentionally for a specific reason and purpose, just like all of those animal's innocent blood, during that old testament time period, was intentionally shed to cover mankind's sins; Jesus's blood was also intentionally shed for the remission of mankind's sins, for the separation of mankind's sin, and for the forgiveness of mankind's sins. So to completely fulfill that part of God's law for the remission of sins, that there is no remission of sins, no separation of sins, and no forgiveness of sins unless innocent blood be shed and applied to that sin; and since the first part of that law for the remission of mankind's sins was completed and accomplished by Jesus shedding His innocent blood; The second part of that law for the remission of sins is where Jesus has to be able to come into your spirit and soul and apply His innocent blood to all of your sins. And this final part where Jesus comes into your spirit and soul with His innocent blood, is that final part of God's salvation plan that actually separates and removes that binding hold that all of your sins have on you. And once this binding hold between you and your sins is broken and completely removed. You are now free to go in one direction completely separate from your sins and your sins can now be picked up by God the Father and cast into hell, independently, and they will no longer have any hold on you to pull you to hell. And this is what completes this beautiful salvation plan of God the Father, that none should perish, but all should come to repentance unto eternal life.

282 But this last part, where Jesus needs to be able to come into your spirit and soul with His innocent blood, to apply and completely baptize your spirit and soul with His innocent blood, to complete God's salvation plan in you, to break that binding hold that your sins have on you, so that your sins can then be legally separated from you, cannot be completed without your permission. Jesus will not come into your spirit and soul by force. He will only come in by faith. Jesus will, continually, stand outside the door of your heart knocking and waiting for you to give Him permission to come in and baptize your spirit and soul with His innocent blood. Jesus will not violate your free will. You can freely choose to answer that knocking by Jesus, at the door of your heart, and let Him in; or you are free to make that choice to reject and not answer that knocking by Jesus and refusing His salvation plan to remove your sins. You have to believe by faith that you are a sinner and that you need total forgiveness of all of your sins. You have to believe and accept by faith that Jesus had come and died for your sins and that God the Father had raised him back to eternal life and that Jesus had accomplished everything that was needed to have all of your sins completely removed and separated from you, legally, so that you can then be free and clear to enter into God's heaven without any sin. But your sins will not be removed from you until you give Him permission to come into your spirit and soul with His innocent blood, so that Jesus can complete that last part of God's law for the remission of all of your sins, by the application of His innocent blood, that He was willing to purposely shed for this very reason, so that He would be able to come into your heart to apply His innocent blood to all of your sins, so that all of your sins can then be legally removed from your spirit and soul by God the Father and picked up and cast into hell by themselves independently, completing that salvation plan of God the Father, and fulfilling the will of God the Father that you should not perish but come unto repentance through His Son Jesus the Christ to which He was willing to send for this

very reason and purpose.

283 The whole time that you are alive on this earth, starting at that very second that you were conceived in your mother's womb, and until the very second that you cease to exist or die from this world, Jesus will be standing and knocking at the door to your heart, wanting to come in and complete His salvation plan in you. And the Holy Spirit is also continually trying to get you to accept this, salvation, plan of God; by placing angels, ministers, preachers and other believers across your path during your life here on earth. And all of these ministers, preachers, and other believers will be claiming the same message; that you must be born again; saved by the blood of Jesus so that you won't go to eternal hell, which is eternal separation from the True and Living God and His eternal heaven. In other words, what is meant to be "born again" is that you are first born physically into this world of sin and death; you are physically born into Satan's family of sin and death. In order to be placed into or become part of the family of God, you must be born again spiritually. You cannot see the kingdom of God unless you are born again, spiritually, into the family of God; that which is flesh, is flesh, and that which is spirit, is spirit. When you are of Satan's family of sin and death, you are his child. And if you do not accept God's offer and salvation plan, you will inherit Satan's kingdom, eternal hell. But if you accept this offer of God's salvation plan; you will be adopted into that family of God, without any of your sins, and all Satan will be left with, is just all of your sins and not you. But this offer of God's salvation plan, to remove all of your sins from you, is only on the table of your life, while you are alive, on this earth physically. Once you die your physical death, of your life, here on this earth, that's it.

284 That offer of God's salvation plan, to have all of your sins removed and separated from your spirit and soul, is no longer available. This offer is

only on the table of you physical life here on earth. By rejecting that offer of God's salvation plan, your sins wasn't separated and removed from your spirit and soul by that innocent blood of Jesus. And since all of your sins wasn't removed from you, all of your sins will forever be a part of you, and you will forever be a part of your sins. You died your physical death with all of your sins still attached to you. This is the first death, the physical flesh and blood death of this life here on earth. God's law of sin and death or the wages of sin is death, is now, on the table, of your eternity. And since you did not accept or agree to that death penalty that Jesus had paid in full for you, your own death will be used to pay that death penalty instead of Jesus's death. That death penalty by God's law, of the wages of sin is death will demand that that death penalty be paid in full by your own death. And at this second death is where God the Father will pick up all of your sins and cast them into hell. And since your sins are still attached to your spirit and soul, and as God the Father picks up all of your sins and cast them into hell, all of your sins will pull you to hell with them. And since there wasn't any innocent blood to separate and remove all of your sins from you, your sins will forever hold you in eternal death and hell for all eternity separated from God's eternal heaven and eternal life. And God the Father will not be able to raise you to eternal life on the third morning because of your own sins that are in your spirit and soul. Not only will you not be able to come back out of your own grave, but all of your sins will pull you to hell and hold you there for all eternity.

285 In other words, God had accomplished everything that was needed to legally have that death penalty paid in full by Jesus's death and have all of your sins separated and removed by Jesus's innocent blood. There is nothing you can do on your own to make yourself righteous and sinless. If you are wanting, or you are trying to get to heaven on your own, you are wasting your time and it's a serious gamble that you will lose. For the hea-

ven that you may be trying to go to on your own is not your heaven, but God's heaven. Yes, it's God's heaven, and He has one main rule and requirement for any of mankind's entrance into His heaven. You cannot come into His heavenly kingdom with any sin attached to you. Jesus is the only way, the truth, and the eternal life to God's heaven. You must go through Jesus to get to heaven. You must have Jesus come into your spirit and soul, to have all of your sins removed and separated from your spirit and soul; you have to put on the righteousness and obedience of Jesus Christ to which the Father is well pleased with; and you can only be escorted into heaven by Jesus. God had accomplished everything that was needed by God's salvation plan, through His only Son Jesus Christ, to take away all of your sins so that you can be free and clear to enter God's heaven, all you have to do is accept it by letting Jesus come into your heart to wash away all of your sins, that's it. And it only takes approximately thirty seconds to accept this salvation plan of God, letting and giving Jesus permission to come into your heart to wash away all of your sins from your spirit and soul, taking you out of the family of Satan's sin and eternal death, and adopting and placing you into the family of God and His eternal life, becoming a child of the Lord and Savior Jesus Christ. For by the Grace of our Lord and Savior Jesus Christ are we saved from an eternal torment in Satan's eternal hell, and not by any works of you trying to get to heaven on your own, lest anyone should boast.

286 Jesus had accomplished everything for your salvation to have all of your sins separated and removed from your spirit and soul. Your sins were punished while they were upon Jesus; His innocent blood was intentionally shed for you; And even though Jesus was not worthy of any death penalty upon Himself; He was willing to lay down His life for you as your friend, Jesus was willing to carry all of your sins upon Himself and taste the death of all of your sins in your place for you, paying in full that death penalty that

was due to you and your sins; knowing that He would be buried with all of your sins for three days and three nights; And Jesus had known that on the third morning that God the Father would be able to raise Him back to Eternal life out of His own grave without any of your sins; God the Father had remove all of your sins that were upon Jesus and set them aside in that grave of Jesus and they wasn't cast into hell at that time for a reason. And the main reason is that Jesus had accomplished everything for your salvation approximately two thousand years ago before you were even born into this world with your physical life, and before you were alive, to commit any, and all of your sins. This offer of God's salvation plan to have His only begotten Son and Savior Jesus Christ to be able to come into your heart and be able to wash away all of your sins can only be placed as an offer on the table of your life here on earth when you are alive. So the very second that you are conceived in your mother's womb and until the very second that you die your physical death of this life here on earth, is when this offer of God's salvation plan is continually set before you on the complete table of your life here on this earth. In other words, Jesus will be standing at the door to your heart, knocking, and waiting for you to give Him permission to come into your spirit and soul with His innocent blood so that He can baptize your spirit and soul in His innocent blood to separate and remove all of your sins from you, and then God the Father will pick up all of your sins that was still in that grave of Jesus approximately two thousand years ago; and the Father will cast all of your sins into hell by themselves, independently from you, and then you are free, and clear, to enter God's heaven.

287 For by Grace are you saved, through faith, and not of any works that you can do on your own. Everything that Jesus had did to accomplish and complete the Father's salvation plan for all of mankind's, our, salvation from eternal separation and eternal punishment in hell, is that free gift of

our salvation that is offered to us and all we have to do is just accept it by faith. For we are saved by hope: but hope that is seen is not hope: for what a man seeth, why doth he yet hope for? But if we hope for that we see not, then do we with patience wait for it. Now faith is the substance of things hoped for, the evidence of things not seen. Knowing that a man is not justified by the works of the law, but by the faith of Jesus Christ, even we have believed in Jesus Christ, that we might be justified by the faith of Christ, and not by the works of the law: for by the works of the law shall no flesh be justified. I am crucified with Christ: nevertheless I live; yet not I, but Christ liveth in me: and the life which I now live, in the flesh, I live by the faith of the Son of God, who loved me, and gave himself for me. I do not frustrate the grace of God: for if righteousness comes by the law, for then Christ death is in vain; For as many as are of the works of the law are under the curse: for it is written, Cursed is everyone that continueth not in all things which are written in the book of the law to do them.

288 But that no man is justified by the law in the sight of God, it is evident: for, the just shall live by faith. And the law is not of faith: but, the man that doeth them shall live in them. Christ hath redeemed us from the curse of the law, being made a curse for us: for it is written, Cursed is every one that hangeth on a tree: that the blessing of Abraham might come on the Gentiles through Jesus Christ; that we might receive the promise of the Spirit through faith. But what saith it? The word is near thee, even in your mouth, and in your heart: that is, the word of faith, which we preach; that if you shalt confess with your mouth the Lord Jesus, and shalt believe in your heart that God has raised him from the dead, you shalt be saved. For with the heart man believeth unto righteousness; and with the mouth confession is made unto salvation. For the scripture saith, whosoever believeth on him shall not be ashamed. For there is no difference between the Jew and the Greek: for the same Lord over all is rich unto all that call

upon him. For whosoever shall call upon the name of the Lord shall be saved.

289 And this is the very basis to your salvation, that if you will confess with your mouth and believe in your heart that you are a sinner, and that you need forgiveness of your sins by God; And you believe that Jesus had died for all of your sins; and that God had raised Jesus back to eternal life from the dead; and you give Jesus complete authority and permission to freely come into your spirit and soul with His innocent blood, thereby letting Jesus come into your spirit and soul to apply His innocent blood to your spirit and soul, cutting that stronghold, that your sins had on your spirit and soul, freeing you of all of your sins, completing and fulfilling that salvation plan of God in you, and pleasing God the Father that you should not perish but that you would accept His salvation plan through repentance unto eternal life through His Son Jesus Christ. And then God the Father will pick up all of your sins that were still in that grave of Jesus, and with great joy, God the Father will then cast all of your sins into hell by themselves and they won't be able to pull you to hell with them; and all of your sins will remain in hell by themselves and with Satan for all of eternity; and you will now be free and clear of all of your sins and will now be able to enter God's heaven. For even though God is a God of Love, He is also a God of perfect justice and in no wise can He just clear the guilty and let them come into His heaven with their sins. And since there was nothing that we could do on our own to punish our sins, to pay that death penalty, or have innocent blood shed and applied to our sins to break that stronghold of our sins that God's laws would demand; this is why God the Father was so willing to send His only begotten Son to accomplish everything that was needed by God's own law to fulfill everything that was needed to free us from our sins, legally, and all we have to do is just accept what Jesus had accomplished for us in our place. And this is done by confessing with your

mouth or saying a thirty second prayer that will complete and give Jesus that permission He needs to come into your heart and remove all of your sins, and all you have to do is to repeat this prayer below, out loud or with your normal voice:

Jesus I come to you right now in prayer by faith: I hereby confess to you that I am a sinner; I am asking you to forgive me of all of my sins: I repent of all of my sins: I believe that you had died in my place for all of my sins; And that you were willing to be in your grave for three days and three nights with all of my sins; And I believe that God the Father had raised you from your grave back to eternal life; And that you have been standing at the door to my heart, wanting to come in, and wash away all of my sins. I hereby give you complete permission and authority to come into my spirit and soul with your innocent blood and wash away all my sins with your innocent blood. I now confess that you are now my Lord, my Savior, and my God. I thank you for your salvation plan and accept it by faith. And I now praise you as my Lord and My God. In Jesus name I pray, Amen.

290 Now if you had just repeated this sinner's prayer above out loud, you had just completed that one tenth of one percent that we each must do to complete and give Jesus permission to come into our spirit and soul to completely baptize your spirit and soul with His innocent blood, purging and separating all of your sins from your spirit and soul, so that you are no longer a part of your sins, anymore, and all of your sins are no longer a part of you, to the point that now God the Father will reach down into that grave of Jesus and He will now picked up all of your sins, and with great joy, cast them all into hell where they will remain there for ever by themselves and they will not be able to pull you to hell with them, and you are now free and clear of any and all of your sins, and you at the same time

had put on the righteousness and the obedience of Jesus Christ. In other words, before you had prayed that sinners prayer above, and as Jesus was continually knocking at the door to your heart; The Holy Spirit was bringing you under conviction of your sins to the point that you were willing to pray that prayer above. For you see that Jesus wants to come into your spirit and soul with His innocent blood to wash away all of your sins so that you will be free from all of your sins. And the Holy Spirit also wants to come into your spirit and take up permanent residence in your spirit forever. But the Holy Spirit will not come into your spirit by force; and He will not come into your spirit because of your sin. For if the Holy Spirit would come into your spirit with your sins still in your spirit, the very righteousness of the Holy Spirit would immediately consume that sin and you would drop dead on the spot and you and all of your sins, would immediately be sapped to hell. So the Holy Spirit has also been waiting patiently, and has been continually trying to bring you under the conviction of all of your sins that you will answer that knocking of Jesus at the door of your heart and let Him in.

291 And when you had actually prayed that sinner's prayer, giving Jesus complete authority and permission to come into your spirit and soul with His innocent blood to wash away all of your sins from your spirit and soul; and as Jesus had entered into your spirit and had completely baptized your spirit with His innocent blood, rendering your spirit now sinless, the Holy Spirit had followed right behind Jesus and moved into your spirit and was able to take up permanent residence in your spirit for all your eternal life. For before you had given Jesus and the Holy Spirit permission to come into your spirit and soul; Your spirit was just this flickering little flame of a candle unto the Lord, that Satan was constantly trying to extinguish so that you would not be able to go to heaven. But now that the Holy Spirit had come into your spirit to take up permanent residence in your spirit for

all eternity; your spirit is no longer that flickering little flame of a candle, but is now the Eternal Light of the Holy Spirit, that Satan can never extinguish or destroy. And as Jesus had moved from your spirit and into your soul, Jesus had also completely baptized your soul with His innocent blood, also rendering your soul now sinless. And then Jesus had pulled out your filthy rag of unrighteousness and replaced it with a piece of His own righteous cloth, to which, the Father is well pleased with. So, now, as God the Father looks into your soul, and He sees the perfect righteousness of His Son Jesus now in your soul, you are now also my beloved son or daughter to which I am also well pleased; And because Jesus was totally obedient and without any sin, that obedience is counted as righteousness. For the law of God had found only obedience to the law in Jesus; for Jesus did not come to do away with the law, but He fulfilled it in one word, Love; For all the laws of God hang upon only two laws, and both of these laws are basically the same; for the first law states that we are to love the Lord your God with all of your Heart, mind and soul; and the second is like unto the first, That you are to love your neighbor as yourself; for upon these two laws hangeth all of the other laws. And since Jesus did not do away with the law but fulfilled the law in the obedience of only one word, the action, and passion of His everlasting and perfect Love. For the righteousness of Jesus, is because of His perfect obedience, to all of the laws and commandments of God; that Adam, and Eve, should have continued in that same obedience that God had made them with. So we put on the obedience and righteousness of Jesus Christ, or we put on that obedience that Jesus Christ had did, for we are disobedient and we have no obedience; and we also put on that righteousness of Jesus Christ, for we have no righteousness of our own.

292 Now to Abraham and his seed, one seed, were the promises made. He did not say; and to seeds, as of many seeds; but as of one, seed, and

to thy seed, which is Christ. In other words, Now to Abraham and his seed, (one seed, not many), were the promises made. This promise by God wasn't made to seeds, as in the plural sense, to the many seeds, but as in the singular sense, one seed, but to thy seed, the seed of Jesus, that was also promised by God, to Eve that the savior will come out of her seed, and not seeds; And, that promised seed, of Eve, was through Abraham, through Isaac, through Jacob, through David, to that one seed of Jesus, for Jesus was that one promised seed that was to come and take away all of the sins of mankind. And this I say, that the covenant, that was confirmed before of God in Christ; the law, which was four hundred and thirty years after, cannot disannul, that it should make the promise of none effect. For if the inheritance be of the law, it is no more of promise: but God gave it to Abraham by promise. Wherefore, (why), then serveth the law? It was added because of transgressions, till the seed should come to whom the promise was made; and it was ordained by angels, in the hand of a mediator. Now a mediator is not a mediator of one, but God is one. Is the law, then, against the promises of God? God forbid: for if there had been a law given which could have given life, verily righteousness should have been by the law. But the scripture hath concluded all are under sin that the promise by faith of Jesus Christ might be given to them that believe. But before faith (Jesus) came, we were kept under the law, shut up unto this faith, (Jesus), which should afterwards be revealed. Wherefore the law was our schoolmaster to bring us unto Christ, that we might be justified by faith (Jesus). But after that faith (Jesus) is come, we are no longer under a schoolmaster; for you are all the children of God by faith in Christ Jesus. For as many of you as have been baptized into Christ have put on Christ. There is neither Jew nor Greek, there is neither bond nor free, there is neither male nor female: for you are all one in Christ Jesus. And if you be Christ's, then are you Abraham's seed, and heirs according to the promise. Even so we, when we were children, were in bondage under the elements of the world: But when the fullness of the time was come, God sent forth his Son, made of a woman, made under the law, to redeem them that were under the law, that we might receive the adoption of sons. And because you are sons, God hath sent forth the Spirit of his Son into your hearts, crying, Abba, Father. For you were in bondage to sin, a slave to sin, a servant to sin; therefore you are no more a servant, but a son; and if a son, then an heir of God through Christ.

293 For it is written, that Abraham had two sons; the one by a bondwoman, the other by a freewoman. But he who was of the bondwoman, was born after the flesh; but he of the freewoman, was by promise. Now we, brethren, as Isaac was, are the children of promise. So then, brethren, we are not children of the bondwoman, but of the free. Stand fast therefore in the liberty wherewith Christ hath made us free, and be not entangled, again, with the yoke of bondage (the law); Behold, I say unto you, that if you be circumcised, Christ shall profit you nothing. For I testify again, to every man that is circumcised, (self righteousness through obeying the law), that he is a debtor to do the whole law. Christ is become of no effect unto you, whosoever of you that are justified by the law; you are fallen from grace; for we through the Spirit, wait for the hope of righteousness by faith. For in Jesus Christ, neither circumcision (obedince to the law) availeth anything, nor uncircumcision (disobedience to the law); but faith which worketh by love. For all the law is fulfilled in one word, even in this; Thou shalt love thy neighbor as thyself. Walk in the Spirit, and you shall not fulfill the lust of the flesh. For the flesh lusteth against the Spirit, and the Spirit against the flesh: and these are contrary, the one to the other; so that you cannot do the things that you would. But if you are led of the Spirit, you are not under the law. Now the works of the flesh are manifest, which are these; Adultery, fornication, uncleanness, lasciviousness, Idolatry, witchcraft, hatred, variance, emulations, wrath, strife, sedition's, heresies, envy-

ing, murders, drunkenness, raveling's, and such like: that they which do such things shall not inherit the kingdom of God. But the fruit of the Spirit is love, joy, peace, longsuffering, gentleness, goodness, faith, meekness, temperance: against such there is no law. And they that are Christ's have crucified the flesh with the affections and lusts. If we live in the Spirit, let us also walk in the Spirit. Let us not be desirous of vain glory, provoking one another, envying one another. Be not deceived; God is not mocked: for whatsoever a man soweth, that shall he also reap. For he that soweth to his flesh shall of the flesh reap corruption; but he that soweth to the Spirit shall of the Spirit reap life everlasting. For in Christ Jesus neither circumcision (obedience to the law) availeth anything, nor uncircumcision (disobedience to the law), but a new creature ,through, and by faith in Jesus.

294 When God had created and made all of the Angels of heaven; Archangel Lucifer and his position of the greatest power and authority that was above all of the other Archangels and angels of God's heaven; may have been purposely and intentionally made, and created by God, to help control and rule over the multitude of the angels of heaven. But when Lucifer had sinned and rebelled against God and was removed from his position and was expelled or kicked out of God's heaven; leaving that greatest Archangelic position of the greatest power and authority vacant, empty and void. But God is not going to have any void and empty positions in His heaven; any and all void and empty positions will be filled. And since Archangel Michael's position of power and authority had now become the greatest Archangelic position of power and authority, temporarily, until that position that was Archangel Lucifer's is refilled; Archangel Michael's position of power and authority didn't just cover his normal two thirds control over the remaining two third angels of heaven, but he had also become a great and powerful fighting army of angels for God against Satan and all of his now demons and evil spirits. And to refill that void and empty section of

heaven, God had decided to create a newer type of creation that would have the very image of himself; a man that He had named Adam, and a helpmate, and a woman named Eve to be that replacement.

295 And this long term plan and intended purpose of this man Adam, was that God had originally created him to refill that void and empty position of power and authority that Satan had held as Archangel Lucifer. And at the same time that God had created this man Adam; He had also made this man Adam with male reproductive organs and his female mate, wife, and woman with the female reproductive organs, so that this man would be able to reproduce and multiply after himself; and then God was going to use all of Adam's children or descendants as the replacements to refill all of those void and empty positions that all of Satan's demons and evil spirits had held as Archangel Lucifer's angels. But God had purposely and intentionally created this man Adam outside of His eternal heaven, and God had placed him on this earth and in that Garden of Eden as a temporary placement to perform a complete test of his obedience or disobedience before he would permanently place this man Adam into that void and empty position, that was Archangel Lucifer's, and bring and restore all of that one third section of heaven back into God's eternal state of His heaven. But God's original plan and agreement or first Testament was broken by Adam's disobedience and sin.

296 So God had let the first agreement or first Testament run its course, but He had immediately invoked the second agreement or second Testament by His promise that He would send His only Son to come into man's world of sin and death to remove all of man's sins. But not only was this second agreement or second Testament between God and mankind, was to remove all of mankind's sins and was mankind's salvation from eternal death in hell to God's eternal life in His heaven; but this second agreement

and Testament was also the complete fulfillment and replacement of all of those void and empty positions that Satan and all of his demons and evil spirits had held as one third of the angels of heaven, but was removed and expelled from heaven. For not only was Jesus the savior of mankind and their sins; but He was also that righteous and obedient man that the man Adam should have remained. Basically, Jesus was the replacement, or the second Adam, that had fulfilled and completed and passed that test of complete obedience to the True and Living God of heaven and completely rejected every temptation test by Satan.

297 This also had qualified this obedient man Jesus to be the perfect and permanent replacement to that void and empty position that Satan had held as Archangel Lucifer. And Jesus is the spiritual head of his church, and all of mankind that choose and accept this salvation plan of God through Jesus Christ will become the body of believers of his church. Satan is the spiritual head of his church, and all of mankind that rejects this salvation plan of God through Jesus Christ will become the body of unbelievers of Satan's church. Jesus is the spiritual head of his spiritual body of believing Christians; and Satan is the spiritual head of his spiritual body, of unbelieving Anti-Christians. But, remember that when Adam and Eve had fallen from their righteous path of obedience and eternal life with the True and living God in heaven, to the unrighteous path of disobedience, sin and eternal death with the false god, (Satan), of eternal death in hell: all of mankind was transferred from the family of the True and living God of heaven to the family of a false and dying, (technical), god, (Satan), of hell. This is why Satan may have at first believed or thought that all of mankind had then belonged with him in hell because they had also received the same sinful nature that Satan and all of his demons and evil spirits had received when they all had sinned and rebelled against God in heaven.

298 In other words, Adam and Eve and all of their children or descendants were intentionally and purposely made and created by God as a newer type of a replacement to refill all of those void and empty positions that Satan and all of his demons and evil spirits had held as one third of the angels of God's heaven. All of mankind, starting with Adam and Eve, was intentionally made to refill that void and empty Archangelic position that was Lucifer's; and all of those void and empty angelic positions would have been refilled by all of Adam and Eve's children or descendants as mankind would multiply through God's intended design of the human male and female reproductive, sex organs and its natural and intended process to reproduce mankind after himself that started with Adam and Eve's first child, Cain. (Two important and true side notes here: There is nothing to express or imply any intended purpose for manmade abortions here: and there is absolutely no expression or any indication of a homosexual lifestyle here either; but only a heterosexual lifestyle instigated, setup, designed and created by God for his purpose; so abortion and the homosexual lifestyles that is being forced and shoved down our throats today, is not from God, but from the pits of hell by Satan.)

299 So you can see, that instead of God making, and recreating new angels to refill that whole one third section of his heaven with new angels again; God had made mankind, starting with this first man Adam and his wife and woman named Eve, as a starting point and as the first test subjects of this newer type creation of mankind. God didn't just restore that whole void and empty section of heaven first and then make and create this first man Adam and then immediately place them into that permanent Archangelic position that was Lucifer's. God wanted to test this new man's obedience to Him by faith; for God had seen and watched one third of his angels that He had made: put their faith, hope, and trust into a created creature, Archangel Lucifer, instead of those angels putting their faith,

hope, and trust in Him, The True and Living God that had made all of the angels of heaven, including Archangel Lucifer. And this is what God wants from all of his created creatures in His heaven from now on; God wants all of these new replacement creatures to put their faith hope and trust in Him. And this is why God wanted to test their allegiance and obedience to Him, by testing this man Adam outside of His eternal heaven first before placing him into that permanent position. God didn't want a similar or same sinful and rebellious event repeat itself again in His heaven.

300 And this test of this new creation of the first man Adam, and his wife and woman Eve, was a very simple test of their obedience to the True and Living God that had made them; for God had wanted this first man of all of mankind to put their faith, hope, and trust in Him. And this is why God had restored only this earth from a destructive state, instead of restoring all of the other planets and this whole universe. That's why when we look at all of these other empty and lifeless planets that we see today is because we are still in that void and empty section of God's heaven that Lucifer and his angels was expelled from and kicked out of heaven; that had become Satan and his demons and evil spirits; that are still in this void and empty section of heaven that this earth is located in, even to this very day. And if Satan and all of his demons and evil spirits had their way; they would surround and destroy this earth and everything on it and in it. And since Satan could not destroy the true and living God; he would have great pleasure in destroying the very image of God, all of mankind, if God's hand wasn't in the way. And this is why God had slammed back all of evil forces of Satan and his demons and evil spirits at the restoration of this earth; and has been held back ever since then. But the more mankind keeps rejecting and refusing to worship the True and living God and worship Satan and his idols; the closer Satan and all of his demons and evil spirits are allowed to reposition themselves to this earth. And there is a time specified in the

book of Revelation that an angel of God will declare Woe! Woe! Woe! to the inhabitants of the earth, for Satan has come to this earth to dwell amongst you!

301 Also, another side note here; to those that may believe in UFO's or flying saucers; they are from Satan and are very dangerous. God doesn't need a flying machine to move anywhere through His heaven: but Satan will try and eventually succeed in having mankind set up a one world government here on earth; forcing worship of Satan as God; that he will cause both small and great, rich and poor, free and bond, to receive a mark in their right hand, or foreheads: and that no man would be able to buy or sell anything, except all of those that would receive Satan's mark in their right hand or forehead, or the name of the beast, or the number of his name. And by accepting that mark, name, or number of Satan would permanently seal their doom to and with Satan and all of his demons and evil spirits in hell for all eternity. And any or all governments that may be secretly making contact with what they may be deceived into thinking or believing that these are Aliens of a higher and more advanced intelligence than mankind, but will be nothing more than demons and evil spirits, of Satan, disguising their real appearance and identity; which will be nothing less than Satan's evil and lying attempt to steal, kill, and destroy all of mankind by getting them to worship him instead of the True and Living God of heaven. But to cover this, UFO's, Flying Saucers/Aircraft, Aliens, and the like, and how they relate to the Biblical truth of Satan and the true and living God, may be the topic of another book.

302 But when the man Adam and his wife and woman Eve, didn't pass, but they failed that second part of that obedience test by Satan's evil deception and lies; and even though they both had fallen from eternal righteousness to eternal unrighteousness, and from eternal life to eternal

death because of their faith, trust, and hope in the obedience to Satan's commands instead of the true and living God's Commands: God had immediately invoked that backup plan of His second agreement to redeem all of mankind from their sins; to remove all of mankind's sins, legally, by and through God's only Son Jesus Christ. When Adam and Eve had fallen into sin, they had not only sentenced themselves to eternal death and punishment in hell, but they had also sentenced all of their children or descendants to that same eternal death and punishment in hell too. So we do not have to choose to go to hell; for we are already sentenced to eternal death and punishment in hell. If God didn't provide His glorious offer of the grace of His salvation plan for all of mankind; we would not have had any choice to choose from. But because of the grace of God the Father that none of us should perish but all should come to repentance unto salvation to eternal life; that God had set before all of mankind, starting with Adam and Eve, a salvation plan provided by God that completely accomplishes everything that was needed to legally remove all of mankind's sins from them; so that all of mankind's sins, on an individual basis, can be removed from man's spirit and soul and cast into hell by themselves without any of your sins pulling you to hell with them. Even though God is a God of Love; God is also a God of perfect justice, and in no wise can He just clear the guilty and let all of mankind into His heaven with their sins still attached to them. Either have your sins removed by God's salvation plan and have just your sins cast into hell by themselves, so you can freely enter God's heaven sinless, or reject God's free offer to have all of your sins removed, keeping your sins that keep you from entering God's heaven, and you will be pulled into hell by your own sins as God picks them up and casts them into hell; for God will still cast all of your sins into hell, and all of your sins will pull you to hell with them and they will forever hold you in hell.

303 So when God had explained the judgment upon Adam, and then upon Eve, and then upon the serpent, and then upon Satan; and as God had cursed that serpent, He had also cursed Satan's evil deeds at the same time; for God had said that I will put enmity between you and the woman, and between your seed and her seed; It, (This man Jesus), shall bruise your head, and all you will be able to do is cause him, (Jesus), to just bruise his heel. This is where God had made His public promise that a savior would come somewhere out of one of the descendants of Adam and Eve, that would not only take away all of the sins of mankind, but He would also destroy that power of death that Satan had over all of mankind. Even though that the will of God the Father, was that all of mankind would come to repentance unto His salvation plan through His son Jesus Christ unto eternal life in heaven; God had seen that some of the descendants of Adam and Eve did not, and would not, accept this free offer of God's salvation plan, but had, and will, reject it because of unbelief.

304 This free offer of God's salvation plan can only be accepted, by the grace of God, through faith, hope and complete trust in Him, the True and living God, and not Satan, and not by any works that you could do on your own; for God's only Son Jesus Christ had accomplished everything that was needed, legally, to have all of your sins completely removed and separated from your spirit and soul; so that all of your sins can, and will be picked up by God the Father, and he will, with great joy, cast just all of your sins only into hell by themselves and they won't be able to pull you to hell with them; for that innocent blood that Jesus had intentionally shed, for this purpose, to fulfill that law that there is no remission of your sins, no separation of your sins, and no forgiveness of your sins unless that innocent blood that Jesus had shed is applied to all of your sins of your spirit and soul: for this innocent blood of Jesus is the only innocent blood that can be used to cut that hold that all of your sins have on you. And when Jesus fin-

ishes separating and releasing all of your sins from your spirit and soul; then this is why God the Father is now able to pick up all of your sins, that He had intentionally set aside in that grave of Jesus when He had removed them from Jesus on that third morning, for this reason; and since all of your sins are then no longer a part of you and you are no longer a part of your sins; all of your sins can then be picked up by God the Father, separately from you, and cast them into hell, and all of your sins, that no longer have that hold and pulling power, are now powerless to hold you in your own grave, even when you do die your physical death; and they also no longer have any hold and pulling power to pull you to hell either.

305 God is going to eventually pick all sin and cast them into hell. No sin will be allowed into God's heaven. Hell was purposely created by God as a temporary place to cast all sin into until the final judgment of sin would take place, then death and hell will eventually be cast into that eternal lake of fire; that is eternally separated from the eternal and living God of heaven. There are two spiritual bodies that are being formed out of the descendants of the first man Adam and his wife and woman Eve. Every descendant of Adam and Eve will each be continually offered that free gift of that salvation plan of God, by God, through His ministers, preachers, teachers, Christians, disciples, and by and through His word of the bible; while they are each alive, in this physical life, here on earth. This free offer of God's salvation plan is only on the table of the timeline of your physical life here on earth. In other words, this salvation plan of God is going to be continually offered freely to you at every second that you are physically alive on this earth: for Jesus will be continually standing at the, spiritual, door to your spirit, soul, and heart, knocking and waiting for you to hear and see Him knocking, and waiting for you to answer His knock and let Him come into your spirit and soul with His innocent blood to purge your spirit and soul of all of your sins.

306 If you accept this salvation plan of God, you will then be taken out of that family of Satan's sin and eternal death in hell, and you will then immediately be placed into God's family of eternal life in heaven; you will also be placed into that spiritual body of Jesus Christ; you are taken off of that path of eternal death in hell, that was that eternal death sentence that you were conceived with and was passed unto you from Adam and Eve at your conception in your mother's womb; and you are no longer a child of Satan, but you are now a child of the True and living God. When you accept that salvation plan of God by letting and giving Jesus permission to come into your heart, spirit, and soul to complete that salvation plan of God in you; you are giving Jesus that permission that he has been waiting for you to give to Him; for Jesus will not violate your free will; He waits patiently for you to hear and answer His knocking; and verbally give Him that legal permission to come into your heart, spirit and soul; so that Satan won't be able to accuse Jesus of violating your free will. And this verbal confirmation is basically of the heart; for God can speak to and hear every man's heart, even if they can't speak or hear physically.

307 And when you pray that sinner's prayer, you are exercising and putting your faith, hope, trust and belief into God the Father, and into God the Lord and Savior Jesus, (both the man Jesus and God the Lord Jesus), and into God the Holy Spirit; that they have done and will do and accomplish everything that they say they will do, even though, you will not see it take place immediately; and you won't actually see or feel Jesus come into your spirit and soul and wash away all of your sins with His innocent blood. We just believe, trust and hope through faith that we are actually saved from eternal death in hell and we have eternal life in heaven with God for all eternity. And God wants anyone of Adam and Eve's descendants that will put their Faith, Hope, Trust, and belief in Him and not Satan. God wants all of you or none of you. You can't have both God and Satan at the

same time; you can't be in both hell and heaven at the same time; and you cannot be in complete darkness and complete and total light at the same time. God has said; I have set before you darkness, and I set before you Light; I myself would rather you choose the light over the darkness; But none the less, therefore, choose you this day of whom you will serve; for the darkness is already yours by birth; but the light is an offer of a choice, by God and from God, as a free gift, that you can freely choose to accept or reject. The choice is yours to choose. God will not violate your free will of choice.

308 And the only way that you go to God's heaven is through God's only Son Jesus; for Jesus is the only Way, the Truth, and the Life; no man can come into God the Father's heavenly kingdom, except you go through, and by Jesus, the Christ, the Messiah; and the only thing that you have to do, is to pray this thirty second-to-one minute prayer here below and confess it with your mouth and believe it with your heart by faith, that's it; that's all you have to do to complete God's salvation plan in you and to become a child of God:

Jesus I come to you right now in prayer by faith: I hereby confess to you that I am a sinner; I am asking you to forgive me of all of my sins: I repent of all of my sins: I believe that you had died in my place for all of my sins; And that you were willing to be in your grave for three days and three nights with all of my sins; And I believe that God the Father had raised you from your grave back to eternal life; And that you have been standing at the door to my heart wanting to come in and wash away all of my sins. I hereby give you complete permission and authority to come into my spirit and soul with your innocent blood and wash away all my sins with your innocent blood. I now confess that you are now my Lord, my Savior, and my God. I thank you for your salvation plan and accept it by faith. And I

now praise you as my Lord and My God. In Jesus name I pray, Amen.

309 If you had just prayed this above prayer and out loud; You had just allowed Jesus to come into your spirit and soul and apply His innocent blood to your spirit and soul; and God the Father at the same time had reached down into that grave, that Jesus was buried in, and picked up all your sins, and now had cast all of your sins into hell by themselves, and you did not go with them; for that innocent blood of Jesus had just separated your sins from you, so that you are no longer a part of your sins and your sins are no longer a part of you and therefore they cannot pull you to hell with them; and now Jesus had just pulled out your filthy rag of unrighteousness and then He had replaced it with a piece of His righteous cloth, to which God the Father is well pleased.

310 For you see, you had no righteousness of your own, and the righteousness of Jesus is the only righteousness to which God the Father is well pleased; and since you now have in you the righteousness of Jesus Christ; God the Father will now say that this is also now my beloved child in whom I am well pleased! And also, since Jesus was in total obedience to all of the laws of God; for Jesus did not come to do away with the law but He had fulfilled it in one word, "LOVE": for the first commandment states that "Thou shalt LOVE the lord thy God with all thy heart, all thy mind, and all thy soul"; and the second commandment is like unto the first: "Thou shalt LOVE thy neighbor as thyself": for upon these first two commandments hang all the laws of God. And since Jesus has now taken up residence in your soul; His obedience to the law, His righteousness, and His eternal life is now in you; and since Jesus was sent by the Father to do His will on earth and Jesus did not do His own will but He did as He saw the Father doing, and spoke as he heard the Father speaking, thereby, it

was God the Father walking in the flesh and blood body of Jesus; and this is why Jesus had said that if you have seen me you have seen the Father; for my Father is in me and I am in my Father; for I and my Father are one and the same; therefore, since Jesus is now in your soul; so now is the Father also; and the Holy Spirit is now in your spirit.

311 God the Father has now taken up residence in your soul along with God the Lord Jesus; and God the Holy Spirit has taken up residence in your spirit: This flesh and blood body will not inherit the kingdom of heaven, for dust it was made and dust it shall return; The life that is in you is not your own but is God's eternal life that was originally breathed into Adam and has been past unto all of us at conception; and this life of God that is in you will one day be called back to God from which it had come from and will return to him; and since you do not have any life of your own, the body without that life of God, dies; But also, since you had let Jesus come into heart with his innocent blood and he washed away your sins; and now the Father and Jesus are in your soul and the Holy Spirit is in your spirit; your spirit, soul and that life of God in you is one and the same; so now when God calls his life back to himself that is in you; The body without that life of God still dies and will turn back to dust from which it came; but your spirit and soul are part of that life of God and that life of God is now a part of your spirit and soul; as God calls his life back to himself in heaven, your spirit and soul will go with it; and as you enter heaven you will pass through a Veil and receive a new eternal and heavenly body to replace that sinful flesh and blood body that did not go to heaven; and at the same time that you get your new heavenly body; Jesus transfers from your soul to your new body; thereby, God the Father will dwell completely in your soul; and God the Lord Jesus Christ will dwell completely in your new heavenly body; and God the Holy Spirit will dwell completely in your spirit; and that the eternal presence of God the Father and God the Lord

Jesus Christ and God the Holy Spirit will now flow in an around you that you will not be able to see your nakedness for you will be clothed with the eternal presence of God.

312 And this is how God has brought us back to the original created form and appearance of Adam and Eve's created form and appearance that they were originally created with by God and before they had fallen into disobedience and sin. And since God the Lord Jesus as that flesh and blood man named Jesus had finished and completely filled that void and empty archangelic position that was Lucifer's: God will still be able to use all of Adam and Eve, and all of their descendants that accept God's salvation plan by faith, becoming the believing body of Christ that will be used by God to refill all of those void and empty positions that were Lucifer's angels. This is why you can do nothing on your own to get to God's heaven; for it is God's heaven and not your heaven; it's not God wanting you to let Him into your heaven, but it's You that is wanting and needing to go to God's heaven; God wants you to go to His heaven and hopes that you will make that choice and decision; but God doesn't need you, but it's You that need Him; You can go to God's heaven only by that free gift of His Salvation plan that is freely offered to you every second that you are alive on this table of the timeline of your physical life here on earth, all you have to do is just accept it, that's it!

Choose The Salvation Plan of God That Is Freely Offered To You

This is the Prayer that complete's that salvation plan of God that will give that legal permission for Jesus to come into your heart, spirit, and soul, to wash away all of your sins from you, so that your sins will be separated from you and cast into hell by themselves, so that you can be free and clear of your sins to enter God the Father's heavenly kingdom. And all you have to do is just confess this prayer here below with your mouth and believe in your heart and that's it; you are then immediately saved from an eternal death in hell to an eternal life in heaven with God the Father, and God the Lord, and now your Savior Jesus Christ and God the Holy Spirit, and all Satan gets it all of your sins only.

The Sinner's Prayer Of Confession To Eternal Life.

<u>Jesus I come to you right now in prayer by faith: I hereby confess to you that I am a sinner; I am asking you to forgive me of all of my sins: I repent of all of my sins: I believe that you had died in my place for all of my sins; And that you were willing to be in your grave for three days and three nights with all of my sins; And I believe that God the Father had raised you from your grave back to eternal life; And that you have been standing at the door to my heart wanting to come in and wash away all of my sins. I hereby give you complete permission and authority to come into my spirit and soul with your innocent blood and wash away all my sins with your innocent blood. I now confess that you are now my Lord, my Savior, and my God. I thank you for your salvation plan and accept it by faith. And I now praise you as my Lord and My God. In Jesus name I pray, Amen.</u>

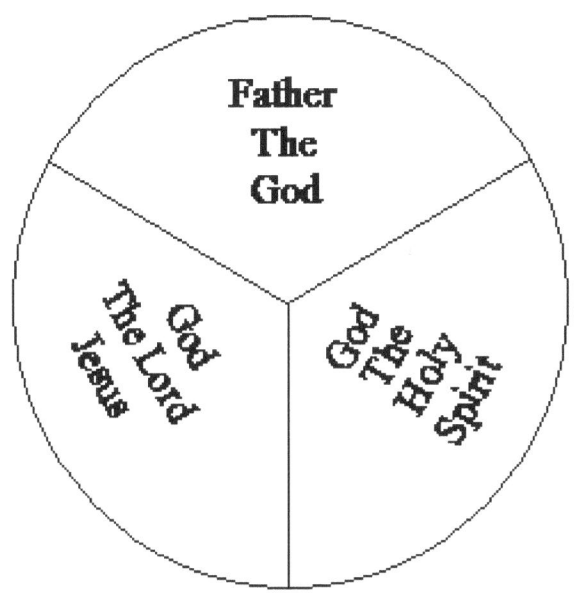

Drawing #1 From Page 16, Paragraph 15

A graphical outline of God's throne would be similar to drawing a circle on a piece of paper and then divide that circle into three equal sections such as one would cut a whole pie into three equal pieces. And I had made this circle with the three sections on a piece of paper so that one section, or one piece of the pie was at the top; and one section or one piece of the pie was down and over to the left of that top section; and one section, or one piece of the pie was down and over to the right of that top section: And in that top section of that circle I had put God the Father: And in that section of that circle that was down and over to the left, I had put God the Lord Jesus: And in that section of that circle that was down and over to the right, I had put God the Holy Spirit. Now this is not an actual picture of God's throne, but a graphical outline of God's throne.

Drawing #2 From Page 31, Paragraph 37

The three sections that were inside that circle had now extended or continued outside of that circle or outside of God's throne; dividing God's one heaven now into three separate individual sections of heaven matching the three sections of God's throne. Inside of that circle is still God's throne and outside of that circle is still God's eternal heaven; but now with three separate individual sections of heaven to match or coincide with the three sections of God's throne, with one section belonging to God the Father; and one section belonging to God the Lord Jesus; and one section belonging to God the Holy Spirit.

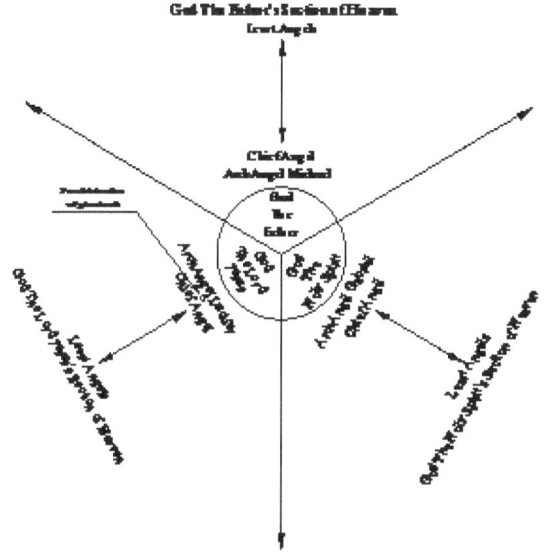

Drawing #3 From Pages 38 & 39, Paragraph 47

God the Holy Spirit's section of heaven is laid out so that Archangel Gabriel's position of power and authority is placed close to and just outside of the throne of God the Holy Spirit. And directly under Archangel Gabriel's position is the position of power and authority of Archangel Gabriel's Chief Angel; And under Gabriel's Chief Angel is all of the other angels in that section of heaven of God the Holy Spirit, ranking from the greatest angels to the least angels. And God the Father's section of heaven is also laid out so that Archangel Michael's position of power and authority is placed close to and just outside of the throne of God the Father. And directly under Archangel Michael's position is the position of power and authority of Archangel Michael's Chief Angel; And under Michael's Chief Angel is all of the other angels in that section of heaven of God the Father, ranking from the greatest angels to the least angels. And God the Lord Jesus's section of heaven is also laid out so that Archangel Lucifer's position of power and authority is placed close to and just outside of the throne of God the Lord Jesus. And directly under Archangel Lucifer's position is the position of power and authority of Archangel Lucifer's Chief Angel; And under Lucifer's Chief Angel is all of the other angels in that section of...........

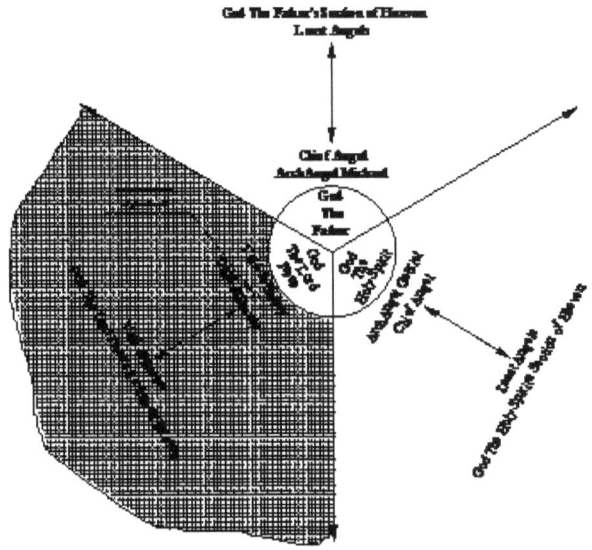

Drawing #4 From page 68-69, Paragraph 85

And again as God had removed himself and his presents from this now dark section of heaven, His eternal life was also removed and replaced by eternal death. So now this dark section of heaven is also now void of any life. And God's perfect Love was also removed from that dark and void section of heaven, replacing it with pure and total hate. And God's perfect order had also been removed from this now dark, empty, void and full of a pure hate, section of heaven; and now it has been replace with total chaos; and so on and so on. In other words, all that God is was removed from that section of heaven; and that section of heaven had now become the very opposite image and reflection of who God is and the very image and reflection of who Satan and his demons and evil spirits have become. This dark and void section of heaven that is now separated from the eternal state of God's heaven has now become the first physical realm in all of God's eternal kingdom; and has now become a..........

Study Notes

Study Notes

Study Notes

www.ingramcontent.com/pod-product-compliance
Lightning Source LLC
Chambersburg PA
CBHW071655090426
42738CB00009B/1539